Learn the FACTS about:

- Telepathy
- Clairvoyance
- Occultism
- Hauntings
- Split-brain Research
- Poltergeists
- Spiritualism
- Mind Links
- Paranormal Crime Detection
- Psychic Archeology
- And More . . .

For centuries, the occurrence of psychic phenomena has been surrounded by mystery and controversy. Now, in this fact-filled, in-depth survey, author Colin Wilson challenges the skepticism with documented evidence.

Be prepared to learn the startling truth.

Enter a world beyond your imagination, beyond the realm of ordinary science. The world of . . .

THE PSYCHIC DETECTIVES

COLIN WILSON is the author of more than fifty novels, plays and essays. His first book, *The Outsider*, was greeted with extraordinary critical acclaim. His work covers a wide spectrum of topics—from philosophy to mysticism, from the criminal to the psychic—and includes *The Occult, The Mind Parasites, Lifeforce,* and *Poltergeist*! He currently lives in Cornwall, England with his family.

COLIN WILSON

THE PSYCHIC DETECTIVES

The story of psychometry and paranormal crime detection

BERKLEY BOOKS, NEW YORK

**For
Andrija Puharich**

This Berkley book contains the complete
text of the original hardcover edition.
It has been completely reset in a typeface
designed for easy reading and was printed
from new film.

THE PSYCHIC DETECTIVES

A Berkley Book / published by arrangement with
the author

PRINTING HISTORY
Pan Books edition published 1984
Mercury House edition published 1985
Berkley edition / August 1987

ISBN: 0-425-10015-4

A BERKLEY BOOK ® TM 757,375
Berkley Books are published by The Berkley Publishing Group,
200 Madison Avenue, New York, New York 10016.
The name "BERKLEY" and the "B" logo
are trademarks belonging to Berkley Publishing Corporation.

PRINTED IN THE UNITED STATES OF AMERICA

10 9 8 7 6 5 4 3 2 1

ACKNOWLEDGEMENTS

I owe a considerable debt of gratitude to the Society for Psychical Research, and particularly to its secretary Eleanor O'Keefe, for providing me with a vast amount of material that would have otherwise been unavailable. Its librarian, Nick Clark Lowes, also showed great patience in duplicating for me hundreds of pages from the SPR *Journal* and *Proceedings*. The College of Psychic Studies was equally helpful, and I am immensely grateful to Brenda Marshall for allowing me to keep Denton's *The Soul of Things* on almost indefinite loan.

I would also like to acknowledge the help of many friends in the United States who sent me a great deal of material—particularly Dennis Stacy, Jerome Drost, Pat Bruneni and Arthur M. Young. Rhea White, of the Psi Centre, New York, was kind enough to provide me with invaluable information on Joseph Rodes Buchanan—I am grateful to the American Society for Psychical Research for providing me with this lead. I also wish to thank Joe Gaute who, many years ago, presented me with a copy of Stephan Schwartz's important book *The Secret Vaults of Time,* as well as providing me with details of the Joy Aken case. Professor Marcello Truzzi provided me with an enormous amount of information on modern psychics, for which I am doubly grateful because his own attitude towards them is distinctly sceptical. I would like to thank Robert Cracknell and Suzanne Padfield for giving so generously, both of time and material. I am also grateful to Andrija Puharich, Uri Geller, Greta Woodrew, Benson Herbert, Eddie Campbell, Joe Cooper, Brian Marriner, David Flint, Leonard Boucher, and my cousin Mrs. Pat Aldaya, for providing important information, while the encouragement of Guy Playfair has been, as always, an enormous stimulus. Finally, many thanks to my wife Joy for preparing the index.

Colin Wilson

CONTENTS

ANALYTICAL TABLE OF CONTENTS

Cicero's Roman villa. Mrs. Denton "sees" the dictator Sulla. The Porcelain Tower near Peking. Melrose Abbey. A description of life in Pompeii. The last days of Pompeii. Visual hallucinations. The power of "eidetic imagery," or photographic memory. Berdyaev's hallucination. Visions of Mars and Jupiter. Sherman Denton's visit to the sun. What went wrong? Swedenborg and his visions. The great fire of Stockholm. Hypnogogic states. Maeterlinck's theory of "the unknown guest." The general's wife dreams of his death. Split-brain research. We have two people in our heads. The "hidden self." Thomson Jay Hudson's *Law of Psychic Phenomena*. The "subjective mind" and the "objective mind." A hypnotized subject talks with Socrates. The illiterate girl who spoke Greek, Latin and Hebrew. The nature of genius. Limitations of the subjective mind. Does it cause psychic phenomena? Hudson attacks Denton. Calculating prodigies. Photographic memory. Jung and "active imagination." How far is psychometry "active imagination"?

3 White crows and black sheep

The 1890s: the age of optimism. Sidgewick and Myers found the Society for Psychical Research. William Crookes investigates spiritualism and admits it to be genuine. "I didn't say it was possible—I said it was true." Alfred Russell Wallace investigates hypnotism and telepathy. T. H. Huxley: "I cannot get up interest in the subject." The dowser Jacques Aymar solves a murder case. Baring-Gould dismisses dowsing as superstition. William Barrett investigates telepathy. "The Willing Game." The Rev. Creery and his four daughters. How the SPR was launched. William James has an attack of depression. Renouvier's definition of free will. James's "white crow," Leonore Piper. Richard Hodgson denounces Madame Blavatsky. Hodgson takes over the American SPR. Mrs. Titus dreams of a drowned body. Myers's theory of "the Subliminal Self." Rose Foster's body found through a dream. Andrija Puharich's theory of telepathy. The case of Jack Sullivan. The drowning of Willie Mason. The body located by a "psychic." The death of Richard Hodgson. Hodgson "returns" through Mrs. Piper. James's "psychometric theory" of spiritualism. Can a gramophone record answer questions? Psychical

4 The Akasic records

5 Spirits high and low

Allan Kardec launches French spiritualism. Eugène Osty and "supernormal faculties in man." Mme. Morel psychometrizes a photograph. Visions of Baalbek. The missing brooch. Mme. Morel foretells an aeroplane accident. Ludwig Kahn and the "empty chair test." How does precognition work? Mme. Morel finds a missing body. Michael Shallis and *deja vu*. Richet's "sixth sense." Pagenstecher and Maria de Zierold. Pagenstecher confirms Denton's theories. What is a poltergeist? Guy Playfair's "spirit theory" of poltergeists. *Spirit-Psychometry*. Olwen's visions of the past. Is psychometry due to spirits? Max Freedom Long and *The Secret Science Behind Miracles*. The theory of the superconscious mind. Man's "three souls." Long's explanation of psychometry: the *"aka* thread." How to contact "George." Why dowsing works—the split-brain theory. Does hypnosis depend on will power? The Abbé Mermet.

6 The Mind Link

Maximilien Langsner solves a murder case by telephathy. Von Osten and Clever Hans Pfungst reveals unconscious signalling. The Elberfeld horses. Maeterlinck finds them genuine. Telepathy and "psi" powers. Animal telepathy. Hans Brick and his lion. Eddie Campbell's lions. My own experience of telepathy. Rider Haggard's dog. Upton Sinclair's *Mental Radio*. The experiments of Tischner. Sigmund Freud admits his belief in telepathy. Hettinger and the "ultra-perceptive faculty." Hettinger's subjects show precognition. Gustav Geley and Eva C. "Protoplasmic substance." *Aka* threads? The murder of Maria Marten. "Dream telepathy." The murder of Mona Tinsley. Estelle Roberts "sees" the body in water. The curse of Tutankhamun. Telepathy? Edward Russell's T-fields. The "curse" on the Great Eastern. Tom Lethbridge and psychometry.

7 Psychic archaeology

The career of Stefan Ossowiecki. Ossowiecki identifies a portrait of Copernicus. Ossowiecki "reads" a prehistoric flint tool. His experiments in "psychic archaeology." Frederick

Bligh Bond and the Glastonbury Scripts. The "visions" of Edgar Cayce. Cayce and the story of Atlantis. Cayce's prophecies of the future. Norman Emerson and George McMullen. McMullen and the carved head. Charles Garrad sees dead Indians. Herman Hilprecht solves an archaeological problem in a dream. The "god of archaeology." James Scott-Elliot discovers a prehistoric site through dowsing. Geoffrey Goodman has a dream. The psychometry of Aron Abrahamsen. The discovery of ancient man in America. David Jones and psychic archaeology. The well of Chichen Itza. The psychic telephone of the Montagnais Indians.

8 The art of psychic detection

Peter Hurkos falls off a ladder. Hurkos discovers his vocation. The murder of van Tossing. Hurkos impresses Andrija Puharich. The Miami murders. The crimes of Melvin Rees. The Boston Strangler case. One of Hurkos's failures? Croiset the clairvoyant. The career of Gerard Croiset. The murder of two children. The case of Edith Kiecorius. The Pat McAdam case. Robert Cracknell and the Genette Tate case. The "psychic detectives" in Aylesbeare. The Janie Shephard murder case. Cracknell predicts the arrest of the Yorkshire Ripper. Uri Geller and the Bronfman kidnapping. Matthew Manning and Greta Woodrew. Suzanne Padfield and psychometry. Benson Herbert's Paraphysical Laboratory. A haunted Deanery. The case of Alison Chadwick. Suzanne Padfield solves a Moscow murder case. The brain-scale of Dr. Oscar Brunler.

Postscript

Pierre Janet's "paleoscope." The problem of "heightened consciousness." Alan Vaughan's experience of precognition. Why scientists reject psychical research. The "over-all pattern." Is psychical research a failure? Gustav Geley's *From the Unconscious to the Conscious*. Conclusions.

FOREWORD

A survey by Christopher Evans published in 1973, by *NEW-SCIENTIST*, a British publication whose circulation is drawn from the scientific community, asked readers to state their feelings about what was called Extra Sensory Perception. Of the 1500 who did so, sixty-seven percent considered ESP to be an established fact or, at the least, a strong probability. Eighty-eight percent of the 1500 considered psychic research to be a legitimate area for scientific inquiry. In the United States, the Gallup organization carried out its own survey and found that, "Slightly more than half of those polled in the general American population believe in ESP, but the figure rises to nearly two-thirds for those people with a college background."

Such insights into the attitudes of educated men and women in the English speaking countries attest to the compelling nature of psi-phenomena. What makes these survey conclusions all the more interesting is the fact that they exist in spite of strong, and exceptionally hostile opposition, from a well-publicized community of critics. This group, which has carried out virtually no actual research in parapsychology, objects largely on philosophical grounds; feeling that anomalous events do violence to the physicalist-materialist world view, because their existence cannot yet be fully explained. In spite of a large and internally consistent body of research being produced by university and independent foundation laboratories, the idea that consciousness may extend beyond the confines of the brain itself remains, for the physicalist scientist, a difficult concept to accept.

However, as it has in the past, science is slowly changing to accommodate ever more rigourous and broadly based data. In addition to accumulating experiment results these explorations are also beginning to address the need for a conceptual framework. Physicists are actively working toward the theoretical framework within which to view these studies. In the biological sciences similar theoretical hypotheses are also being advanced, notably the Morphogenic field theory of Sheldrake. Within the medical field, the concept of the Collective Unconscious, first advanced by the psychiatrist Carl Jung, has begun to take on a new dimension. The result of all this work seems destined to establish a solid new foundation to underpin a class of phenomena that have previously resisted integration into the scientific mainstream.

Thus, although the controversy about the existence of psi-functioning will probably persist for a number of years, this conflict is an issue of concern to a strident but shrinking minority, and the time has come to consider something of the applications to which this research can be put. To ask how best to work with this intuitive source of information, even as we continue seeking to explain and understand its potential and limitations.

Even a cursory glance at the literature involving intuitive information in criminology strongly suggests that many law enforcement professionals, indifferent to the psi-controversy, have already made an *ad hoc* decision that psychically derived data can make substantial contributions. Professor Marcello Truzzi of Eastern Michigan University, a sociologist who is also the Director of the Center of Scientific Anomalies Research, carried out a survey of what had been published *only up to 1981* in the West and compiled—what to his and other researchers' astonishment—became a bibliography containing 327 published articles on the subject. If this is what had been reported in print stopping four years in the past, from the time I write this in the spring of 1985, it seems reasonable to assume that more cases have reached print since then, and that the actual number is far larger. Clearly, on an individual or departmental level a great deal of manpower, time, and money is already being committed to the use of psychics in criminology. One can only infer that there must be some pay-off that makes it seem worthwhile.

So large is this effort, in fact, that its size is perhaps the most compelling argument possible for carrying out a serious overall study. What can legitimately be done with this information in law enforcement? There is no competent thorough answer to this question presently available, only semi-informed speculation.

Colin Wilson has assembled some of the more interesting examples to be recorded, in which intuitively derived data has been useful in criminology and the related applications field of archaeology. Because the book is at least one generation removed from primary research it is heir to the always present difficulty of repeating errors, and cannonizing them through repetition. Complicating that, some of the primary research recounted here, for example the archaeological work reported on in Arizona, is itself the subject of intense controversy, which may not be clear to readers not fully familiar with parapsychological research literature. However, the gain paid for by that cost is to give readers some sense of the breadth of what has been tried, and an awareness of the large cross-section of the scientific community that has been intrigued by the issue of extraordinary human performance—which is what we are studying when we talk about psychic functioning in any manifestation.

Wilson also provides a critically needed sense of the commonality of vision about these phenomena that has developed in every human culture. Modern western science may be the most sophisticated and useful intellectual tool ever developed, but it is not the only door into the human psyche. There is a cultural chauvinism implicit in almost any discussion of one culture by another. It will be hard for us to fully appreciate the range of human accomplishment until we acknowledge our western biases, just as the non-technological older cultures of humanity have a dreadfully difficult time integrating western science and modes of thought into their established interpretations of reality.

Ultimately, real understanding will come from some combination of arm's length replicatible research and direct personal experience. The sooner the marriage is consummated the more likely we are to survive as a species.

STEPHAN A. SCHWARTZ
The Mobius Society
Los Angeles, California

© Foreword, Stephan A. Schwartz, 1985

INTRODUCTION

In the summer of 1981, shortly after I had finished writing a book called *Poltergeist,* I came upon a story that made me want to kick myself. It was in the *Leicester Mercury*, the evening newspaper of the city where I was born, and told an extraordinary story about Bodmin, Cornwall, a town which is about thirty miles from where I now live. James Pencarrow, a prosperous builder from nearby Liskeard, died in a Plymouth hospital in 1946. He had left no instructions about his funeral, and his eldest son Harold decided that he should be buried in the churchyard of St. Mark's, Bodmin, where Pencarrow's own parents had been buried. Harold knew this was against his father's wishes: Pencarrow had detested his mother and had no wish to be buried near her. Nevertheless, St. Mark's seemed the obvious choice. The coffin was placed on two trestles in front of the altar. Later that evening, the Rev. Basil Bradley looked into the church, and found that the coffin was now lying in the aisle, about twelve feet from the altar. Assuming that vandals were responsible, he summoned the churchwarden and lifted it back. But as he turned to leave, the coffin rose up from its trestles, and floated back down the aisle. The church suddenly became icy cold.

The Rev. Bradley told Harold Pencarrow what he had seen, whereupon Pencarrow admitted that his father had asked not to be buried in St. Mark's. They decided to respect his wishes and bury him elsewhere in Bodmin. Just before the burial service, the churchwarden noticed that the coffin was surrounded by a kind of blue haze. Then a pile of hymn books jumped off a shelf and fell with a crash on the floor; as the man started to pick them up, the Bible fell off the lectern.

But the service passed without incident. The coffin was carried from the church, and placed on the lawn near the church gate while they waited for the hearse. Ever since then, says the Rev. Basil Bradley, not a blade of grass has grown on that piece of lawn . . .

It was frustrating—having missed such a marvellous tale of poltergeist phenomena. But I felt it might be useful for some future occasion. So the next time my wife went to Bodmin, I asked her to call at St. Mark's church, see if there was still a patch of dead grass near the gate, and if the vicar could give her any more details about the case. But when she enquired for St. Mark's in Bodmin, she was told there was no such church. A check with the Diocesan Records Office in Truro revealed that there is no St. Mark's church in all Cornwall; moreover, no builder named James Pencarrow ever lived in Liskeard.

I was now feeling slightly irritable with the writer of the story, Mr. John Macklin. If I *had* used the story, I would have been left feeling rather a fool. Accordingly I wrote a letter to the *Leicester Mercury*, asking for an explanation. In due course I received a reply from Mr. Macklin's literary agent, who explained that "members of the family involved" had stipulated that there should be no precise identification. That might explain why the builder's name had been changed. But surely there could be no possible reason for also disguising the church? Meanwhile, my sister in Leicester had sent me more of Mr. Macklin's stories—they were apparently syndicated nationwide. The first was about a "cursed field" in north Cornwall and about a family of farmers who met dire misfortune by ploughing it. I checked on the name of the family in the Cornwall telephone directory; it was not there. This time I addressed a letter direct to Mr. Macklin, pointing out that it was hardly ethical to write "true" tales of the paranormal in which all the names were changed so that no one could check up.

Under this persecution he became distinctly waspish. He replied that in twenty years of writing for newspapers, mine was the first serious complaint he had ever received. He went on: "Despite being provided with verification for the two articles you have queried, you continue to attack my work and motives." He had not, of course, offered any kind of "verification." Sadly, I decided to drop the correspondence.

I tell this story to illustrate the difficulties facing a writer who attempts a serious assessment of psychical phenomena. To some extent *all* stories are bound to be second-hand, unless the writer happens to be a psychic himself (which I am not). But it is obviously the writer's first duty to offer the reader access to the same information that he used himself. If he does not do so, then he lays himself open to the accusation of dishonesty, and he deserves it.

This rule applies as much to journalists as to professors of parapsychology writing up their results for technical journals. And Mr. Macklin is far from being alone in breaking it. Dr. Lyall Watson, a respected zoologist, has written a number of excellent books that have attempted to bridge the gap between modern science and the paranormal; his basic method is to see how far subjects like astrology, palmistry, alchemy, the "human aura," have some kind of scientific justification. But his book *Lifetide* begins with a personal experience: how, in Venice, he encountered a five-year-old girl named Claudia, who could cause a tennis ball to turn inside out—without breaking it—by merely stroking it with her fingers. He explains that he took the everted tennis ball back to his hotel, and pondered what it all meant for our narrow, materialistic view of reality.

Now, if this had happened, it would probably be one of the most important events in human history. It would demonstrate quite clearly that our consciousness is somehow limited to our three-dimensional world, but that there exists a fourth —or fifth—dimension beyond our understanding; just as, if a completely flat, two-dimensional creature could exist, it would be unable to understand how a cook can turn a pancake by tossing it into the third dimension.

Lyall Watson is a friend, so I wrote to him to ask for further details. I also criticized his previous book, *Gifts of Unknown Things,* for moving into a kind of semi-fictional field, pointing out that the very essence of scientific evidence is to guard against the slightest intrusion of embroidery or dramatization.

He wrote me back a long letter, explaining his own changing attitude to the paranormal, and his recognition that it is almost impossible to remain open-minded *and* rigidly "scientific." He went on to say that he had not given further details about Claudia because he was unwilling to see her "embroiled in that kind of controversial circus." In any case, he said, she is not doing "strange things to tennis balls any more." And her everted tennis balls always turned themselves the right way round after forty-eight hours—which answered my question about what had happened to the one he had taken back to his hotel.

My own feeling is that he should not, in that case, have included the story in the book. He is relying on the reader's kindness and indulgence, and placing himself in the same position as Erich von Däniken who, in *Gold of the Gods,* describes a visit to a mysterious underground library in South America, and was later forced to admit that he had never set foot in such a place.

The question is not whether an indulgent reader is willing to give him the benefit of the doubt. It is a question of the rules of scientific evidence; and no serious researcher has any *right* to ask for the benefit of the doubt. By doing so, he not only exposes his own honesty to question; he exposes the flank of every other serious investigator of the paranormal. And there is at present such an atmosphere of bitter hostility between orthodox scientists and paranormal investigators that this is downright suicidal.

It all began, of course, with Uri Geller, and his exploits in "metal bending" in the early 1970s. It is true that there had always been a number of scientists ready to denounce "pseudoscience"—meaning Wilhelm Reich, J. B. Rhine, Immanuel Velikovsky, or whoever. But the rise of a new interest in "the occult" in the 1960s had made everybody more irritable, and Geller's worldwide publicity brought an explosion of fury. A group of scientists, scientific popularizers and stage magicians orchestrated the fury by demanding that all serious intellectuals should close ranks to resist what Freud had once called "the black tide of occultism." These included "the Amazing Randi," John Wheeler, Carl Sagan, Christopher Evans and Martin Gardner (who was writing the Mathematical Recreations page for the *Scientific American*). At this early stage, things were not particularly bitter. Martin Gardner was a friend of mine, I was in friendly correspondence with Marcello Truzzi, editor of the sceptical *Zetetic Scholar* (and still am), and had collaborated with Christopher Evans editing a series of books on the paranormal. Gardner was the author of a brilliant and amusing book called *Fads and Fallacies in the Name of Science,* covering every form of intellectual dottiness from the Flat Earth Society to people who believe the earth is hollow. Yet in spite of my admiration for the book, I had always felt a little uneasy about Gardner's tone of condescending superiority. Once a scientist begins to decimate the cranks, he tends to generate an emotional head of steam that ruins the tone of scientific detachment. Could Gardner be *quite* sure that no sane person could ever question Einstein, or that dowsing for water is a laughable superstition?

It was unfortunate that the Geller controversy caused an increasing polarization between hard-line scientists and those who felt that the paranormal is at least worth investigating. Polarization is never good for intellectual freedom; it generates negative emotion and fanaticism. The hard-liners formed a Committee for the Scientific Investigation of Claims of the Paranormal, and the tone of its public utterances became increasingly intolerant. At the annual meeting of the American Association for the Advancement of Science in 1979, the eminent physicist John Wheeler caused a stir by demanding that researchers in parapsychology should be ejected from the Association. His battlecry was: "Drive the pseudos out of the workshop of science!," and members of the Committee for investigating the paranormal cheered. In Martin Gardner's collection of reviews, *Science, Good, Bad and Bogus* (1981), all the good humour has vanished and been replaced by a hectoring tone: "Dermo-optical perception is still being taken seriously by yahoos of the paranormal . . ."

But the Committee was soon to be split by a kind of Watergate scandal. In 1975, the sceptical magazine the *Humanist* had published an attack on Michel Gauquelin, a statistician who had looked into the claims of astrology and discovered some interesting supporting evidence—for example, that an unusual number of sports champions tend to be born under Mars, actors under Jupiter, scientists under Saturn, and so on. (His figures had even convinced the confirmed sceptic, Professor Hans Eysenck.) Dr. Dennis Rawlins, a physicist (and later one of the founders of the Committee), read this attack and realized that it was incompetent and inaccurate. He was asked to try to "disprove" Gauquelin himself; but in fact, his computer analysis tended to support Gauquelin. Still convinced that Gauquelin was basically wrong, he tried hard to get his sceptical colleagues to move on to firmer ground. They ignored him; instead, there was a "cover-up," and (as Rawlins wrote) "one's willingness to go along with the cover-up (to protect the cause) became a test of loyalty." His fellow Committee members became increasingly irritable at Rawlins' insistence that Gauquelin should be fought with honest arguments, not with arguments they now knew to be based on error. And Rawlins finally became so embittered at being treated as a leper for acting on principle that in 1981, he blew the whole gaff in a pamphlet called *sTARBABY*, whose cover states its basic theme: "They call themselves the Committee for the Scientific Investigation of Claims of the Paranormal. In fact, they are a group of would-be debunkers who bungled their major investigation, falsified the results, covered up their errors, and gave the boot to a colleague who threatened to tell the truth.'' The pamphlet begins: ''I used to believe it was simply a figment of the *National Enquirer*'s weekly imagination that the Science Establishment would cover up evidence for the occult. But that was in the era BC—before the Committee . . . I am still sceptical of the occult beliefs [the Committee] was created to debunk. But I *have* changed my mind about the integrity of some of those who make a career of opposing occultism.

''The irony of all this particularly distresses me since both in print and before a national television audience I have stated that the conspiratorial mentality of believers in occultism presents a real political danger in a voting democracy. Now I find that the very group I helped found has partially justified this mentality.''

To which it is tempting to reply: ''Of course it has.'' For the moment a Committee begins to generate the witch-hunting mentality, it has turned its back on the kind of open-minded curiosity that has led to all great scientific discoveries. The moment one group of people begins to develop ideas about the wrong-headedness of another group of people, the shadow of the concentration camp appears on the wall. And in science— or in *any* form of intellectual discovery—this is disastrous. The investigator who was once driven solely by enthusiasm begins to look nervously over his shoulder to see whether he is about to be denounced as a crank. And the fear of being denounced creates the same atmosphere in the scientific community as it did in Hitler's Germany or Stalin's Russia. *Any* sensible person must see that this is not the way to get at truth.

The right way is to be open-minded, to state the facts as you see them, and to be willing to acknowledge it frankly if you are shown to be wrong. And, above all, to remain good humoured.

In this book I have tried to state the facts about psychometry. Some of them may later prove to be wrong; but I have tried to be as accurate as possible. The aim is to lay out as much of the evidence as I can, so it can be seen and assessed. The occult means ''the hidden''; and in that sense, I am also an anti-occultist.

COLIN WILSON

1

Telescope Into the Past

WHEN A PRETTY eighteen-year-old typist, Myrna Joy Aken, failed to return home from the office in Durban, South Africa, her parents decided to notify the police. They knew Joy had been anxious to get home early; she intended to go to a dance, and had even laid out her dress on the bed.

The officer assigned to the case, Sergeant N. J. Grobler, made enquiries at Joy's office. On the evening of her disappearance—2 October 1956—Joy had left work at about six. A colleague thought she had seen her climbing into a light-coloured Ford Anglia outside the post office. Another girl in the office described a man who had come to see her on two occasions; he was good-looking and several years older than Joy, and seemed to be on familiar terms with her. After his second visit, Joy had seemed upset. But she had not told anyone who he was.

A week after her disappearance, there were still no leads. At this point, her brother Colin suddenly thought of a neighbour —Nelson Palmer, the father of his schoolfriend Jack. Palmer, a retired headmaster, had a reputation as a "clairvoyant," and had apparently helped the police to track missing persons. According to his son, he could hold some object in his hands, allow his mind to become a blank, and then give details about the person to whom the object belonged. Colin was inclined to scepticism; but the family was in such a state of desperation that anything seemed worth trying.

Eight days after Joy's disappearance, Maud Aken and her

son called on Nelson Palmer. They took with them, at Palmer's request, some of Joy's underwear—two slips, a bra and some knickers. The grey-haired clairvoyant drew the curtains and placed the clothing on the table in front of him. He rested his hands on it, closed his eyes, and began to breathe regularly. After a few minutes, he began to speak. Joy was dead, he said. Her body lay in water in a culvert several miles away—Palmer described the surrounding countryside. And when he opened his eyes and drew the curtains again, he told them that he thought he could lead them to the body.

A group of searchers, including Colin Aken, drove south out of Durban. About sixty miles away, near the village of Umtwalumi, Palmer told them to stop in a valley between two hills. He climbed down off the road, to a sluggish watercourse, and peered into a culvert. Before the others could join him, he told them: "You had better fetch the police . . ."

Joy's naked body had been rammed head first into the culvert. The lower part of her abdomen had been mutilated. But the gunshot wounds in the head suggested that she had been dead when this happened.

Now the police were convinced they were dealing with a demented sex criminal, although medical examination showed that Joy had not been raped. And a check on every light-coloured Anglia in Durban had finally brought a promising lead. The owner of a radio shop mentioned that his Anglia had been used by a radio engineer named Clarence Van Buuren, who had returned it on the day after Joy's disappearance. Since then, Van Buuren himself had disappeared. Van Buuren, it seemed, lived only a hundred yards from the Akens's house in the suburb of Pinetown, and had even been there on two occasions to repair the radio. Therefore, Joy might well have accepted a lift home in his car . . .

Nearly a hundred police officers were involved in the search for Van Buuren, and everybody in Pinetown knew that he was suspected of the murder of Joy Aken. On 11 October, a gardener reported seeing a man creeping on all fours into some shrubbery; he reported it to the police. They located the man and challenged him; he ran away, and a policeman fired warning shots at him. As they approached, the man threw away a pistol. It was Clarence Van Buuren. He was taken to the police station and told he was wanted in connection with Joy Aken's murder. In his possession police also found a .22 pistol. One of the bullets that had killed Joy Aken was a .22.

Clarence Gordon Van Buuren had a police record—he had been in prison for theft and forgery. He had been married three times—the two earlier wives had left him when they found out about his crimes. But the latest marriage was apparently a happy one.

The suspect's story was unconvincing. He admitted picking Joy Aken up in front of the post office. But then, he insisted, they had sat together talking about domestic problems, and she had told him about her disagreements with her father. According to Van Buuren, he had invited her for a drink, but she had refused; so he went into a hotel on his own, and spent an hour drinking, leaving her in the car. When he went out, the car was missing, and he assumed she had driven away. He had more drinks, then found the car parked nearby. On the floor, in the back, lay the dead body of Joy Aken. Aware that he might be a prime suspect, he drove around with her for most of the night, then hid the body in the culvert near Umtwalumi. The story, understandably, struck the police as absurd. Would a man leave a pretty redhead seated in his car while he went off for a drink on his own?

The problem, they had to admit, was total lack of motive. Joy's parents insisted that she scarcely knew Van Buuren. But a jury found him guilty of the murder, and in 1957 he was hanged—still insisting on his innocence, and expressing the hope that the real murderer would forever have it on his conscience.

The trial brought Nelson Palmer some unwelcome notoriety, and many requests for help in finding missing objects and animals; most of these he refused, being of a retiring disposition (although a few weeks later he located the body of a doctor who had committed suicide). But one interview he gave to a crime reporter a few years later may explain the mystery of why Joy Aken was murdered. Through her clothing, Palmer had sensed that Clarence Van Buuren and Joy Aken were lovers, and that she hoped to marry him. They used to drive to a distant "lovers' lane" to make love. When Joy disappeared, she believed she was pregnant. This could explain why she was upset after his second visit to the office. It would also explain the mutilations to her abdomen—her murderer had hoped to destroy all signs of her pregnancy, which might provide the police with a motive, and in turn, with a suspect. In that respect, at least, he seems to have been successful. If the body had never been found, Van Buuren would almost certainly have been acquitted.

The faculty employed by Nelson Palmer is known in the field of paranormal research as "psychometry," meaning soul-measurement—a word invented by a professor of medicine called Joseph Rodes Buchanan. Palmer was almost fifty years old before he accidentally discovered that he possessed this curious ability. Since then, he had used it sparingly and reluctantly, since it often involved glimpses of tragedy. But, in 1953, he had agreed to use it to try to help the parents of a six-year-old boy, Leon Cohen, who had been kidnapped in Durban. The parents received a ransom demand for $10,000. A friend of the family, who also knew Palmer, persuaded Palmer to see if he could help. Again, he handled underclothing that had been worn by the kidnapped boy the day before his disappearance. He was able to describe a large apartment building with a neon light, which a policeman was able to identify as a new building in downtown Durban. His description of the man and woman who had seized Leon Cohen on his way home from school was so precise that one police officer murmured "John Kramer" as Palmer spoke. He was already known to the police for other criminal enterprises. They located the building, discovered that a man and woman had recently taken a third-floor room, and unceremoniously burst in by kicking open the door. The weeping child was lying on a bed, guarded by John Kramer and his wife Violet. The boy was unharmed. Kramer received fifteen years in gaol, and his wife ten.

The task of tracing a commercial traveller named Johannes Britz in 1955 was more difficult, since Britz had vanished somewhere along the 1200 miles between Durban and Cape Town. When a two-month search had yielded no result, Palmer agreed to try. He handled some of Britz's clothing, then told the police that the man was dead. He could "see" him in a car on a lonely road, and a black man creeping up with a revolver. The black—who had a piece missing from his left ear and only three fingers on his left hand—forced Britz to walk into the brush beside the road, then shot him in the head. The man robbed the body, then drove off in the car, which he abandoned near Cape Town, taking a bus. (The car was found by the police.) Palmer "saw" the murderer enter a large house with wrought-iron gates, owned by a white-haired old man.

Palmer's description of the place where the murder took place—with mountains to the west—was accurate enough for the police to narrow down their research to a particular stretch of road. Spots of oil where a car had been parked led them to search the bushes; police dogs located the decomposed body of the salesman, killed by a gunshot. A long search of Cape Town finally located a big house with wrought iron gates, owned by white-haired old man. He was able to tell them that their description—missing fingers and part of the ear—fitted a Zulu servant named Samson Mabala, who had returned to work from a holiday the day after Britz disappeared. When Mabala saw the police officers, he turned and fled, trying to get rid of a wristwatch and fountain pen as he ran. They proved to have belonged to Johannes Britz. Mabala was hanged in Pretoria Central Prison.

Nelson Palmer was convinced that there was nothing "supernatural" about his faculty of psychometry, and that it had nothing whatever to do with the spirits of the dead. He was simply receiving impressions in the same way that a radio set receives electromagnetic waves. In this respect, he was in total agreement with the man who "discovered" psychometry.

Joseph Rodes Buchanan, who taught medicine at the Eclectic Medical Institute of Covington, Kentucky (and later became its Dean), was still in his twenties when he stumbled on his discovery. Buchanan had been an infant prodigy, studying astronomy and geometry at the age of six and taking up the law when he was twelve. In the introductory chapter of his *Manual of Psychometry* (1885) he describes how this came about.

In his early twenties, Buchanan became fascinated by the mysteries of the human nervous system. He was inclined to accept the view of the famous—or rather, notorious—Dr. Franz Anton Mesmer (who had died in 1815, the year after Buchanan was born) that the whole universe is permeated by some "magnetic fluid," and that the stars and planets cause "tides" in this fluid. These tides, in turn, cause health—or sickness—in human beings, for we are also full of a magnetic fluid, generated by the nerves, which flows around the body. Mesmer called this nerve-fluid "animal magnetism." When it is blocked, we become ill. (In fact, modern practitioners of acupuncture accept an almost identical theory.) Mesmer believed that this magnetic fluid could be moved around the body by means of magnets, and—since all living beings possess "animal magnetism"—by other living beings (including trees). This practice became known as "mesmerism." A pupil of Mesmer's, the Marquis de Puységur, accidentally discovered hypnotism when he was trying to "mesmerize" a young shepherd tied to a "magnetized" tree, and the youth fell into a hypnotic trance.

All this excited the young Buchanan, who was convinced that the world was on the brink of some tremendous medical discoveries. He recognized, of course, that the secret of the "nerve aura" lies in the brain, not in the nervous system, for the brain is its central control box. But in the 1830s, almost nothing was known about the anatomy of the brain. What *was* known was that different parts of the brain seem to govern our instincts—protectiveness, tenderness, aggression, selfishness, and so on. The great physiologist Joseph Gall discovered the basic structures of the brain in the late eighteenth century, and his pupil J. K. Spurzheim went on to try to locate various areas of the brain that were connected with human emotions—destructiveness, love, acquisitiveness, cheerfulness, egotism, and more than twenty others. Spurzheim was convinced that when any of these areas becomes highly developed it causes a bump on the skull, which can be felt with the fingertips. The science of these "bumps" was called phrenology, and it soon became the happy hunting ground of all kinds of quacks and charlatans.

Buchanan studied these new developments with enthusiasm. Nowadays a man who held his beliefs would be shunned by his colleagues as a crank; but in that less sophisticated—and less narrow-minded—era, he was simply regarded as a brilliant young experimenter. He was excited to discover that when a patient was hypnotized, he would respond with the appropriate emotion if various "bumps" were gently touched—anger, love, joy, grief and so on. This notion became known as "phreno-mesmerism" and Buchanan claimed to be its discoverer—with some opposition from other followers of Mesmer and Spurzheim. He was only twenty-four years old when he located what he believed to be the "region of sensibility" in the brain. And it was in this region that he later decided that the power of psychometry resided.

Three years later, Buchanan had a fateful meeting that was to determine the course of his whole life. It was with a newly consecrated bishop of the Episcopal Church named Leonidas Polk, who had abandoned the army in favour of the church, and whose diocese included practically the whole of the American south. (He later became a Civil War general, and was killed at Marietta in 1864.) The bishop happened to mention casually that he could instantly detect brass when he touched it—even in the dark—because it produced an offensive metallic taste in his mouth. Polk allowed Buchanan to feel his "bumps," and Buchanan was delighted to discover that his region of sensibility—governing the physical senses—was abnormally developed. (It is important to note that phrenology—usually dismissed as a pseudo-science—could be astonishingly accurate, and that modern science has verified some of its claims.)

The bishop was so transparently honest that it never occurred to Buchanan to doubt his word—but neither, apparently, did he ask Polk to submit to scientific tests. Instead, he decided to test others and see whether they might also have the same highly developed sensibilities. Any one of his students whose head showed an unusual bump of sensibility was roped in, and Buchanan was gratified to discover that this faculty of "sensing" brass through fingers was relatively common. In fact, his subjects could distinguish various metals, and substances like sugar, salt, pepper and vinegar.

There was nothing very odd about this, as far as Buchanan was concerned. After all, the tongue has precisely this power —so why not the finger-ends, which are equally important for sensing objects? Besides, scientists of the nineteenth century were aware of a power that modern science has forgotten— that of "seeing" with other parts of the body beside the eyes. This sounds absurd, yet precise descriptions of scientific experiments leave no doubt that it happened, and that it could still happen. Dr. Justinus Kerner, whose book *The Seeress of Prevorst* was a nineteenth-century best-seller, described how the "seeress," Friederike Hauffe, could read with her stomach; he made her lie down with closed eyes, placed documents on her bare midriff, and listened to her reading fluently from them. Later in the century, Professor Cesare Lombroso, the founder of scientific criminology, carefully tested a girl who was able to see through the tip of her nose and her left ear, and who could smell through her chin and—later—through her heel.* Modern paranormal research has identified people who can "see" colours through their fingertips, but modern science still regards the case as nonproven. In Buchanan's day it was regarded as a perfectly normal possibility.

Buchanan also observed that people in warm climates could "sense" metals and other substances better than those in cold ones. That was also logical, for in warm climates, we sweat more, and sweat-dampened skin is more sensitive—for example, to wind—than a dry skin. This, says Buchanan, is "a fact which I now consider as well settled and familiar as any other in medical science." And when he imparted this fact to his students, he took care to disarm scepticism by an immediate demonstration. Various chemicals were carefully wrapped in paper, and given to the students to hold. Some of the substances were strong stimulants or narcotics, some emetics, some even cathartics. Out of a class of eighty-six, half the students experienced definite effects from the substances they held—some holding the emetic had hastily to put it down to avoid being sick. (He does not mention what happened to those holding laxatives.) Buchanan got the forty-three who experienced these effects to sign a testimonial, which he includes in his book.

His next thought was that if a mere substance could affect a "sensitive" so strongly, then living people would produce an even stronger effect. He selected his best sensitives, and asked them to try placing the hand on the head or body of another person, then to concentrate on the effect. Again, his sensitives showed by their reaction that they were somehow picking up the feelings of the other person. When the hand was placed on the stomach of a person suffering from a disease of that region, a "morbid impression" was produced. Buchanan claims that he himself became so good at sensing the diseases in patients in this way that he would feel ill after a few minutes and have to break the contact.

One of Buchanan's best sensitives was a man named Charles Inman. He could experience the mental states of patients by lightly running his fingers over there "bumps." But could it have been telepathy? Or even mere auto-suggestion? Bu-

---

*For a longer account of both cases see my *Poltergeist*.

chanan decided to try a simple experiment. He selected from his correspondence files four letters written by people with strong characters, and asked Inman if he could discover anything about the character of the writers by merely holding their letters. The result, he says, surpassed all his expectations; Inman began to talk about the letter-writers with as much insight as if he had known them personally.

Two of the letters were from a surgeon named J. B. Flint and a doctor, Charles Caldwell, who had founded the college at Louisville. These men had once been friends, but had become bitter enemies. Inman immediately sensed their mutual detestation, and their negative emotions affected him so powerfully that he had to put the letters down. Buchanan asked him which of the two he thought would win in a conflict; Inman held up Caldwell's letter and said: "This one would crush the other." It was, in fact, true—Caldwell's efforts had resulted in Flint being removed from his chair of surgery.

One of the other letters was from an eminent politician, and Inman was able to say that he was a man of considerable mental and physical power. What could happen, asked Buchanan, if Dr. Caldwell and the politician met in a head-on collision? Inman shook his head. That would be highly unlikely, he said, because both were too courteous and dignified. Buchanan insisted—suppose the unthinkable happened and they *did* clash? Reluctantly, Inman gave his opinion. The two men would never reach the stage of open hostility, but if some disagreement *did* break out, the politician would probably handle the situation by some tactful rebuke that would immediately check the doctor. Since Buchanan had seen that precise event take place, he was deeply impressed.

But what did it all mean? For a "sensitive" to identify a metal or a chemical—or even someone's illness—was one thing; but surely to pick up someone's character from a letter was quite another? Buchanan did not think so. Photography was a fairly recent invention—the photographs of the period were known as daguerreotypes, after the inventor Daguerre. A daguerreotype, Buchanan reasoned, is nothing more or less than a "light painting," a painting made on sensitive chemicals by the light reflected from its subject. Well, human beings seem to emanate "nerve aura," and this seems to vary according to their strength of character. So why should a sensitive not be able to pick up the nerve aura from letters?

If this reasoning strikes us as specious, it is mainly because Buchanan has missed out a step in the argument. A bloodhound can tell the difference between two human beings by the scent on their clothes. Buchanan regarded sensitives like Charles Inman as human bloodhounds who can pick up the "scent" of the nerve aura. And if his precise character-readings sound improbable, we have to reflect that such processes as sound-recording and television transmission seem equally unlikely. A gramophone record is a series of bumps on a disc of plastic or wax; when a needle travels over these bumps, it reproduces the sounds that originally made the bumps. But any bright child will immediately raise the question: how can a few bumps record *all* the instruments of the orchestra? Surely at least there ought to be a separate row of bumps for each instrument? Sound recording is a preposterous miracle which, in any well-ordered universe, ought not to be allowed to happen. And any scientist in 1842—the year Buchanan performed these experiments with Inman—would have stated with certainty that it *could* not happen. Buchanan's nerve aura daguerreotypes are no more or less absurd than a long playing record.

We may, of course, feel that Buchanan was deceiving himself with his own enthusiasm and excitement. But reading his careful and precise accounts of his experiment, it is hard not to feel that any reasonable person would have found them just as exciting and just as convincing. He describes, for example, how he called upon a clergyman in Boston, the Rev. Kent, whom he describes as having an active mind but a feeble constitution. (Many later experimenters discovered that sick people made the best "sensitives.") Kent thought the whole idea preposterous, but agreed to cooperate. Buchanan tried handing him a letter that had been written to him "by a gentleman of strong character and ardent emotions, immediately after the death of his wife." The Rev. Kent described his sensations in an account of the experiment. After placing his right hand on the folded letter:

> I felt nothing in my frame at the moment, but very soon an increasing, unusual heat in the palm of my hand; this was followed by a prickling sensation, commencing in my fingers' ends and passing gradually over the top of

my hand, and up the outside of my arm. I felt for nearly a minute no change in my mental condition, and stated this. Dr. Buchanan had given no hint of the nature or author of any letter he had with him—and I had no bias or subject on my mind from the day's experience to influence me. A rush of sadness, solemnity and distress suddenly came over me; my thoughts were confused and yet rapid—and I mentioned, there is trouble and sorrow here . . .

Buchanan next handed Mr. Kent a letter by General "Stonewall" Jackson, written to Buchanan's father-in-law during an election campaign "in a spirited style."

My first sensations were sharper and stronger than before, passing up in the same manner from my fingers' ends. In less than a minute my whole arm became violently agitated, and I yielded to an irresistible impulse to give utterance to my thoughts and feelings. A determined, self-confident, daring and triumphant feeling, suggested the language I used, and it seemed to me that I could have gone on triumphantly to the accomplishment of any purpose, however subtle or strong might be the opposition to be overcome. My whole frame was shaken, my strength wrought up to the highest tension, my face and arm burned, and . . . when I retouched the letter, after repeated removals of my hand by Dr. B., in consequence of my great excitement, it was like touching fire, which ran to my very toes.

We can see why Buchanan, watching the clergyman's mood change from scepticism to intense excitement, should have been totally convinced. Further experiments—he carried out literally hundreds in those first two years—deepened his certainty that he had made one of the major scientific discoveries of the age. In his "Original Sketch" of psychometry, written in 1848, he wrote exultantly:

If, then, man, in every act, leaves the impression or daguerreotype of his mental being upon the scenes of his life and subjects of his action, we are by this law furnished with a new clue to the history of our race; and I think it highly probable that, by the application of this principle, the chasms of history may be supplied, and a glimpse may be obtained of unrecorded ages and nations whose early history is lost in darkness. The ancient manuscripts, paintings and other works of art . . . are doubtless still instinct with the spirit that produced them, and capable of revealing to psychometric exploration the living realities with which they were once connected. At present these relics are barren of significance. Their hidden meaning lies waiting for the future explorer, as the hieroglyphics of Egypt awaited the arrival of Champollion . . .

The Past is entombed in the Present! The world is its own enduring monument; and that which is true of its physical, is likewise true of its mental career. The discoveries of psychometry will enable us to explore the history of man, as those of geology enable us to explore the history of the earth. There are mental fossils for the psychologist, as well as mineral fossils for the geologist . . . Aye, the mental telescope is now discovered, which may pierce the depths of the past, and bring us in full view of all the grand and tragic passages of history . . .

It is easy to sympathize with his excitement. He was no mad enthusiast or religious crank, but a respectable man of science. If he was correct, as he had not the slightest doubt that he was, then his name would rank with the greatest discoverers and explorers in human history. It was surely impossible that his findings could fail to arouse wide interest . . . The unfortunate Buchanan had no way of knowing that history was about to make him the butt of one of its cruellest jokes.

Before we proceed with the story of psychometry, it is important to consider an interesting parallel development on the other side of the Atlantic; an idea that, by that revolutionary year 1848, had already made its discoverer famous. It was called: the Odic force.

Karl Reichenbach was one of those dynamos who seem born for wealth and success. Born in 1788, he had flung himself into the bold and venturesome spirit of the age, and built his first ironworks when he was twenty-six. A sugar beet factory followed; then there were blast furnaces in Moravia and a steelworks at Ternitz in Austria. He purchased vast estates, including a castle. Turning to the study of tar derivatives, he discovered paraffin, creosote and a blue aniline dye.

He was approaching fifty when his business partner, Count Hugo zu Salm, died, and Reichenbach found himself involved in tiresome legal battles with the count's sons. He won; but the litigation filled him with longing to turn his back on the world of quarrelsome human beings. When, in 1839, he was created a baron (*Freiherr*), he decided to retire to his castle at Reisenberg, near Vienna, and plunge into the peace of scientific research. But he was no longer concerned with organic chemistry. He now felt free to pursue an old dream, which was connected with the mysteries of the human mind.

When he was in his early twenties, Reichenbach had been excited by the researches of the poet Goethe into the nature of light. Goethe had decided that Newton was wrong in believing that white light is made up of the seven colours of the spectrum—a conclusion he reached by looking at a white wall through a prism and observing that the rainbow colours only appeared around its edges. If white light was really multicoloured, why did not the whole wall turn into a rainbow? Goethe decided that colours are created by the mechanism of the eye, pointing out that if you rub your eyes vigorously in the dark, you see vivid flashes of colour. Goethe's results had been dismissed by scientists as muddle-headed; but Reichenbach suspected he might be right after all. If so, it would be one more proof that the human mind is more complex than we think. And it was this possibility that fascinated Reichenbach.

Like most other scientists in Europe in 1839, he was interested in mesmerism and hypnotism (usually known as "somnambulism"). It is also certain that he was aware of a mystery that was still causing speculation all over Europe: that of the youth called Caspar Hauser, who had been murdered by an unknown assailant a mere seven years earlier. Hauser had first walked into the town of Nuremberg on Whit Monday 1828, apparently unable to speak a word. His feet were bleeding, and proved to be so white and tender that it was obvious he had never walked on them. A letter he was carrying, addressed to an army captain, stated that he was a foundling who wished to serve his king and country. He wrote his name on a piece of paper in crude and childish letters: Caspar Hauser. And it soon became clear that the unfortunate youth—who seemed to be about sixteen—had spent his whole life in darkness, chained to a bed in some unknown dungeon. He had no memory of who he was; his mind was totally unformed. Yet he proved to be intelligent and, under the tutelage of a local schoolmaster, soon learned to speak.

Because he had been raised under such abnormal conditions, Caspar proved to have an extraordinary sensitivity. His sight and hearing were abnormally acute; he could see in the dark, and demonstrated his ability by reading aloud from the Bible in a completely black room. His sense of smell was so keen that he began to vomit if coffee, beer or any other strong drink was in the same room. The mere smell of wine literally made him drunk. The static electricity in the air during a thunderstorm caused him intense suffering. His teacher, Mr. Daumer, soon discovered that Hauser could instantly detect copper or brass as soon as he came into a room, even if it had been carefully hidden. Moreover, he could distinguish between various metals—exactly like Buchanan's subjects—simply by holding his hands above the cloth that concealed them.

Hauser was also something of a human magnet—another phenomenon that has never been explained by science. Some people can build up such a powerful electric charge that anyone who touches them receives a severe shock. Hauser was not actually "electric," but he attracted metal, and when he was on a horse, the stirrups stuck to his feet. He responded strongly to magnets; the north pole gave him a different sensation from the south pole, and he seemed to perceive different colours at either end.

In 1829 an unknown man entered Daumer's house when Hauser was alone and stabbed him. He recovered; but in 1832, the same man stabbed him again in the public gardens, and this time it proved fatal. The criminologist Anselm von Feuerbach published a paper in which he argued convincingly that Hauser was a prince of the house of Baden, a brother of the queen of Sweden who, for reasons of political intrigue, had been kept alive by those who were ordered to murder him. (His brothers, Feuerbach maintains, *were* murdered soon after birth.) Feuerbach was bitterly attacked for his views—for in those days of petty princelings, royalty was regarded as above criticism—and died soon after Caspar Hauser's murder. The mystery still remains unsolved.

Whether because of the Hauser case, or because of some more general interest in abnormal sensitivity, Reichenbach began to repeat some of Mesmer's experiments with magnets —which, according to Mesmer, could cause small tides in the universal ether, and move it around the body. Then, in 1844, he heard about a girl named Mary Novotny, daughter of a tax collector in Vienna, who suffered from general debility and cataleptic attacks—like Justinus Kerner's famous patient, Friederike Hauffe, "the Seeress of Prevorst." Herr Novotny was asked if he would take a large magnet—no doubt supplied by Reichenbach—into his daughter's bedroom in the middle of the night, and see if she responded to it. The results were far more striking than he had expected. Around the poles of the magnet, the girl saw a fiery glow, a kind of aurora borealis, reddish-yellow from the south pole and bluish-green from the north. Could this have been auto-suggestion? Reichenbach got his assistant to go into the next room and point the magnet at her through the wall; she immediately detected its presence. Blindfolded, she could tell when the armature was moved from the end of the magnet. And, like Caspar Hauser, Miss Novotny proved to be a kind of magnet herself—at least, her hand stuck to the magnet as if her skin was made of iron.

Two months later, Reichenbach heard about another sick girl, Angelica Sturmann. He had, meanwhile, been experimenting with "magnetized" crystals, and found that they also affected sensitives. But for his first experiment with Miss Sturmann, he took a large piece of ordinary mountain crystal. He hid this in a dark room, then asked for the girl to be brought in. Within moments she had pointed out the crystal; she said that it was glowing and emitting sparks, and that a blue light was streaming out of its peak. When Reichenbach turned it upside down, she saw a kind of red and yellow smoke around the bottom.

His tests with sensitives revealed that they enjoyed holding their fingers in the blue light, which they found cool and pleasant, while the reddish-yellow light produced a warm, slightly nauseating, sensation. Metals like brass and copper produced this same unpleasant sensation; so did quicksilver, which seemed to explain why many of his "sick sensitives" could not stand mirrors. When he threw a spectrum on a wall with a prism, and placed glasses of water in the blue and the yellow light, the sensitives could tell the difference; the "blue" water tasted faintly lemony, the "yellow" bitter and sickly —one sensitive vomited after tasting it.

His sensitives could also see plants and flowers in the dark—they seemed to be surrounded by a dim light. In fact, so were animals and human beings. And when a bell was rung, its vibrations produced a colour which gradually died away. The light from human beings was dim and smoky, except around the hands. These had clear colours streaming from the finger-tips—blue from the right hand, yellowy-red from the left. A blindfolded sensitive could tell which hand he was touching her with according to whether it produced a cool or a warm sensation. "You see," remarks Reichenbach, "that a man is polarized from right to left . . . in the same way as a crystal"—anticipating one of the most interesting discoveries of modern brain physiology.

All this seemed to support Mesmer's conclusions about animal magnetism; but, oddly enough, Reichenbach dis-agreed. This was surely not some "etheric" fluid that pervad-ed all space, but some mysterious energy that was common to magnets, crystals and living creatures. Reichenbach called this energy "Od" or "Odyle," and it became generally known as the "Odic force."

Here it becomes possible to see the error in Reichenbach's reasoning. Our senses are all tuned to different kinds of energy; our ears vibrate to sound, our eyes to colour, our skins to warmth. The range of our senses is limited, apparently by survival needs; it would be of no particular use to us to be able to see the sun's ultra violet rays, or the infra-red radiation from a hot stove. It sounds very much as if Caspar Hauser's years in darkness developed his senses to a point where he could perceive far beyond the normal range, just as some of Reichenbach's sick sensitives could see the vibration of a bell or a violin. They were not perceiving "Od," but ordinary energy. The force that animates living beings seems to have little in common with heat and light, although we now know that all living creatures generate a weak electric field—which its discoverer, Harold Burr, called the "L-field." Whatever the nature of this life-force, it is certainly not Reichenbach's "Od." Reichenbach, like Goethe, had been led astray by his enthusiasm and his desire to find some simple uniting principle behind all phenomena. He would have done better to be con-tented with multiplicity.

Nevertheless, by the year 1848 Reichenbach had achieved European celebrity. His "Od" theory was regarded as the latest scientific advance, and most scientists were willing to preserve an open mind about it—Reichenbach's descriptions of the precautions he took against auto-suggestion were so impressive. Others were beginning to take up his ideas and repeat his experiments. It seems a reasonable assumption that, even if Buchanan had never discovered psychometry, one of Reichenbach's followers would have done so.

But the year that saw so many political revolutions in Europe saw the beginning of another kind of revolution in America, and the end of Buchanan and Reichenbach's hopes of being taken seriously.

During the last days of March 1848, the Fox family of Arcadia, New York, was kept awake for several nights running by loud rapping noises. John Fox and his wife Margaret had been in the house for less than six months, and the previous tenant—so they later discovered—had left it because he had been disturbed by noises. It was a windy March, and at first they were not unduly bothered. But on the night of Friday 31 March, the bangings and rattlings were so loud that John Fox made a thorough search of the house, watched by his two daughters, Margaret, fifteen, and Kate, twelve. He tried shaking the window sashes, to see if they could be responsible, and Kate observed that as her father rattled the windows, the sounds seemed to reply, like an echo. Mrs. Fox was convinced that she had heard footsteps walking downstairs on the previous night. Now, worn out by lack of sleep, they decided to go to bed at about eight o'clock and try to get a good night's rest.

All four slept in the same room, and the noises soon began again. Kate tried snapping her fingers in imitation of the raps; then she said perkily: "Mr. Splitfoot, do as I do," and clapped her hands. The raps promptly imitated her. Margaret, just as unconcerned, said: "No, do as I do and began to count as she slowly clapped. The raps imitated her. The children suddenly remembered that tomorrow would be April Fool's Day, and concluded that someone was playing a joke. Mrs. Fox thought of a test; she asked the unknown knocker to rap her children's ages; it did so correctly, convincing her that this was not some mischievous neighbour's child. She asked: "Is it a human being who makes these raps?" There was no sound. "Is it a spirit?" There were two raps. "If it is an injured spirit, make two raps." The two raps were so loud that the house shook.

By questions, Mrs. Fox obtained the information that the knocker was thirty-one—or had been at the time of his death—and that he had been murdered in the house and buried in the cellar. She asked if the "ghost" had any objection to her calling in the neighbours. It said no. Within an hour, the house was crowded with neighbours who listened breathlessly to the noises. Most of them did not dare to venture into the bedroom. One of the braver participants, a Mr. William Duesler, not only went into the bedroom, but continued to question the knocker. He was told, by a code of knocks, that the man had been murdered in the east room of the house, by having his throat cut; this had happened five years earlier, and the murderer was the man who then lived in the house, a Mr. Bell. The murder had been committed for the $500 carried by the man, who was a pedlar. It also rapped out Duesler's own age correctly, that of his wife, and of various other people in the neighborhood.

By means of an alphabetical code, the "spirit" later identified itself as Charles B. Rosma. A maid named Lucretia Pulver, who had worked for the Bells, could recall the pedlar's arrival, and how she was sent off to her parents' home for the night. When she came back the next day, she was told the pedlar had left.

Mr. and Mrs. Bell had moved to Lyon, New York, and he indignantly denied the accusation, producing a testimonial to his good character signed by his neighbours. The spirit had already prophesied that he would never be brought to justice.

The Foxes tried digging in the cellar, but at a depth of a few feet the hole began to flood with water. At a later date, when the water had subsided, they tried again. Five feet down they encountered a plank, and underneath this, in quicklime and charcoal, human hair and a few bones. But there was not enough of these to justify a charge of murder against Mr. Bell. It was to be another fifty-six years before, in November 1904, the collapse of a wall in the cellar revealed another wall a few feet behind it. This time, digging between the two walls revealed most of a human skeleton, and a pedlar's tin box. It looked as if someone had dug up the body from its original burial place, buried it close to the wall, then built another wall to confuse searchers.

The Foxes soon found their house uninhabitable. From the east bedroom, there were nightly sounds of a death struggle with gurgling noises, and the sound of a body being dragged across the floor. Mrs. Fox's hair turned white. The two girls were sent to stay elsewhere—one with her brother David at his home in Auburn, one with her sister Leah in Rochester. The manifestations followed both of them and made life unpleasant. A lodger at Leah's house—a man named Calvin Brown—took an unsympathetic view of the unknown spirit, which began throwing things at him. When they tried to pray, the spirit stuck pins in them. The manifestations had now become typical poltergeist phenomena, as recorded down the ages.* Poltergeists have been called the knockabout comedians of the spirit world; they are noisy, mischievous and sometimes—as in this case—spiteful; but they seldom do any actual harm.

At this point, a visitor named Isaac Post decided to try communicating with the spirit. His first question brought a barrage of raps, as if it was relieved that someone had finally decided to behave sensibly. Soon afterwards, there followed a message that stated: "Dear friends, you must proclaim this truth to the world. This is the dawning of a new era; you must not try to conceal it any longer. God will protect you and good spirits will watch over you." After this, the communications continued, but they ceased to be violent. Tables moved, guitars were played by unseen fingers, which also touched people lightly, and objects were transported around the room. The Fox family obediently passed on the message to all who would listen. The result was that on 14 November 1849, the first "spiritualist" meeting took place in the Corinthian Hall in Rochester. Margaret and Kate soon found themselves famous. But they were inevitably accused of fraud; on one occasion they were almost lynched. Other members of the spiritualist circle discovered that they were also "mediums"—the name coined to designate one who acted as intermediary between the physical world and the "spirit world."

There were those who said that all this was merely a revival of witchcraft, and they were not entirely wrong. Throughout

*See my book *Poltergeist*.

the ages, witches and "magicians" have produced manifestations very similar to those of the spiritualist mediums; in past centuries, mediums were known as "scryers," meaning, "descryers of spirits." Dr. John Dee, the famous Elizabethan magician, wrote a lengthy work *A True and Faithful Relation of What Passed Between Dr. John Dee and Some Spirits* (1659), describing the spirits who communicated through his scryer, Edward Kelley. Witches throughout the ages have claimed to perform their magical acts through the intervention of spirits of the dead (hence the word "necromancy"). Whatever our views on the existence of these spirits, the one thing that seems clear is that the manifestations seldom take place without the presence of a medium or scryer—the common assumption being that the medium somehow provides the necessary energy. Poltergeists are usually associated with children or adolescents, who play the part of unconscious mediums; as we have seen, there were two such in the Fox household.

So, in historical perspective, we can see that spiritualism bore a close relation to the witchcraft that had caused so much bloodshed and persecution in earlier centuries, and may infer that some of the furious resistance it aroused was not based upon entirely rational considerations.

The career of the poet Browning provides a case in point. In 1864, Browning published the poem "Mr. Sludge the Medium," a scathing attack on spiritualism. Mr. Sludge, the fake medium, was based on a man Browning detested, Daniel Dunglas Home—one of the few mediums of the period against whom, in fact, there had never been any imputation of fraud. Browning remained all his life an impenitent sceptic. Yet in the 1850s, he had been confronted with personal proof that "clairvoyants" are not always frauds. He had been introduced in Florence to an Italian nobleman, Count Giunasi, who professed to have powers of "second sight." Browning handed the count one of a pair of gold cufflinks he was wearing. The count held it for a moment, then said: "There is something here that cries in my ear: Murder, murder!" Browning was impressed. The links had belonged to his uncle, who had been murdered by his own slaves on the island of St. Kitts, in the West Indies; he had been wearing the links in his nightshirt at the time of his death. Browning went on to ask Giunasi about the situation of the murder, and again had to acknowledge the accuracy of the count's statement that it took place in a bedroom. But Browning's emotional prejudice was too strong to allow this to influence his attitude to spiritualism. Years later, asked about this experience by a psychical researcher, Walter Franklin Prince, Browning replied that he was convinced that Giunasi had "read" the facts about the links from his face and eyes—failing to explain how the notion of a bedroom can be conveyed by a facial expression.

By the early 1850s, spiritualism had swept across America, and even reached Europe. At seances, musical instruments played in mid-air, tables floated up to the ceiling, and ghostly figures materialized and addressed the audience. Almost without exception, scientists took the attitude that it was all a fraud. So when, in 1852, Buchanan published his first accounts of psychometry in his own *Journal of Man,* and Reichenbach brought out the definitive edition of his book on the Odic force, they were already too late. They were quickly tarred with the same brush as the spiritualists, and nothing they said could persuade scientists to take them seriously. To open the door even as wide as a crack might admit hordes of occultist lunatics into the sacred halls of science. This is why two of the most remarkable discoverers of the century spent the rest of their lives in relative oblivion.

2

The Unknown Guest

BUT BUCHANAN HAD at least one enthusiastic ally.

His name was William Denton. He was nine years Buchanan's junior, and was the professor of geology at the University of Boston. In 1853, he came upon Buchanan's original papers on psychometry, published in the *Journal of Man*—the second of which contained the remarkable passage about the past being entombed in the present. Buchanan has a fine paragraph about geology:

> And why should not the world be filled with the monuments and unwritten records of its past history? . . . The geologist finds, in the different strata of the earth, in its curiously mingled and irregular structure, and in the fossil remains which it conceals in its bosom, the history of its various changes of surface, and of the antediluvian races of animals which have long been extinct. The huge saurian monsters, which he portrays from their fossil relics, rise before the eye as incredible chimeras. And over this fertile region, now occupied by prosperous States, he revives, by the magic power of science, the antediluvian seas and their strange inhabitants . . .

Denton was carried away by Buchanan's daguerreotype theory. He also liked an experiment performed by G. H. Lewes, husband of the novelist George Eliot. Lewes laid a wafer on a surface of polished metal, and breathed on it. Then he allowed his breath to evaporate, removed the wafer, and breathed on the plate again. The image of the wafer appeared on the surface. It was still there months later. It even remained there when he carefully brushed the metal surface with a camelhair brush. Is it not conceivable, Denton reasoned, that nature is full of such daguerreotypes of past events?

His sister, Anne Cridge, seemed a suitable subject for experiment, since she was "highly impressible." Denton began by trying Buchanan's experiments with letters. Mrs. Cridge revealed herself to be an excellent psychometrist; "She saw and described the writings of letters he was examining, and their surroundings, telling at times even the colour of hair and eyes correctly."

The next step was to try her with a geological specimen. Denton selected a piece of limestone which he had picked up near Quindaro, Kansas, on the Missouri River; it was full of tiny fossil shells. His sister was not told anything about the specimen, and it was wrapped in paper so she could not tell what it was. Her response was:

It seems to me there is a deep hole here. Oh, what shells! small shells; so many. I see water; it looks like a river running along. What a high hill almost perpendicular; it seems as if the water had cut it in two; it is not so high on the other side. The hill is covered with sand and gravel.

This was an excellent beginning. Denton admitted that, as far as his memory served him, it was a very accurate description. "This piece of rock had taken in the pictures of the turbid Missouri that swept past it, the hill that hung over it, and the country in general around it, and, to the eye of the psychometer, they became apparently as plainly visible as to a spectator on the spot."

His wife, Elizabeth Denton, also proved to be a good psychometer. When he handed her a piece of quartz from Panama, she received an impression of a huge insect, with antennae nearly a foot long, resting its head against a quartz rock, and could see a snake coiled in the wiry grass. She remarked that the country seemed much warmer than North America, with tropical vegetation.

These experiments were encouraging. But the result of the next was spectacular. He handed his sister a fragment of volcanic lava from Kilauea, on Hawaii, wrapped in paper. Mrs. Cridge had an impression of an ocean, with ships sailing on it, and could tell that it was an island. Then she saw "an ocean of fire pouring over a precipice and boiling as it pours. I see it flow into the ocean, and the water boils intensely." The vision was so real that it shattered her nerves, and the feeling of fear remained for the next hour. Denton knew that the piece of lava had, in fact, been ejected in the eruption of 1840, so the vision of ships was probably accurate.

At this point, Denton took a precaution which reveals that he was a genuine scientist, determined to rule out all possibility of auto-suggestion. He tried wrapping several specimens in separate sheets of paper, then mixing them up, so he had no idea which was which. Then he handed his wife one of them. She had a vision of a volcano, with molten lava flowing down its side. "The specimen must be lava," said Mrs. Denton, and she was right.

Denton's precaution seems to us merely common sense. But we have to bear in mind that in 1853, telepathy was virtually unknown. The word itself was not even invented until 1882 (by F.W.H. Myers, one of the founders of the Society for Psychical Research). Before that, most psychic faculties were bundled vaguely together under the general heading of "clairvoyance," which included the ability to see ghosts, glimpse what was happening elsewhere, and foretell the future. Once the Society for Psychical Research began to investigate telepathy, it became clear that it is probably the commonest of psychic faculties. (Most married couples, for example, have had experiences of starting to say the same thing at the same time.) Professor Gilbert Murray, a determined rationalist, was so good at it that he treated it as a party game, leaving the room while the company thought up a subject from life or literature, then coming back in and telling them what they had decided upon. ("Jane Eyre at school standing on a stool and being called a liar by Mr. Brocklehurst . . .") By 1949, telepathy was so widely accepted, even by scientists, that Sir Alister Hardy could say, in his presidential address to the zoological section of the British Association: "I believe that no one who examines the evidence with an unbiased mind can reject it"—a statement that would have brought catcalls half a century earlier.

When we consider many of Buchanan's experiments, we

often feel that the results could be explained by telepathy—particularly when the psychometer is his own wife. With Denton, this is ruled out from the early experiments, since he usually took the precaution of making sure that he himself had no idea what was wrapped in the paper.

Denton was understandably elated. "From the first dawn of light upon this infant globe, when round its cradle the steamy curtains hung, to this moment, Nature has been busy photographing every moment." It was—and is—a perfectly reasonable hypothesis. We now know that matter and energy are the same thing; matter is frozen energy. Energy from space—light, heat, cosmic rays—falls upon us in a continuous cosmic hail, knocking electrons from the surface of everything it strikes. Light falling on a sheet of metal "evaporates" electrons as sunlight evaporates a sheet of water, producing the "photo-electric effect," an electric current. So there can be no doubt that everything that happens in daylight *is* "photographed" by the surrounding objects. But the "film" is double- and treble- and multiple-exposed, so that even if it could be developed, it would be useless. In a science fiction novel, *Before the Dawn* (1934), the mathematician E. T. Bell invented a "light decoder" that could sort out the various exposures and then "play back" the resulting record of the ages like a film projector; since then, the invention of the computer has made the notion rather more plausible, since sorting out the exposures *would* be largely a matter of computer analysis. But the human brain is thousands of times more complex than any computer; so the assumption of Buchanan and Denton—that the mind has its own inbuilt decoder—is easier to accept today than it was in 1860.

Denton went to considerable lengths to rule out self-deception. For example, he would try the same specimen on the psychometer more than once, with an interval of weeks in between, to see whether it produced the same impressions. From a fragment of bone obtained from a piece of limestone, Elizabeth Denton's first impression was:

. . . a long, smooth beach . . . On that beach are quadrupeds of some kind. One is large, heavy, thick-skinned, dark coloured and thick necked; the flesh is not fibrous, but soft. Its head is broad, and horns rise up from its nose. I see another with a long neck and a head nearly as large as a sheep's, but in appearance like that of a snake, though it is a quadruped.

This sounds like a plesiosaur, the species to which the fabled Loch Ness monster is supposed to belong. She was impressed by rocks covered with bright green moss.

Denton tried the same specimen on her a month later, making sure she had no idea of what it was (although this time, he took no precaution against telepathy). Again she saw water, with water weeds that looked like moss; but this time she saw birdlike creatures with membranous wings in the shallow water. We know that pterodactyls fed on fish, so it seems conceivable they spent part of their time in the water, like seagulls.

On other occasions, Denton himself had no idea of what the psychometrist was examining; he would cover the table-top with various minerals and fossils, and the psychometrist would pick up one of them with closed eyes. When she described in detail a scene under the sea, the specimen proved to be a piece of Silurian coral. A tiny fragment of a mastodon's tooth, so small that it could not be recognized, immediately produced an impression of "a perfect monster with heavy legs, unwieldy head, and very large body." Various fragments of limestone produced magnificent and detailed descriptions of prehistoric landscapes. A small fragment of chamois horn produced a fine description of the Alps. A fossil from Cuba brought a description of a tropical island with some accurate geographical details. A piece of Indian pottery brought an immediate image of Red Indians. Fragments of meteorites —tried on several psychometrists—always brought visions of empty space, sometimes of the earth seen from a great height. A pebble from a glacier produced an immediate impression of being frozen in a great depth of ice. A fragment of rock from Table Rock, Niagara, brought an impression of looking down from a mountain into a "deep hole" with something boiling up from it—the psychometrist thought it was a hot spring with steam, although she could hear the noise of a torrent, and see the Niagara River. Later in the experiment she recognized that "the water makes that smoke; it looks like a rain-cloud or mist." A fragment of stalactite brought a picture of "pieces of rock hanging down; they look like icicles."

When Denton tried his wife with a piece of hornstone

brought from the Mount of Olives, the result was a description of a dry land with low rocky hills, "so poor . . . they could not raise enough to eat," and horses, sheep and goats. She then went on to describe a large church, and a city with a wall and iron gates. Finally, by inference, she guessed she was looking at Jerusalem.

On a later occasion, Denton took the same fragment out of a box of mixed specimens without knowing what it was. Again, there followed a description of a walled city and a barren landscape, with the comment: "I think the Bible might have been written here." It was only when she had finished that Denton looked more closely at the rock and identified it as the hornstone he had used previously.

As the psychics became more skilled, they began to be able to distinguish different periods in the history of the specimens. One of these cases is among the most impressive Denton recorded. He handed his sister a fragment of mosaic pavement that had been dug up in 1760 and brought to England. It came from the villa of the Roman orator Cicero. Denton was hoping for a description of Cicero—or at least, of some ancient Romans. Instead, Mrs. Cridge began by describing a prehistoric forest with a beast like a mastodon. Denton asked her to come forward to more modern times. Now she saw a country house standing in its own grounds, and an old man in knee breeches and a swallow tailed coat. This sounds like the house to which the fragment had been brought in 1760.

Denton decided to try it on his wife. She immediately sensed that her sister-in-law had already psychometrized it. Then she described a garden with a cascade which she felt to be landscaped ("there is human influence about this"). She went on to describe a sick-room scene in the house. All this was rather disappointing.

Some days later, Denton decided to try her again. This time she immediately saw a distinctly Roman scene, with a large building with pillars and steps leading up to it. In a room with uncomfortable furniture ("if furniture it can be called") the walls were hung with crimson velvet. She saw lines of helmeted soldiers, then a "fleshy man with a broad face and blue eyes." He wore a "dress like a gown" (presumably a toga). "He is majestic, yet has a good deal of geniality about him too. He regards himself as superior, and withdraws from others

. . . It seems to me that he has something to do with those troops . . ."

Cicero *had* been a successful military commander at one point in his career; but he was tall and thin. Denton concluded that the man might have been Cicero, and ended his notes on the experiment ". . . at all events, we have a description in harmony with the time and people of the days of Cicero."

By the time he came to republish the book—with an additional two volumes—in 1888, he had made an important discovery. The previous owner of Cicero's house had been the dictator Sulla, and his wife's description was altogether closer to what we know of Sulla (who died in 78 BC). He was one of the few Roman dictators who succeeded in dying in his bed. While some of his measures were ruthless and unpopular, he was known as a convivial man who was fond of his friends. His soldiers called him "lucky Sulla." Mrs. Denton had apparently focused on Sulla rather than Cicero—an indication (like Mrs. Cridge's eighteenth-century garden) that Denton's expectations had little or no influence on the psychometers. (In fact, most modern paragnosts would say that if they want to receive telepathic impressions, then they have to focus on the person whose mind they want to read; if they want psychometric impressions, they concentrate on the object.)

When Denton handed his wife a fragment of the Porcelain Tower, near Peking, he knew nothing whatever about it, except that it came from a place called the Porcelain Tower in China. His wife described a place like a temple, with massive walls and large urns; she saw a bell-shaped roof and spire. After writing down her description, Denton checked in the *Iconographic Encyclopedia* to find out what the Porcelain Tower was used for (for all he knew, it was simply a monument like the leaning tower of Pisa). He discovered that it was a temple, with walls twelve feet thick.

If we can make the assumption that Denton's own knowledge of the objects had no telepathic influence on the psychometrist, then the experiments he describes in the first volume of *The Soul of Things* are stunningly impressive. Again and again they were able to pin down the place from which the object came. A piece of a limestone slab from Nineveh brought an impression of a vast temple; a Greek coin (kept unseen) brought a detailed description of the mint; a

piece of curtain from the House of Representatives brought a
large council chamber, and an impression of some members
talking glibly and superficially; a piece of sandstone from
Melrose Abbey in Scotland brought a description of an abbey
with arched doorways, Gothic windows and an aisle. Three
months later, Mrs. Denton was handed the fragment a second
time—with no knowledge that she had handled it before.
Again she saw arches and a "place of worship," but this time
with some conference going on there. "These people are ignorant and bigoted." A check with an encyclopedia revealed
that Melrose Abbey was "usually involved in the rancorous
events of border feud and international war." ("Ignorant and
bigoted" is an admirable description of the Scottish religious
temperament of earlier centuries.) A piece of mosaic from a
Roman bath brought a detailed description of a Roman bath,
with an atmosphere of "gaiety and voluptuousness."

A piece of mosaic from Pompeii brought an interesting
description of an ancient town with narrow streets, and a
populace in the grip of war fever; Denton had hoped for some
mention of the destruction of Pompeii. But a piece of volcanic
rock from Pompeii brought far more satisfying results. It was
the size of a small bean, and the psychometer was not allowed
to see it. (Denton does not explain how he did this, but presumably it was wrapped in paper or cloth.) Mrs. Denton saw
coloured figures on a wall—frescoes—and observed that the
building overlooked the sea. Out of the window, she could
look towards the mountain top, and see smoke and cinders rising up in a column. The black cloud of dust was spreading
across the countryside. From a situation higher up the mountain she was able to observe the eruption. "I feel the influence
of human terror that I cannot describe." The land below finally became a desert of cinders. Watching crowds fleeing
from Pompeii (in fact, most of the population escaped before
the final catastrophe) she is surprised that it resembles a
modern town more than she had expected.

One interesting observation was that the volcano had also
vomited water. In fact, Pompeii was engulfed by a kind of
mud, not by molten lava. Bodies found encased in the hard-
ened material were unscorched. A description of the eruption
by Pliny the Younger describes a tree-like column of smoke
rising from the volcano, then spreading out like branches—or
a mushroom-cloud—which then descended and covered the

town. Elizabeth Denton's description was startlingly close.

Almost a decade later, Denton returned to the subject of Pompeii. By now, his son Sherman was in his mid-teens; he had been practising psychometry since he was a child, and was in some ways more sensitive than his mother. The tests Denton conducted occupy more than fifty pages of his second volume, and they provide a remarkably rich and complex picture of life in Pompeii.

Sherman's first session—with a piece of plaster from the "House of Sallust"—immediately brought one remarkable "hit." Over a doorway, Sherman "saw" a painting of two winged children drawing a cart with another winged child riding in it. Denton later discovered an engraving of the painting in a book on Pompeii (which, he insists, neither he nor Sherman saw before the test), and he reproduces it in his text.

When Sherman spoke of wide streets, Denton was dubious; most streets in Pompeii were hardly six feet across. But he later discovered that the House of Sallust was not in the residential section, but on a square, in an area with wide streets. Sherman described a Pompeiian boat with a prow like a swan's head and neck. Denton found engravings from nearby Herculaneum (also engulfed in the eruption) of the *cheniscus*, a birdlike head and neck attached to the prow of Roman vessels.

Sherman also comments: "The labouring people seem to hate the rich. Where there is a number of them together, the rich pass them quickly, and seem to regard them as a man would a snake." Denton makes no attempt to verify this statement. But from a modern book, *Pompeii and Herculaneum* (1960) by Marcel Brion, we learn that the walls of Pompeii contained such graffiti as "The city is too rich" and "I propose a share-out of the public wealth among the inhabitants." The attitude of the rich must have added fuel to this feeling of social injustice; in the hall of the House of Vedius Siricus there was an inscription, *Salve Lucrum*—"Hail, Profit!" It also, comments Brion, meant "Welcome to money," addressed as a welcome to other moneyed people who came to the house. The Pompeiians, it becomes clear, took money-making very seriously indeed. In her earlier examination of a fragment from Pompeii, Mrs. Denton had commented on the difference she sensed between the Pompeiians and the ancient Egyptians: that for the Egyptians, religion was inherent in their way of life, while for the Pompeiians, it was largely a matter of forms and observances. But the wealthy had statues of Mercury in their houses to bring luck to their business and ward off evil spirits that might harm it. "Hail, profit!"

Another of Sherman's comments was that women seemed to play a prominent part in the life of Pompeii; Brion remarks that in Pompeii the women took a hand in business; even a rich woman advertised that she had shops to let.

Sherman's description of a theatrical performance makes it sound more like a circus with clowns and acrobats, and makes no mention of the kind of things a modern reader would expect—comedies by Plautus, Statius and Terence, Greek tragedies and so on. Denton remarks that his son's description of acrobats and comics sounds very modern. But Marcel Brion comments that the favourite form of dramatic entertainment at this time was the *atellanae,* popular farces that took their name from their town of origin, Atella; originally intended to relax the audience after performance of tragedies, they became so popular that they were performed on their own. Brion says of these performances: "they might be compared to music hall numbers of a rather low level, interspersed with dancing, clowning, obscenities, feats of skill and athletic exhibitions, the whole ending with a procession of nude girls." Apart from the nude girls (which Denton would no doubt have censored out) this is a fairly accurate summary of Sherman Denton's lengthy description of a theatrical performance in Pompeii.

The descriptions of Pompeii are certainly the highlight of Denton's second volume; but there are other impressive things. By this time, Denton had become aware of the possibility of mind-reading, although he was inclined to discount it simply because he had noticed that his own expectations failed to influence the "visions" of the psychometrist. But he devised one interesting experiment to show that the visions could be just as accurate when all possibility of mind-reading had been excluded. He had made the interesting discovery that the psychometer could look at a map, then close his eyes and experience a sensation of flying through the air until he came to the place he had seen. This faculty is known as "travelling clairvoyance," and has been the subject of a great deal of modern research (for example, at Stanford University in the mid-1970s where, under laboratory conditions, the psychic

Ingo Swann was able to demonstrate his ability to travel mentally to other places and describe accurately what was happening there). They chose at random the island of Socotra in the Gulf of Aden, and Mrs. Denton was first asked to describe it. She stated that it was a rocky island, "almost a rock in the sea," with one coast high and mountainous and the other—the inhabited coast—low. There seemed to be two types of people. Those inland, the natives, were poor, and "there seems to be a wandering disposition about them." Near the coast the people were "yellowish" and engaged more in business. All this proved (from an encyclopedia article on Socotra) to be remarkably accurate. The geographical description is precise. The population consisted of two types—the original inhabitants, Bedouins, who lived inland and who were nomadic, and Arab traders and agriculturalists who lived near the coast.

By comparison, Sherman Denton's description sounds vague and inaccurate; he described it as a green island without mountains (in fact, the mountains are five thousand feet high), and continued with descriptions of natives who lived a hand-to-mouth existence. But the fact that Denton includes this relative failure is a testimony to his honesty.

These first two volumes of *The Soul of Things* are both impressive and exciting; with their long descriptions of past ages, they read almost like a novel. Denton was as convinced as Buchanan that psychometry was a normal human faculty, a "telescope into the past" that could be developed by anyone who was willing to take the trouble. He gives the impression of being a rather better scientist than Buchanan, more anxious to exclude possible error, and to explain psychometry in terms of scientific theory. For example, he devotes a chapter to the psychological curiosity that is now known as "eidetic imagery" or photographic memory—the ability some people (especially children) possess to look at some object, then to project an exact image of it on to a blank sheet of paper. Newton discovered that, during his optical experiments, the image of the sun (seen in a darkened glass) kept returning like a hallucination. It would vanish when he forgot about it; but he only had to call it to mind to make it appear in front of him. Denton discovered many other descriptions of the same phenomenon: not just of simple images like the sun, but of whole scenes. He quotes Professor Stevelly who, after watching bees swarming from hives, continued to have visual hallucinations of swarms of bees for days afterwards. A doctor named Ferriar described how, in the evening, he could conjure up in detail some scene he had looked at during the day—an old ruin, a fine house, a review of troops; he had only to go into a darkened room to see it as if in a coloured photograph. The geologist Hugh Miller had a similar ability. He wrote:

> There are, I suspect, provinces in the philosophy of mind into which the metaphysicians have not yet entered. Of that accessible storehouse, in which the memories of past events lie arranged and taped up, they appear to know a good deal; but of a mysterious cabinet of daguerreotype pictures, of which, though fast locked up on ordinary occasions, disease sometimes flings the door ajar, they seem to know nothing.

More than a century later, Dr. Wilder Penfield proved the truth of this observation when, during a brain operation, he touched the patient's temporal cortex with the electric probe, and the patient suddenly "replayed" precise and lengthy memories of childhood, all as minutely detailed as if they were happening in the present.

It is difficult to see at first what connection Denton saw between these visual hallucinations and psychometry—after all, they seem to have little enough in common. But it slowly becomes clear that his wife and sister—and later his son—actually *saw* these visions of the past; if the cinema had been invented at the time, he might have compared it to a mental film show. These experiences of hallucination seemed to offer a clue to this strange faculty of psychometric vision. Particularly interesting is Newton's observation that he could make the image of the sun reappear before his eyes by *imagining* it. What is suggested here is that the image was so vividly imprinted on his brain that it could be "projected" like a film by merely wanting to. This also seems to explain Stevelly's visions of the swarming bees and Ferriar's of old ruins of fine houses. The philosopher Berdyaev has a passage in which he describes his own hallucinatory vision of a woman called Mintslova, a disciple of Rudolph Steiner, whom he regarded as a pernicious influence.

• • •

I was lying in bed in my room half asleep; I could clearly see the room and the corner opposite me where an icon was hanging with a little burning oil lamp before it. I beheld the outline of Mintslova's face: its expression was quite horrifying—a face seemingly possessed of all the power of darkness. I gazed at her intently for a few seconds, and then, by an intense spiritual effort, forced the horrible vision to disappear.*

It is significant that Berdyaev was half asleep, so that what might have been merely a dream-image was projected as a hallucination.

The third volume of *The Soul of Things* makes us aware of the drawbacks of this ability. The frontispiece is a "Map of Jupiter," with a key underneath listing such items as "Houses and city, seen 19 March 1870," "Sugar loaf hills, seen 23 March 1870." And the longest section in the book is a chapter called "Astronomical Examinations," beginning with "A boy's visit to Venus," "Visit to a comet," and including accounts of Mars and Jupiter. Sherman Denton's observations on Venus begin promisingly with the comment that its mountains are higher than those on earth—which is true. But he then goes on to describe giant trees shaped like toadstools and full of sweet jelly, and an animal that was half-fish and half-muskrat. The 1962 Mariner space-probe revealed that the temperature on the surface of Venus is 900°F, hot enough to melt solder, and therefore too hot to support life. Sherman's visit to a comet is equally disappointing; he states that it is a planet that has become a kind of fireball. We are still not sure of where comets originate; but we know that they are of low density, and almost certainly very cold. Sherman's visit to the sun revealed that it is made of molten lava which is hardening in places into a crust. Modern astronomy has shown that the sun is a ball of gas. A visit to Mars revealed that it was much like earth, but peopled with men with four fingers, wide mouths, yellow hair and blue eyes. "It seems warm, like summer weather." (In fact, Mars would be very cold indeed, since it is more than fifty million miles further from the sun than earth is.) Mrs. Cridge and Mrs. Denton also visited Mars, and

Dream and Reality, chapter 7.

described its religion, its art and its scientific inventions. Sherman and Mrs. Cridge both described Jupiter, also peopled by blue-eyed blondes who can float in the air, and whose women all have plaits down to their waists. Modern space probes have revealed that Jupiter is basically a ball of freezing gas with a hot liquid core.

Volume three of *The Soul of Things* is undoubtedly an anticlimax, and no one could be blamed for being inclined to dismiss the whole work as an absurd piece of self-deception. But before we throw the baby out with the bath water, we might recollect the parallel case of Emanuel Swedenborg. That remarkable mystic devoted the first fifty-six years of his life to science and engineering; then he began having strange dreams, hallucinations and trances. In these visionary states, he believed he had visited heaven and hell, and his books contain detailed accounts of the "afterworld," all of which his disciples—who were soon numbered in thousands—accepted as literal truth. A century before the rise of spiritualism, Swedenborg claimed to be able to converse with spirits of the dead. When the queen of Sweden asked him to give her greetings to her dead brother, the prince royal of Denmark, Swedenborg said he would. Soon after, he told her that her brother sent his greetings, and apologized for not answering her last letter. He would now do so through Swedenborg . . . As Swedenborg delivered the detailed message, the queen turned pale, and said, "No one but God knows this secret." On another occasion, in 1761, the widow of the Dutch ambassador told Swedenborg that she was having trouble with a silversmith who was demanding payment for a silver tea service; a few days later, Swedenborg told her he had spoken to her husband, and that he *had* paid for the tea service; the receipt would be found in a secret compartment in his bureau drawer. Swedenborg also mentioned some secret correspondence that would be found in the same drawer. Both the receipt and the correspondence were found where Swedenborg had said.

In July 1759, Swedenborg was able to tell guests at a party in Gothenburg that a great fire had broken out in Stockholm, three hundred miles away. Two hours later he told one of the guests that the fire had been extinguished only three doors from his home. Two days later, a messenger arrived confirming these details.

So, understandably, Swedenborg's disciples believed him

when he described the "spirit realms," and his visits to other planets. Mercury, he said, had a moderate temperature, and its beings were more spiritual than human beings; the planet also had cattle that were a cross between cows and stags. Venus had two races living on opposite sides of the planet, one mild and humane, the other savage and violent—the latter being giants. Martians had faces that were half black and half white, and communicated by a kind of telepathy; they were also vegetarians. The inhabitants of Jupiter—whom Swedenborg claimed to know more intimately than those of any other planet—looked like human beings, but were far more gentle and humane, and naturally moral and virtuous. Those in warm regions went naked—except for a covering over their loins—and were astonished to be told that human beings could be sexually excited by another's nakedness. The inhabitants of the moon had thunderous voices, which were produced by a kind of belching . . .

How can these contradictions be resolved? One answer is suggested by Dr. Wilson Van Dusen in his book *Presence of Other Worlds*. Van Dusen argues that there is strong evidence that Swedenborg's visions were seen in "hypnogogic states," the states in which we linger between sleep and waking. Swedenborg seems to confirm this when he writes: "Once, when I awoke at daybreak, I saw . . . diversely shaped apparitions floating before my eyes . . ." Swedenborg's descriptions of various kinds of spirits—particularly the "damned"—sound as if he is deliberately writing in parables; but the descriptions are as precise and detailed as those of a novelist. The most probable answer is that Swedenborg had developed a faculty very similar to that discussed by Denton in the chapter on Newton, Hugh Miller and others who experienced visual hallucinations. The severe mental crisis that changed him in his mid-fifties from a scientist to a visionary allowed the unconscious mind to erupt into consciousness; he could, in effect, dream with his eyes open.

But if the visions of planets—and probably of heaven and hell—were self-deception, then how do we explain the accuracy of the vision of the Stockholm fire, and the information about the secret drawer and the queen's letter? The answer is that, unfortunately, the possession of genuine "clairvoyant" or mediumistic faculty is no guarantee of the truthfulness of other kinds of vision. In fact, the best clairvoyants and psychometrists have always been willing to admit that they can be confused by telepathic impressions from other people.

Then what, precisely, is the difference between the kind of clairvoyance involved in Swedenborg's vision of the Stockholm fire, and his visions of Mars and Venus? Or Mrs. Denton's vision of an erupting volcano on Hawaii and the climate on Jupiter?

This is, in fact, one of the most important of all questions in paranormal research. The Belgian dramatist and philosopher Maurice Maeterlinck raised it in his book on the paranormal, *The Unknown Guest* (1914), whose title is a three-word summary of his own answer. Inside every one of us, says Maeterlinck, there is an unknown entity that lives "in a sort of invisible and perhaps eternal palace, like a casual guest, dropped from another planet, whose interests, ideas, habits, passions have nothing in common with ours." In fact, we harbour a kind of "second self" whose presence is hidden from the "first self"—the person you call "you." We might label this "the unconscious mind," but if we do so, we shall be in danger of missing its whole significance. Most of us feel that we know all about the unconscious. I try to recall what I did with a book I was looking at ten minutes ago, then I find I have put it back on the shelf; I say I did this "unconsciously." I have a nagging feeling that there is something I have forgotten; then I remember that it is my wife's birthday; I say that my unconscious was trying to remind me. I want to wake up at 6:30, and I open my eyes at precisely that time; I say that my unconscious alarm clock has awakened me. These examples tend to domesticate the unconscious, to turn it into a familiar old grandmother who sits quietly in the corner. And this is not at all what Maeterlinck means by "the unknown guest." In fact, most of the functions mentioned above are carried out by a part of us that might be called the "robot" or automatic pilot, a habit of mechanism. The powers of the unknown guest are apparently far wider. For example, it can foretell the future. Maeterlinck cites the case of the wife of the Russian general Toutschkoff, who woke up one night dreaming that she was at an inn in an unknown town, and that her father came into the room to tell her "Your husband has been killed at Borodino." When the dream had been repeated a third time she woke her husband and asked him "Where is Borodino?"

He had no idea and they had to look it up on the map. But when Napoleon invaded Russia later that year, General Toutschkoff was killed at the battle of Borodino, and her father came into the room at the inn where she was staying to give her the news.

In fact, modern brain research has placed this notion of the "unknown guest" on a scientific basis. The brain is divided into two identical halves, like the halves of a walnut, and the part of it that presses against the top of the skull is called the cerebrum; it is larger than in any other animal, and is the part of the brain that makes us human. The two halves of the cerebrum are joined by a bridge of nerves called the corpus callosum. If this is cut—as it is sometimes to prevent epilepsy —then the patient becomes two people. Each half of the brain controls one side of the body (and, for some odd reason, the right side controls the left half of the body, and vice versa). One "split-brain" patient tried to hit his wife with one hand while the other defended her. Another tried to unzip his flies with one hand while the other tried to do them up. A patient who was given some wooden blocks to arrange into a pattern tried to do it with his right hand, and the left hand continually tried to interrupt him; finally, he had to sit on his left hand to make it behave.

But the most significant point to emerge from split-brain physiology is that the person you call "you" *lives in the left cerebral hemisphere*. This is the half of the cerebrum that deals with language and logic. It could be regarded as a scientist. The right half seems to work in terms of patterns and insights; it is basically an artist. And it seems to be a "second self." It was natural for the patient to try to solve the wooden block pattern with his right hand (connected to the left brain), because the doctor had asked *him* to do the puzzle, and the conscious, everyday self lives in the left brain. If he had not been a split-brain patient, the right brain would have quietly helped him to solve the puzzle by "putting ideas into his head," and he would not even have been aware of it.

So what is it like to be a split-brain patient? The unexpected answer is that most of them do not even notice it. And if we reflect for a moment, we can see that this makes sense. If I try to solve some puzzle—say a Rubik cube—after a few glasses of alcohol, my "insight" refuses to function. This is because alcohol seems to interfere with the connection between right and left. It has, in fact, given me a kind of instant split-brain operation. Yet I hardly notice this. My conscious self is so accustomed to coping with reality that it hardly notices when the "other self" withdraws its help. But if I attempted to write this book after several glasses of alcohol—or when I was so tired that the "two selves" had lost contact—I would instantly realize that something was wrong. For writing is an act of close cooperation between the two selves. The right takes a "bird's eye view," surveying all the possibilities; the left chooses between them and decides which of them to turn into words. If the right fails to do its half of the job, the left stares blankly at the sheet of paper and wonders what to say.

Is the right cerebral hemisphere "the unknown guest"? That might be going too far. We still know so little about the brain and its working that it would be better to preserve an open mind. But we can safely say that the right hemisphere is the entrance to the "invisible palace" of the unknown guest.

When Maeterlinck coined that term, he was apparently unaware that the idea of a "hidden self" had been anticipated by more than two decades. In 1893, a book called *The Law of Psychic Phenomena* caused widespread discussion all over America. Its author, Thomson Jay Hudson, was a Detroit newspaper editor and an official of the Patent Office. Like Buchanan and Denton, his name has now been almost forgotten; yet, like them, he deserves to be regarded as one of the most original figures in the early history of paranormal research.

Hudson, like Buchanan and Denton, was fascinated by the phenomena of mesmerism and hypnotism. These were far more remarkable than is generally realized. There is strong evidence that many people developed clairvoyant powers under hypnosis. A young Frenchman named Alexis Didier could go into a hypnotic trance, then tell visitors where they had been, what they had been doing, and what their homes looked like. This could have been telepathy; but on one occasion, he was able to tell an official whose clerk had absconded with the funds that the man had gone to Belgium, and to describe his route in detail; he was also able to predict, correctly, that when the man was arrested he would have gambled away all the money. The psychologist Pierre Janet was able to hypnotize one of his patients—a woman called Leonie—at a distance of several miles by merely thinking about her, and induce her to come to his house. The Russian L. L. Vasiliev later demonstrated that distance was unimportant, and hypnotized some of his own patients at a distance of thousands of miles. Dr. Julian Ochorowitz studied a woman who, under hypnosis, could describe what was going on behind her back, and other subjects who could correctly call out the identity of cards that they could not see.

Thomson Jay Hudson started from the observation that people under hypnosis can often perform feats that would be impossible for them in a state of wakefulness. He was present in Boston when Professor William B. Carpenter placed a young man—whom he calls C—in a state of trance, then told him that he was about to introduce him to the spirit of Socrates. C looked awe-stricken, and bowed reverently to an empty chair. At Carpenter's request, he then proceeded to hold a conversation with Socrates and to ask him questions. Carpenter explained that he was unable to hear what Socrates said, and asked C to repeat it aloud. The result astonished everybody. C proceeded to expound "a wonderful system of spiritual philosophy." It was so clear, so plausible, and so perfectly consistent with itself and the known laws of Nature that the company sat spellbound through it all, each one almost persuaded . . . that he was listening to a voice from the other world." In fact, some people present became convinced that C really *was* talking with the ghost of Socrates.

C was introduced to the spirits of many later philosophers. His manner changed with each one, and the ideas were presented in the language appropriate to the philosopher. "If the person themselves had been present," says Hudson, "their distinctive peculiarities could not have been more marked." And the philosophy expounded continued to be impressive— Hudson calls it "one of the grandest and most coherent systems of spiritual philosophy ever conceived by the brain of man."

By way of testing whether C might actually be speaking to the spirits of the dead, one of the philosophers was asked where he died; he replied, "In a little town near Boston." This was a mistake; the man had lived in a little town near Boston—a fact that was known to C—but he had died abroad. Equally conclusive was a dialogue between C and the spirit of a pig, which delivered a discourse on the subject of reincarnation, a subject that C had recently been studying in the works of the Theosophists. Naturally, the pig's view echoed those of the Theosophical Society.

Maeterlinck would have said that C's powers under hypnosis emanated from the "unknown guest." Hudson preferred to call it "the subjective mind." Human beings, according to Hudson, have two minds. The "objective mind" is the part of us that deals with everyday life and copes with practical matters; the subjective mind is concerned with our inner powers and energies. It is as if the mind had two faces; one turned towards the outside world, the other turned towards the inner worlds of memory and intuition. For practical purposes they are rather like a husband and wife; the husband—the objective mind—assertive and aggressive, the wife shy and taciturn, inclined to doubt her own judgement in the face of her husband's superior forcefulness. Under hypnosis, the husband is put to sleep, and the wife, no longer tongue-tied with self-doubt, can exercise her powers of intuition without fear of criticism. As a result, she can perform far more remarkable feats than when her domineering partner is awake. She seems to have remarkable powers over the body, so that a man under hypnosis can not only have a tooth extracted without pain, but will even obey an order not to bleed. He becomes capable of feats of strength that would be impossible if he were awake—an old favourite of stage hypnotists is to tell a man that he is about to become as stiff as a board, then make him lie between two chairs while someone jumps up and down on his stomach.

Hudson is fascinated by these powers of the subjective mind. He cites a case of an illiterate girl who, when in a fever, began to speak Greek, Latin, and Hebrew. A young doctor was so intrigued by this that he investigated the girl's past life, and discovered that, at the age of nine, she had lived with a Protestant pastor who used to walk around the house reading aloud in these languages. Consciously, the girl had not assimilated a single word; but some hidden tape recorder in the brain had preserved everything.

Hudson discusses the mystery of calculating prodigies—usually young boys of no particular talent or intelligence who can perform astonishing feats of calculation within seconds—like five-year-old Zerah Colburn, who once snapped out the answer to the square root of 106,929 before the questioner had finished speaking. He also discusses the power that so interested William Denton—"eidetic imagery"—and describes an artist friend who could conjure up a scene at will and then see it projected in detail on a blank canvas.

Genius, says Hudson, is simply a perfect balance between the objective and subjective minds—as if a husband and wife are in such deep sympathy that the wife has lost all her shyness and pours out her intuitions in the certainty that they will be understood. When this happens, the subjective mind can actually take over, and the result is known as inspiration, a spontaneous outpouring of insights. Hudson cites the example of the great political orator Henry Clay, who was once called upon to answer an opponent in the Senate when he was feeling sick and exhausted. Clay asked the man sitting next to him to tug on his coat-tails when he had been speaking for ten minutes. Two hours later, after a magnificent speech, Clay sank down exhausted, and asked his friend reproachfully why he had failed to interrupt. In fact, the friend had not only tugged his coat-tails; he had nudged and pinched him, and even jabbed a pin deep into his leg. This aspect of the "subjective mind" seems to be what the Spaniards call the *duende,* the "demon" that sometimes takes over great singers or dancers so they seem to be possessed by a force greater than themselves. They *are*, in fact, "greater than themselves," for the ego—as we have seen—is a left-brain entity.

Yet the limitations of the subjective mind are as odd as its talents. Hudson observed that it can reason deductively—from the general to the particular—but not vice versa. Induction is the ability to leap from a collection of facts to the laws underlying them. The subjective mind can be shown any number of trees without noticing that they add up to a wood. It leaves "leaping to conclusions" to its more enterprising and aggressive partner. In fact, the subjective mind is oddly shortsighted and passive. This also explains why it tends to be bad at argument, which involves selecting and reasoning—making choices. Right-brain people—"subjective-minders"—usually become tongue-tied when someone tells them something in an authoritative voice, even when they can see it is nonsense; they find it hard to put their perceptions into words. This also explains, says Hudson, why psychic powers often evaporate when confronted with scepticism. The subjective mind is intensely suggestive, so a mere hint that it is a fraud turns it into a nervous wreck. Hudson cites the case of a clairvoyant named

Bishop, who demonstrated again and again his power to read people's minds and decipher the contents of sealed envelopes. But when the well-known journalist Henry Labouchere denounced him as a fake, and challenged him to read the number of a bank note sealed in an envelope, he failed miserably. He had done the same thing successfully a thousand times; but the aggressive self-confidence of a left-brainer was enough to shatter his self-confidence and paralyze the powers of the subjective mind.

This brings us to what Hudson considered the most important thing about the subjective mind: that it is responsible for all so-called psychic phenomena—including ghosts and poltergeists. This suggestion naturally infuriated the spiritualists; but Hudson argued his case with impressive skill and conviction. He points out that a hypnotist can induce a blister in a good hypnotic subject by suggesting that he had been burnt by a hot iron, and argues convincingly that the stigmata of the saints—bleeding nail holes and wounds—can be explained in the same way. He discusses some of the remarkable cures that have been brought about by hypnosis, and concludes that the subjective mind has immense healing powers. In fact, he became convinced that the miracles of the New Testament were a manifestation of these powers. By way of testing this hypothesis, he decided to try to cure a relative who suffered from rheumatism and nervous convulsions. The method, apparently, was to persuade his own subjective mind that it *could* be done, even though the relative lived a thousand miles away. He informed two friends that he intended to begin the treatment—so that they could bear witness if it worked—and started on 15 May 1890. He decided to try to communicate the healing suggestions by an effort of will just as he was on the point of going to sleep. Some months later, one of the two "witnesses" met the relative, whose health had improved remarkably; the improvement had started, he said, in mid-May. Hudson claimed that he and close associates had made more than a hundred similar experiments, and that not one of them had been a failure.

After discussing healing, Hudson turns to the experiments of William Denton, and the reader expects to be told that psychometry is another striking example of the powers of the subjective mind. Instead, Hudson rejects them as self-deception. All that Denton proved, he says, is the ability of his wife's subjective mind to read his own. Denton was an eminent geologist who already had very clear ideas about his various samples. Both his wife and his sister were intelligent and cultured women. So they had merely picked up his own mental pictures of the past. Hudson acknowledges that Denton had tried hard to exclude telepathy, by wrapping the samples in paper parcels, then mixing them up so thoroughly that he himself had no idea of which was which. But although Denton's objective mind—his conscious self—might have lost track of which was which, the subjective mind, with its incredible memory, would have no trouble in remembering...

This sounds plausible, until we look more closely into Denton's experiments. If the visions originated in his own mind, then why did his wife and sister—and later his son—often produce different pictures from different periods in the sample's history—as with the piece of mosaic from the villa of Cicero? Why did Mrs. Denton describe a man who sounds like Sulla when Denton was expecting her to describe Cicero? And if, indeed, it was Sulla she described, and Denton had no idea that Sulla had lived in the villa, then telepathy would have been impossible.

Hudson could, of course, have countered these objections. If Denton's wife and sister selected different parts of the sample's history to describe, then they were merely selecting from the knowledge in Denton's mind. As to Denton not knowing that it was the dictator's villa, perhaps he *did* know, but had long ago forgotten that he had read it...

But the real objection to Hudson's arguments is that he is willing to credit the subjective mind with powers just as remarkable as psychometry—for example, healing a relative at a thousand miles. If the subjective mind can pick up vibrations from another mind, then why can it not pick up vibrations from a letter or a piece of mosaic? Hudson even credits the subjective mind with the power to foretell the future; he says that its deductive powers are so tremendous that it can calculate every possibility—like some gigantic computer—and select the likeliest one. He gives a great deal of space to the "daemon" of Socrates—the inner voice that would give the philosopher good advice and warn him of impending danger; this, says Hudson, is simply the subjective mind making itself heard as a kind of voice inside the head. (A modern exponent of split-brain theory, Julian Jaynes, believes that the ancients heard "voices" that came from the right cerebral hemisphere.) If the subjective mind possesses these remarkable powers, it seems contradictory to deny it the power of psychometry.

The explanation of Hudson's "tough-minded" attitude is probably that he was unwilling to expose his newborn theory to ridicule by appearing too credulous. In fact, we can see it in retrospect that many of his mistakes sprang out of being too sceptical. His chapter on crime and hypnosis provides two examples. He argues that no one could be made to commit a crime under hypnosis because the prophetic powers of the subjective mind would make it aware that it might lead to disaster. In fact, many crimes have been committed under hypnosis—one of the best known examples being the Copenhagen case of 1951, when a man named Palle Hardrup robbed a bank and murdered the cashier under hypnotic suggestion. Hudson also remarks that committing suicide under hypnosis is as unlikely as committing a crime under hypnosis; in fact, this is precisely what did happen in the Sala case of 1929, when the hypnotist Sigwart Thurneman made a member of his criminal gang commit suicide by hypnotic suggestion.*

Finally, Hudson's "super-telepathy" theory fails to explain the powers of a psychometrist like Nelson Palmer and many other "psychic detectives" whom we shall discuss later. It *is* just conceivable that Palmer located Joy Aken's body by reading the mind of her murderer; but why, in that case, did he need something belonging to the dead girl? If only telepathy was involved, he should have been able to read Van Buuren's mind without the aid of Joy Aken's clothing.

But these criticisms fail to obscure the remarkable nature of Hudson's achievement. *The Law of Psychic Phenomena* is one of the most important contributions to nineteenth-century thought, and deserves to be as well-known as *The Origin of Species* or *Das Kapital*. It was Hudson's bad luck that, within ten years of the book's publication, Sigmund Freud's theory of the unconscious mind had become even more notorious. Freud also believed that the unconscious is far more powerful than the conscious mind; but Freud's unconscious is entirely negative, a kind of gigantic dustbin full of guilt, misery and repressions. Freud seemed even more sceptical and tough-minded than Hudson, and the result was that his more con-

*See *Antisocial or Criminal Acts and Hypnosis* by Paul J. Reiter.

troversial theories won the day, and Hudson's were forgotten.

In fact, modern split-brain research has shown that Hudson's ideas have a sounder basis than Freud's. It is now a matter of scientific fact that we have two "selves" inside our heads, that one is intuitive and the other intellectual, and that genius, as Hudson said, is a close cooperation between the two. So it is important to look again at Hudson's contribution, and give careful thought to some of his insights. His most important recognition is that human beings possess mental powers of which they are unaware. He was right to emphasize the mystery of calculating prodigies; for their abilities seem to defy what we regard as the normal laws of the mind. They often appear out of the blue, in perfectly normal children, and later vanish just as abruptly. Archbishop Whately said that his own powers appeared at the age of six, when he knew nothing about figures except simple addition; suddenly, he could do tremendous calculations in his head. When he went to school three years later, "the passion wore off," and he became a dunce at mathematics. The powers of such prodigies seems incredible. One six-year-old boy, Benjamin Blyth, was out walking with his father when he asked what time he was born. His father told him four a.m. A few minutes later, the child stated the number of seconds he had lived. When they got home, his father worked it out on paper, and told Ben he was 172,800 seconds wrong. "No," said the child, "you have forgotten two leap years."

Most calculating prodigies lose their powers in their teens, when life becomes more complex and difficult, and sexual changes in the body disturb the emotions. But the inference is that our brains have an extraordinary power that few of us ever bother to develop.

Where psychometry is concerned, the power of "eidetic vision" is even more important, as Denton recognized. Modern research has revealed that between 8 and 20 per cent of all children may possess eidetic vision—the power to conjure up an image so powerfully that it looks like a film projection. One test involves the use of "random dot stereograms." Two sheets of paper contain apparently random patterns of ten thousand dots, but when these are superimposed, a picture emerges. Many children can look at one pattern, then move their eyes to the other sheet, and see the two patterns combining into a picture. This is obviously right-brain function—it is the right brain that recognizes patterns and shapes—and again the inference is that we gradually lose it as the left brain becomes more powerful, to "cope" with reality. But if this is correct, then all human beings possess a latent power to "photograph" what they are looking at, and to project the photograph later in all its detail. As we have seen in the cases cited by Denton, this "projection" is a deliberate act of will and imagination. But Hudson's artist friend was able to project purely imaginary scenes on his canvas. And this, again, would be perfectly natural. If we have the latent power to "hold" mental photographs and keep them in some memory-file, then there is no reason why the imagination should not combine them, or simply invent its own mental photographs.

The psychologist C. G. Jung also recognized this power, which he called "active imagination," and he believed that anyone could develop it with sufficient effort. Jung made the discovery accidentally. In 1913, after his break with Freud, Jung was experiencing severe mental problems that made him fear insanity. Sitting at his desk one day, he says, "I let myself drop. Suddenly it was as though the ground literally gave way beneath my feet, and I plunged down into dark depths." There followed a waking dream in which Jung found himself in an underground cave, guarded by a mummified dwarf, and saw the body of a blond youth with a wound in his head float past on a stream.

In his autobiography, *Memories, Dreams, Reflections,* Jung goes on to describe his deliberate development of techniques to enter this realm of "waking dreams."

In order to seize hold of the fantasies, I frequently imagined a steep descent. I even made several attempts to get to the very bottom. The first time I reached, as it were, a depth of about a thousand feet; the next time I found myself at the edge of a cosmic abyss. It was like a voyage to the moon, or a descent into empty space. First came the image of a crater, and I had a feeling that I was in the land of the dead. The atmosphere was that of the other world. Near the steep slope of a rock I caught sight of two figures, an old man with a white beard, and a beautiful young girl. I summoned up my courage and approached them as though they were real people, and listened attentively to what they told me . . .

• • •

Here we can see clearly that Jung had entered a hypnogogic realm in which he remained wide awake whilst at the same time encountering the strange creations of that "other self" inside us. It is, admittedly, difficult for most of us to accept the notion of such an ability; but we should bear in mind that a dog would find it quite impossible to conceive the mental state of a child reading a book, with half his consciousness in the "real world" and the other half in a world of fantasy. Jung's "active imagination" is only a single step beyond this ability that every educated person possesses.

And now at last we are in a position to understand those detailed descriptions of "other worlds" that we find in Swedenborg and Denton. A good psychometer possesses the power to "read" objects in the way that a bloodhound can recognize scents. When this reading becomes second nature, it is accompanied by images—images that are sometimes so detailed and real that they amount to eidetic visions. When Mrs. Denton described Cicero's villa, or when Sherman Denton described the theatre in ancient Pompeii, they were using active imagination as a tool to amplify their readings. But when they tried to "psychometrize" Mars or Jupiter, there were no psychometric impressions to amplify, and the subjective mind—which, according to Van Dusen, is an incorrigible performer that hates to admit defeat—produced elaborate waking dreams.

This tendency of the unconscious to spin its own webs of fantasy certainly complicates the question of psychometry. But, unlike Swedenborg and Denton, we are at least aware of the problem; and this is already an important step toward solving it.

3
White Crows and Black Sheep

WE THINK OF the last quarter of the nineteenth century as an age of occultism and decadence: of Madame Blavatsky and Oscar Wilde, of strange magical societies and poets who drank themselves to death with absinthe. Nothing could be more inaccurate. To anyone with an enquiring intellect, it must have seemed one of the most promising and exciting periods in human history. It was an age of discovery and invention: in the 1890s alone, these included x-rays, electrons, wireless telegraphy, the aeroplane, the film projector, the gasoline automobile, the Diesel engine, the gas and steam turbines, the safety razor, the electric stove, the tape recorder and the submarine. Civilization had advanced more in fifty years than in the previous five thousand; and discoveries were being made at such a rate that it seemed impossible to predict what the world would be like in fifty years' time.

It was typical of that age of intellectual optimism that a small group of thinkers decided that the time was ripe to solve the ultimate "riddle of the universe"—the problem of why man is alive and what will happen to him after death. This audacious project originated one evening in December 1869, when the moral philosopher Henry Sidgwick went for a walk in Cambridge with his ex-pupil Frederick Myers. It was a calm, starlit night, and the two men discussed the great issue that tormented the Victorians: the problem of scientific materialism. Both men had been brought up in devoutly religious households; both had come to reject the Church of

England and, as a consequence, been forced to resign fellow-ships at Trinity. Yet neither could accept the idea that man is stranded in a meaningless, empty universe that has been created by pure chance. And it was Myers who asked, with a kind of desperation, whether, since philosophy has failed to solve the riddle of the universe, there was just a chance that the answer might lie in the realm of ghosts and spirits. If, after all, it could be proved that there was life after death, the philosophy of materialism would vanish like a bad dream . . .

If these hopes strike us as naive, we have to remember that spiritualism was a new phenomenon, and that some of its results were very impressive indeed. Of course, there were plenty of fraudulent mediums, and spirits that played tambourines and trumpets could hardly be taken seriously. But the best mediums produced results that were beyond the skill of any conjuror. Daniel Dunglas Home—the man the jealous Browning had attacked in "Mr. Sludge the Medium"—could wash his face in red hot coals, cause heavy tables and settees to rise up to the ceiling as if they were balloons, and float out of one third-storey window and in at another. His feats had been witnessed by whole committees of sceptical scientists, who were forced to accept the evidence of their own eyes.

The problem was that most scientists became almost hysterical about spiritualism; they insisted, in the teeth of all the evidence, that it *had* to be fraudulent. William Carpenter—who had hypnotized the young man into holding a conversation with Socrates—denounced spiritualism as an epidemic delusion, like witchcraft. Another scientist announced his discovery that all women who believed in spiritualism were suffering from "improperly-angled wombs." The sheer bitterness of the attacks reveals a deep underlying insecurity. More balanced people did their best to be reasonable. Lewis Carroll, the author of *Alice in Wonderland*—who was also a mathematician—agreed that "trickery will *not* do as a complete explanation of . . . table-rapping, thought reading, etc.," and suggested that the answer might lie in "a natural force allied to electricity and nerve force, by which brain can act on brain."

In the early days, the few scientists who dared to look into these forbidden realms soon found they had lost most of their friends. When, in 1871, the eminent physicist William Crookes (later Sir William), discoverer of the element thallium, announced that he intended to investigate spiritualism scientifically, his colleagues welcomed the decision, convinced that he would explode the nonsense once and for all. When Crookes investigated Daniel Dunglas Home and Florence Cook, and finally published a detailed report of his investigations, admitting that he had found them to be genuine, his colleagues instantly decided that he must simply be a less good scientist than they had assumed. At one point in the bitter controversy that followed, Crookes exploded: "I didn't say it was possible—I said it was true." (A modern researcher, Trevor Hall, has speculated that Florence Cook became Crookes' mistress, but there is no evidence whatever for this conjecture.)

The gentle Alfred Russell Wallace, co-discoverer of the theory of evolution, encountered the same hostility. Wallace was widely respected, since it was known that he had voluntarily suppressed his own discovery of evolution when he found out that Charles Darwin was about to publish the theory. In the 1840s, he investigated hypnotism, and discovered that he could place a boy in a trance and then influence him telepathically. When Wallace was pricked, the boy gave a cry of pain and placed his hand on the same part of his own body; when Wallace put a lump of sugar in his mouth, the boy went through the motions of sucking. In 1865, Wallace attended a seance—in broad daylight—in the house of a friend, and heard raps resounding from around the room and watched a heavy table moving and vibrating. Impressed, he invited the sceptical Professor Carpenter to come and see for himself. Carpenter came and sat silently through the phenomena, then went away; he never came again. The great T. H. Huxley, whose own scepticism had been reinforced after a session with a highly unconvincing medium, remarked tolerantly: "I am neither shocked nor disposed to issue a commission of lunacy against you. It may all be true, for anything that I know to the contrary, but really I cannot get up interest in the subject."

To scientists like Wallace and Crookes, such an attitude was almost criminal. It was true that rapping noises were of no particular interest; but some evidence was of a far more dramatic and convincing nature. In his book *Miracles and Modern Spiritualism* (1864) Wallace offers a case in point: the solution of a double murder by the dowser Jacques Aymar, reported in detail in the court evidence of the Procurator

Royal, and witnessed by the Dean of the College of Medicine at Lyon and by a Dr. Chauvin who was present throughout the investigation. This took place in Lyon in July 1692, when a wine merchant and his wife were robbed, and murdered by a hedging tool. There were no clues whatever, and someone suggested consulting the dowser Jacques Aymar, who lived in Crôle, and who had solved a robbery the previous year with the use of his divining rod.

Aymar went to the cellar where the two bodies had been found, and his dowsing rod seemed to pick up the scent like a bloodhound. He announced that three men had been involved in the murder. He walked through the town, holding the rod, which twitched as long as he was on the right track. It took him to the cottage of a gardener, and reacted to an empty wine bottle on a table. The gardener flatly denied that any strangers had been in his house; but his two children admitted that when their father had been out, two men *had* walked in and helped themselves to wine.

The Procurator was now convinced that Aymar was no fraud, but wanted to test him further before pursuing the case. Three hedging bills were borrowed from the man who had made the murder weapon, and all four were buried in a garden. Taken to the garden, Aymar's dowsing rod had no difficulty in locating the murder weapon; it ignored the other bills. A second trial was conducted with Aymar blindfolded, and was just as successful.

Aymar was authorized to continue the investigation. He walked down the left bank of the Rhône, and stopped at a place where the footprints of three men in the sand showed that they had entered a boat. Aymar and the police officers also entered a boat; he apparently found it more difficult to follow the trail on water, but nevertheless made them pull in further downstream, and showed them the place where the three men had slept overnight. Then his rod took them on to a military camp, where his agitation convinced him they had caught up with the murderers. But they could do nothing without authority, and had to return to Lyon.

When they got back to the camp at Sablon, Aymar said the murderers had left. The pursuit continued, on to the town of Beaucaire, and Aymar halted in front of a prison, saying that one of the murderers was inside. Taken into a room with a dozen or so prisoners, he picked out a hunchback who had been brought in an hour previously for theft. The hunchback denied everything; but, taken back along his route from Lyon, he was recognized by many householders as a man who had passed that way recently with two companions. The hunchback made a full confession, but insisted that he was only the servant of the other two men, and had been in another room when the murder was committed.

Aymar returned to Beaucaire, and his rod again led him to the prison. There he learned that a man had been enquiring about the hunchback, and had left hurriedly when he learned that the pursuers were so close. Aymar tracked the fugitives to the frontier, where the chase had to be abandoned. The hunchback was sentenced to be broken on the wheel.

Wallace mentions that this story is related in some detail in a book called *Curious Myths of the Middle Ages* (1869) by the Rev. Sabine Baring-Gould; in fact, this account provides an interesting example of the ambivalence towards the paranormal that made the task of men like Wallace and Crookes so difficult. Baring-Gould cites an impressive list of witnesses to the case—including two abbés—and the court transcript; but then he goes on to refer to Aymar as an "impostor," and speaks of his "exposé and downfall." In fact, all that happened was that Aymar went to Paris and failed various tests—Baring-Gould is willing to concede that being brought among dukes and marquises may have deprived Aymar of his powers by making him over-anxious to get results. Baring-Gould concludes: "I believe the imagination is the principal motive force in those who use the divining rod." Wallace points out that this is simply illogical; if Aymar is to be proved an impostor, then all the witnesses—including the author of the court transcript—have to be shown to be liars; Aymar's failure in Paris is irrelevant. But what strikes the reader of Baring-Gould's chapter as even more odd is that his careful, detailed account sounds as if he is trying to prove the case for dowsing; then he abruptly changes his mind.

A reference to a dictionary of literary biography may help to shed some light on the mystery. Baring-Gould—the author of "Onward Christian Soldiers"—later became known as the author of many books about ghosts and hauntings—even one on werewolves. But at the time he wrote *Curious Myths of the Middle Ages* he had been ordained for only four years. The 1860s were a period when spiritualism was sweeping across

Europe, and arousing intense hostility in both scientists and churchmen. A newly ordained clergyman may have felt that it would be rash to allow himself to be tarred with the same brush as the spiritualists. In 1872, he inherited his family estates in Devon, where he later became rector; it was after this that he began to publish books with accounts of ghosts and spirits. The ambivalence of his chapter on dowsing probably reflects current attitudes towards the "supernatural" in 1869, and his anxiety to appear "impartial."

This is why it required considerable courage for Frederick Myers and Henry Sidgwick to decide to form a society to investigate the claims of spiritualism, as well as such matters as clairvoyance and dowsing. But Myers soon became convinced that, whether or not there was a life after death, spiritualism was not entirely fraudulent. At a seance with the medium Charles Williams in 1873, a large hand materialized, which Myers held in his own; he felt it diminish in size until it disappeared. Soon after this, he started an "informal investigative association," together with Sidgwick, Lord Rayleigh—the physicist who discovered the element argon—and the philosopher Arthur Balfour, who later became Prime Minister. Another associate was a brilliant young classical scholar named Edmund Gurney. Nine years later, their "investigative association" would be relaunched as the Society for Psychical Research.

In 1876, Alfred Russell Wallace, who was a member of the British Association, was chairman of a committee that decided which scientific papers should be published. One of the papers submitted was by the professor of physics at the Royal College of Science in Dublin: William Barrett. It was about hypnotism. Barrett had been staying in the country with a friend who had experimented with the village children. One girl was an excellent subject. When the hypnotist placed his hand over a lighted lamp, the girl withdrew her own hand as if in pain. When he tasted salt, she grimaced; when he tasted sugar, she smiled. It was totally impossible for the girl to see the hypnotist and guess what he was doing. Barrett was fascinated and baffled. The sceptic Carpenter had explained similar results by saying that people under hypnosis can become abnormally sensitive. But that obviously failed to explain how a hypnotized person, sitting with her back to the hypnotist and her eyes closed, could know whether he was tasting sugar or salt. If Wallace had not happened to see Barrett's paper, it would probably have been quietly shelved; as it was, the committee refused to publish it. But Wallace told Myers about it, and made the investigative association aware that they had another potential ally.

In 1881, Barrett had a letter from a clergyman, the Rev. A. M. Creery, of Buxton in Derbyshire, who told him of a curious ability that had been developed by his family. A favorite party game of the period was known as the "willing game"; a person went out of the room, and the others decided on something he should be made to do—find some object, scratch his nose, or whatever. When the person came back, everyone would "will" him to perform the action, and it was often very successful. Creery and his four daughters were so good at the "willing game" that they could even pick up lines of poetry, names of towns or cards drawn from a pack. Barrett called on them, and found them to be a delightful family—the four daughters being between eleven and seventeen. Their skill at the "willing game" was incredible. When flushed with success, they became almost infallible. Myers—who also went to see them—saw them choose seventeen correct cards one after another.

As a result of the experience with the Creerys—which we now recognize as a simple case of telepathy—Barrett called a meeting of the "Cambridge group" in London and suggested setting up a society for the scientific study of such phenomena. Myers and Gurney were not over-enthusiastic, but agreed; the result was the first meeting of the Society for Psychical Research in February 1882. Early members included Crookes, Barrett, Wallace, and the physicists J. J. Thomson (discoverer of the electron) and Sir Oliver Lodge.

We must try to make an effort of the imagination, and grasp the immense optimism that fired these early researchers. They knew that many mediums were fraudulent. But they also knew that the attitude of sceptics like Carpenter and Ray Lankester was sheer prejudice. Barrett had seen a hypnotized girl wince when the hypnotist held his hand above a lamp; Myers had held a materialized hand in his own; Crookes had seen Home materialize a phantom form, which then went around the room playing an accordion. They *knew* these phenomena were genuine. Therefore, the sceptics were mistaken. Therefore, a cool and unprejudiced investigation should establish the facts once and for all. And the result ought to be that, by the beginning of the new century, mankind should know beyond all doubt whether there was life after death, or whether human beings have some strange unknown powers that can cause miracles.

Thomson Jay Hudson, of course, believed that he had discovered the answer: that man's subjective mind gives him the power to perform miracles, and that the miracles in the Bible were, in fact, performed with the aid of this faculty. Hudson believed in life after death, but he could not accept that spiritualism had anything to do with genuine spirits of the dead. He was convinced that the phenomena of spiritualism were due to the subjective mind using its power to perform miracles.

This was a view that was developed independently by another influential psychical researcher, Professor William James, who taught physiology and psychology at Harvard. James had good reason to believe in the mind's power to work miracles. As a young man he had been an invalid, suffering from back pain, eye pains, headaches and permanent exhaustion. In his late twenties he experienced a nervous breakdown followed by deep depression; the "attack" happened quite suddenly as he walked into a room at twilight and recalled a mental patient he had seen, staring blankly into space; suddenly, it seemed to him that he could easily find himself in the same state, and he experienced a "panic attack" and a complete collapse of the will. For months afterwards he woke every day with a deep sense of foreboding; life seemed a meaningless charade.

At this point—in 1868—James came across the writings of the French evolutionary philosopher Charles Renouvier. Renouvier believed firmly in the reality of free will, and he taught that if the individual exercises his free will by striking out on his own, his whole life can be transformed. In his depression, James had ceased to believe in free will; he had come to accept that men are machines driven by desires, and that everything they do is a mere penny-in-the-slot-machine response. A man who believes that, inevitably comes to feel that there is no point in doing anything. But in April 1870, James came upon Renouvier's definition of free will: "the sustaining of a thought *because I choose to* when I might have other thoughts," and saw that it appeared to be irrefutable. I may believe that all my physical acts are "inevitable"; but I can *feel* my own ability to go on thinking about something, or to change my mind and think about something else. James decided that he would accept Renouvier's definition, and think and behave as if he had free will. The result was startling. His illness simply vanished. He accepted an appointment at Harvard as an instructor in physiology, married an attractive girl, and began the work that would bring him fame, *The Principles of Psychology*. James felt he had disproved nineteenth-century materialism by personal experience.

It was in 1885 that James heard about a remarkable Boston housewife, Leonore Piper, who was causing a stir in American spiritualist circles. As a child of eight, she had been in the garden when she felt a sharp blow on her ear, and heard the words: "Aunt Sara, not dead but still with you." It was discovered that Aunt Sara had died at that exact moment. In 1881, at the age of twenty-two, she went to consult a Boston healer, and fell into a trance. It happened again the second time she went to see him; and on this occasion, she took a pencil and a sheet of paper, wrote a long message, and handed it to another person who was present, Judge Frost. It was from the judge's dead son, and the judge said it was the most remarkable he ever received. Greatly against her will, Mrs. Piper was drawn into mediumship.

William James's mother-in-law, Mrs. Gibbens, went to see Mrs. Piper, and was impressed when the medium told her intimate facts about members of the family. The next day, James's sister-in-law went to see Mrs. Piper, taking with her a letter written in Italian. Mrs. Piper pressed the letter to her forehead and went on to describe its writer in detail. (On a later occasion, she was even able to give his name.)

Told by his womenfolk about these remarkable events, the professor of psychology refused to be impressed, and proceeded to advance various practical explanations. But he allowed himself to be persuaded to go with his wife to see Mrs. Piper. He watched her go into a trance; then her "guide," a Frenchman named Phinuit, began to talk in detail about members of the family. James and his wife had recently lost a child named Herman; Mrs. Piper mentioned Herman in her trance state. James went away bewildered. Either Mrs. Piper was a consummate fraud, who had taken the trouble to learn all about his family—or she had genuine paranormal powers.

A few more sessions convinced him that she was perfectly genuine. He also tried testing her with card-guessing games, and with the "willing game." She was no good at either. Her only peculiarity, apparently, was this ability to sink into trances. And what did that amount to? James found it hard to believe that she was really in contact with the spirits of the dead—the trouble being, as he wrote later, "the extreme triviality of most of the communications." That was, and continues to be, the great stumbling block of spiritualism. If the spirits have really passed on to some higher form of existence, which gives them some kind of "bird's eye view" of our life on earth, they certainly show no sign of it in their communications, most of which are on the level of advice to their loved ones not to forget to wear their woolly underwear.

Added to this was the problem that "Phinuit" appeared to be unable either to speak or understand more than a few words of French, in spite of his claim to be a Frenchman. Yet he was by no means an obvious fraud. When he proceeded to lecture James and his wife on their moral and personal short-comings, he revealed a level of insight that was probably far beyond that of the young and relatively inexperienced Boston housewife.

In spite of his doubts and qualifications, James felt that he had encountered something new and strange, and that he would be dishonest if he decided to ignore it. "If you wish to upset the law that all crows are black," he wrote later, "you must not seek to show that no crows are; it is enough if you can prove one single crow to be white." And Mrs. Piper was James's white crow. His interest in her led to his involvement with the American Society for Psychical Research, launched in Philadelphia in 1885 at the suggestion of Professor William Barrett. The American SPR was an altogether more amateur affair than its London counterpart; to begin with, few of its founders were rich enough to finance its operations. James, with his Harvard connections, quickly became its most active member. But even James did not have time to spend investigating mediums and writing reports; so the London SPR sent one of its most brilliant young members, Dr. Richard Hodgson, to take over the running of its American branch. In the previous year, Hodgson had been sent to India to investigate the "miracles" of Madame Blavatsky—particularly the "Mahatma" letters that were supposed to be written by some god-like Master in Tibet, and which materialized miraculously in a shrine next to Madame Blavatsky's bedroom. Hodgson had discovered secret panels in the "shrine" that seemed to explain how the letters "materialized." He denounced her as a fraud, and Theosophy lost many of its devotees as a result of the exposure.

Hodgson lost no time in arranging a sitting with Mrs. Piper. It left him in no doubt that she was genuine. One of the things she—or rather Phinuit—spoke about was Hodgson's cousin Jessie, to whom he had been engaged in Australia (where he was born). Jessie, with whom Hodgson had been in love, died while he was in England. Phinuit was not only able to describe Jessie; he was also able to report a conversation between Jessie and Hodgson that was unknown to anybody else. Hodgson had so far been something of a sceptic about psychic phenomena; it was Mrs. Piper who convinced him that it was not all fraudulent. For Hodgson, as for James, she became a "white crow." He was so impressed that he offered her £200 a year to devote her services to the Society for Psychical Research.

Mrs. Piper was undoubtedly genuine; but, as James recognized, this did not mean that she was really receiving messages from the dead. A far more probable explanation was telepathy. But could that be extended to other psychic phenomena —for example, to "clairvoyance"? A case in point was drawn to James's attention shortly after it took place. At six o'clock on a frosty October morning in 1898, a girl named Bertha Huse left her home in Enfield, New Hampshire, and walked down to the Shaker Bridge that ran across the surface of Mascoma Lake. Her family became alarmed when she failed to return and the search began. By the end of the day a hundred and fifty men had joined in the search, and a local mill owner sent along a man in a diving suit, who investigated the water on either side of the Shaker Bridge.

Two days later, while the search was still going on, Mrs. Nellie Titus, who lived in the nearby village of Lebanon, fell asleep in her rocking chair after dinner. She began to twitch and groan, and, when her husband shook her awake, said: "Why did you disturb me? In a moment I would have found the body."

That night, Nellie Titus screamed in her sleep and tossed restlessly; but her husband did not repeat his mistake. Instead he lit the lamp. Then, in a kind of trance, his wife began to speak. She described how Bertha Huse had walked onto the Shaker Bridge—which was an eighth of a mile long and floated on the lake—and had climbed out on to a jutting beam covered with hoar frost. Her foot slipped, and she went in backwards. Her body was now jammed head downward, caught in the timberwork of the bridge.

The next morning, George Titus told his story to his employer and asked leave of absence. Then he and his wife went to Enfield in a buggy. On the bridge, Mrs. Titus pointed out the beam from which the girl had slipped, and said that the body was in the water below it. They drove to the house of the mill owner who had sent the diver; he was sceptical, but agreed to send for the diver again. The man said that he had already been down below the beam, but Mrs. Titus told him he was mistaken. (Later the diver said: "I was more afraid of the woman on the bridge than of the one down below.") The diver climbed down a ladder, groped around on the bottom, and suddenly found himself holding a foot. The body was jammed head downward in a hole, just as Nellie Titus had said.

Had Bertha Huse committed suicide? Mrs. Titus's statements are ambiguous. At one point she says: "She did not intend to commit suicide." But she also described how the girl had stood on the beam, trying to decide whether to go into the water there, or to go over the hill to a pond. Unless she was intending to go for an early morning swim—which seems unlikely on a frosty morning—it sounds as if she set out with the intention of committing suicide, but died by accident sooner than she intended.

Several witnesses, including the local doctor, the mill owner, the diver and George Titus himself, wrote accounts of what happened; and, since the doctor happened to be a cousin of Mrs. James, these were sent to William James, who published them in the *Proceedings* of the American Society for Psychical Research.*

How could all this be explained? James was inclined to accept a theory that had been developed by Gurney and Myers. In investigating cases of hypnosis, Gurney had reached the conclusion that man possesses "two different strata of con-

---

*They are reprinted in *William James on Psychical Research*, edited by Gardner Murphy and Robert O. Ballou, London 1961.

sciousness, ignorant of each other," and that hypnotic phenomena are due to this "extra consciousness" or second self.
(This was, of course, an anticipation of Hudson's "subjective
mind" theory that appeared almost a decade later.) Myers
preferred to call this second self the "subliminal self," and
was convinced—like Hudson—that its powers were far greater
than those of the "everyday self." And since the everyday self
is ignorant of the existence of the sublimal self, then a telepathic message picked up by this "second self" would remain
unknown to the "everyday self" unless it could be communicated either as a "premonition" or as a dream. In his article
on "The Subliminal Self,"* Myers cites a case that seems to fit
this explanation. On 17 April 1895, a thirteen-year-old girl
named Rose Foster left her home in Smethwick, Staffordshire,
and took shelter under a canal bridge from a thunderstorm—
she was known to be terrified of storms. A boatman heard a
scream and a splash while the storm was at its heights. When
the girl failed to return home, police dragged the canal under
the bridge but found nothing. The following night, Rose
Foster's aunt Mrs. Jefferies had a dream in which she was
walking along the canal, trailing an umbrella in the water,
when she saw the face of her niece rise to the surface. She
caught the girl by the hair, clasped her in her arms, and kissed
her face. Then she woke up trembling.

The next day, Mrs. Jefferies and the girl's father went along
to where the police were still dragging the canal, and Mrs. Jefferies recounted her dream to the sergeant, and showed him
the exact spot where she had seen the body—it was about sixty
yards from where the police were searching. They dragged
there, and almost immediately, the girl's face rose to the surface. Her father leapt into the water, clasped her in his arms,
and kissed her face, just as Mrs. Jefferies had done in her
dream.

Now according to the "subliminal mind" theory, the girl's
terror, at the moment of death, was picked up "subliminally"
by her aunt—to whom she was very close; but the subliminal
mind could only communicate this information through a
dream. The same explanation would apply to the Huse case.
In fact, Nellie Titus mentioned to her husband that she had a
premonition that "something awful is going to happen" on

the day before the drowning. This, according to the telepathy theory, would be her subliminal mind "picking up" Bertha Huse's thoughts of suicide. And at 6:30 the following morning, at about the time of Bertha Huse's death, she told her husband "That has happened." But her subliminal mind could only communicate a vague foreboding—until she fell asleep in her rocking chair, and it could speak more plainly.

There is a great deal of convincing evidence for this theory; in fact, it has been revived in our own time by an eminent scientist, Andrija Puharich, who suggests* that people become good telepathic "senders" when their nervous system is flooded with adrenaline (the state known technically as "adrinergia"), and good receivers when they are totally relaxed (the state known as "cholinergia"). Puharich reinforces his point with a case that took place in 1955, when a welder named Jack Sullivan was buried alive when a trench caved in. He was alone at the time; and, as he lay half-suffocated, tried sending an urgent telepathic message to a friend, Tommy Whittaker, who was on a site five miles away. Whittaker had a vague foreboding that something was wrong and that he ought to go to the other site—although he believed no one was there. He arrived in time to rescue his friend. Whittaker was relaxed, concentrating on his own welding, when Sullivan sent out the telepathic message, so his "subliminal self" was able to pass it on to the "everyday self" in the form of foreboding. If he had been asleep at the time, he would probably have dreamed of the cave-in, just as Nellie Titus dreamed of Bertha Huse's drowning.

As an explanation of clairvoyance and mediumship, the subliminal telepathic theory clearly has great attractions, particularly when buttressed with this notion of adrinergia and cholinergia. But one of the most discouraging things about psychical research is that no sooner have we found a sensible, scientific theory to explain some problem than we discover another case that contradicts it. And such a case is cited by Myers in the same article on "The Subliminal Mind."

In March 1864, a fifteen-year-old boy named Willie Mason, who worked in a drug store in Boston, came home for the weekend to the village of Natick. There he found his eleven-year-old brother Joshua; and, learning that his mother was

* *Beyond Telepathy*, 1962.

due back on the next train, suggested that they should go to the station to meet her. The two boys set off for the station, and then vanished.

Their mother had, in fact, been delayed, and arrived on a later train. When the boys failed to return home she became frantic, convinced that they were probably drowned in the nearby lake—although it was in the opposite direction to the station, and no one had reported seeing them there. When a neighbour called Elizabeth Davis arrived on Monday morning to offer help, the mother asked her to go to Boston to see if she could consult a clairvoyant.

This turned out to be harder than she expected. Two clairvoyants proved to be engaged; it was mid-afternoon when she knocked on the door of a clairvoyant named Mrs. York in Washington Street. The door opened; Mrs. York was just taking leave of a client. When Mrs. Davis said she wanted to consult her, Mrs. York asked her to come back the next day. Mrs. Davis said that would be too late. So the clairvoyant asked her to wait in the parlour while she went out to take a walk—presumably to refresh herself. Mrs. Davis had no time to explain the case. A quarter of an hour later, Mrs. York came back, stood with her back to Mrs. Davis, and said without preamble: "They went east before they went west. They saw the fire and so went to the water." The railway station was to the east of the home of the Mason boys, the lake to the west. On that afternoon, men had been burning brush near the lake.

Mrs. York went on to describe how the boys had gone to a boathouse, scrambled through a hole in its side, and taken out a black, narrow boat. The boat was only intended for one person, and as they got out on to the lake, the eleven-year-old boy fell into the water. His brother tried to save him, and both were drowned. They were, said Mrs. York, in a shallow part of the lake near the shore, to the left of the boathouse. Mrs. Davis hurried off, saying that she thought the bodies might be found before she got back. "No," said Mrs. York, "they will be found five minutes after you reach the lake."

Back in Natick, she repeated what the clairvoyant had told her. The boathouse with a hole in its side was located; a black boat, intended for only one person, was missing. (It was found in a nearby cove two days later.) Two boats set out from the boathouse with grappling hooks, and veered to the left. Within a few strokes of the oar, one of the men shouted "I've got something." It was the body of Willie Mason; his brother Joshua was found minutes later.

It is, of course, conceivable that the clairvoyant unconsciously registered the death of the two boys at the moment it happened, and that she was able to retrieve this information from her "subliminal mind" on her walk. But it would obviously be impossible for her to use telepathy to state that the bodies would be found within five minutes of Mrs. Davis getting to the lake, as they were. This seems to be a case of the most baffling of paranormal powers, precognition. And if we can accept that Mrs. York's subliminal self could catch a glimpse of the future, then it seems slightly absurd to deny it the power to pick up information direct from the scene of the tragedy instead of from someone else's mind.

Yet in spite of its inadequacies, James was inclined to accept the subliminal mind theory as a good basic explanation of psychic phenomena. The next question was then to decide how far the powers of this mysterious "second self" extended—a question that became more insistent as a result of the events that followed the sudden death of Richard Hodgson, at the age of fifty. On 20 December 1905, Hodgson collapsed and died as he was playing handball at the Union Boat Club. That night, Mrs. Piper had a strange dream; she was trying to enter a dark tunnel, but a man with a beard raised his hand to try to prevent her. She saw the hand clearly, and thought it was Hodgson's. When her daughters came into the bedroom at 7:30 she told them about the dream; an hour later, the newspaper arrived with the news of Hodgson's death.

Hodgson had often said jokingly to Mrs. Piper that if he died before she did, he would come back and "control" her as no one had done so far. So news of his death aroused much speculation about whether he would attempt to "return." He did—or someone did—eight days later, causing Mrs. Piper's hand to write the word "Hodgson." Later, he began communicating through Mrs. Piper, and William James and his son, who were present, felt that this was the authentic Hodgson personality. Yet the messages themselves were disappointing. There was the matter of a ring, which had been given to Hodgson by a woman friend, and which was not on his finger at the time of his death. The "spirit" of Hodgson said he had put it in his waistcoat pocket, and that it had been taken by the undertaker. The ring *did* turn up eventually in the waistcoat pocket; "Hodgson" was wrong about the undertaker. He convinced two ladies that he was Richard Hodgson by mentioning jokes he had told them and various other trivial incidents. Yet he seemed muddled and confused, and the evidence was far from satisfying. "Hodgson" was unable to read some words written in a cipher that he had used in one of his own notebooks. When Mrs. Piper went to England in 1906, "Hodgson" failed to recognize some old friends who came to a seance. As a spirit control, "Hodgson" was a bumbling incompetent.

In a paper about these seances, William James did his best to summarize this frustratingly inconclusive case. Even though he had felt convinced that he was in the presence of Hodgson's personality, he was unhappy about the notion that Hodgson had returned from the dead. To James, it seemed more likely that he was confronting some kind of "after-image" of Hodgson, like a gramophone record of his voice or a film of his movements. In fact, he admits that his theory amounts to a "psychometric hypothesis" about "spirits." James is usually an exceptionally clear writer, and the fact that he becomes so muddled and obscure when he talks about his theory indicates that he was not quite sure what he was talking about.

> Now, just as the air of the same room can be simultaneously used by many different voices for communicating with different pair of ears, or as the ether of space can carry many simultaneous messages to and from mutually attuned Marconi [radio] stations, so the great continuum of material nature can have certain tracts within it thrown into emphasized activity whenever activity begins in any part or parts of a tract in which the potentiality of such systematic activity inheres.

But having tied himself in verbal knots, he goes on to suggest that at one of Mrs. Piper's seances, in the presence of some of Hodgson's old friends, the "system of physical traces left behind by Hodgson" could be somehow thrown into gear and "made to vibrate all at once." In other words, the "spirit" of Hodgson that reappeared at the seances was not a genuine ghost, but a kind of combination of a film and a gramophone record. James concludes: "There seems fair evidence for the reality of psychometry, so this scheme covers the main phenomena in a vague general way."

If James was right, this would be one of the most important and exciting theories in the history of psychical research. For it would amount to the simplest and most satisfying explanation so far of some of the most baffling psychic phenomena. We have seen how Buchanan's original theory—about a kind of "nerve aura" that enables a sensitive to sniff out impressions like a bloodhound—has a pleasant air of common sense about it, and how Denton's experiments with geological specimens were a logical extension of Buchanan's discovery. *If* psychometry could really be stretched to include what happens at seances, then paranormal research could certainly begin to claim the status of a science.

Regretfully, it has to be admitted that James's theory will not hold water. A film or a gramophone recording cannot answer questions. Hodgson's "spirit" behaved like a living person, not like a recording. It knew various things that were not known to the sitters or to Mrs. Piper herself—such as that Hodgson had put the ring in his waistcoat pocket because it hurt him when he played handball. Hodgson's communications are so frustrating because they are all so trivial; nevertheless, they sound genuine enough. Years later, in a "Last Report" written shortly before his death, James admitted that he was as far as ever from understanding these infuriating problems. "For twenty-five years I have been in touch with the literature of psychical research . . . Yet I am theoretically no further than I was at the beginning." And he goes on to make a statement that has been echoed by many frustrated researchers: "I confess that at times I have been tempted to believe that the Creator has eternally intended this department of nature to remain *baffling*, to prompt our curiosities and hopes and suspicions all in equal measure, so that, although ghosts and clairvoyances, and raps and messages from spirits, are always seeming to exist and can never be fully explained away, they can also never be susceptible of full corroboration."

If James had known that psychical research would be in precisely the same position seventy-five years later, he would probably have thrown up his hands in despair.

The sad truth is that, even by 1905, those pioneer investigators had come to recognize that their original optimism had been unfounded. Psychical research was simply not going to provide the answer to the "riddle of the universe."

Yet the first few years had been full of promise and achievement. Various committees were set up to deal with mind-reading, apparitions, mesmerism and hypnosis, and what might be called "thought apparitions"—apparitions of living people. The basic aim was to find "white crows." If you wish to establish that people really come back from the dead—or appear to do so—you do not need to prove that every haunted house is genuine. You only need to find one single ghost story that will stand up to stringent testing. Henry Sidgwick's wife Eleanor spent months collecting ghost stories, and authenticating them with as many reliable witnesses as possible. The result was a lengthy survey of "Phantasms of the Dead" in volume three of the *Proceedings*. Mrs. Sidgwick's standards were high. She dismisses one of her most remarkable cases as "collective illusion." It is the narrative of two sisters, who had been to the village church on a foggy evening. They were returning—with the maid—when one of them noticed a man who appeared to be trying to pass her sister. She said, "Let that man pass," and as she did so, the man vanished—apparently into her sister's dress. Then the three women found themselves in the midst of a crowd of people, all walking quite silently. The women wore old-fashioned clothes of a generation earlier. The men seemed to have "sparks" round their faces. All appeared rather short, with the exception of one very tall man who was striding purposefully beside them. They found him frightening, and hoped that he would not enter their gate; but the man strode on, and as they entered the gate, he was now the only form in sight.

Mrs. Sidgwick admits that, if this *is* a collective hallucination, it seems to have been strangely persistent; most ghosts vanish within seconds. So she suggests that it might have been an illusion due to "irregularities in the density of the fog"—in spite of the comment of the witness that they were perfectly real-looking human beings in identifiable clothes.

Denton would have had no difficulty explaining it. He would have said that this was simply another case of "recorded impressions" of the past becoming visible; that what the girls saw was, in fact, a kind of three-dimensional film. The late Tom Lethbridge—of whom we shall speak later—saw a number of "ghosts," and became convinced that they were "tape recordings." Lethbridge suggested that strong emotions —either of joy or sorrow—can imprint themselves on some kind of electrical field, usually associated with water—he noticed that such apparitions were often seen above underground streams, or under damp conditions. Apparitions usually appear singly for the obvious reason that strong emotions are usually experienced by only one person. But if a whole crowd experiences a strong emotion—for example, an army during a battle—then the "recording" may include everyone present. A phantom Roman army has been seen several times on the Norfolk Broads, near Wroxham, and another in an old cellar in York. Charles the First sent a group of officers to investigate stories of a phantom battle of Edgehill that took place regularly on the site of the original battle, and their signed document testifying to witnessing the battle was presented to the king.*

The likeliest explanation of the events witnessed by the three women is that they saw a crowd of people who were all experiencing some strong emotion, and who had been "photographed" by damp conditions—probably a fog like the one in which the sisters saw them. They could have been a holiday crowd on their way to the village fair. But the girls do not describe them as looking particularly festive. It seems more probable that they were, like the girls themselves, on their way back from church after a funeral, or some powerful hellfire sermon that had aroused a strong collective emotion. The sinister tall man was probably merely some local farmer in a hurry to get home, while the others were drifting along in a more leisurely manner. The "sparks" around their faces are difficult to explain until we recall Lethbridge's theory that the medium on which the events are recorded is some kind of electrical field. If the girls had been less alarmed, they would probably have noticed the same "sparks" around hands and light patches of clothing—in the same way that, when an old film is shown, the faces look abnormally pale while the dark patches look more than usually dark.

It was not Mrs. Sidgwick's business to speculate about the mechanics of these phantasms, although various members of the Society for Psychical Research—like Sir Oliver Lodge and Sir Arthur Conan Doyle—were not long in evolving their own

---

*See my *Mysteries*, p. 471

version of the "tape recording" theory, Lodge suggesting that "strong emotions could be unconsciously recorded in matter," so that "on a psychometric hypothesis the original tragedy has been literally *photographed* on its material surroundings . . . and thenceforth in certain persons an hallucinatory effect is experienced corresponding to such an impression." That comment: "in certain persons," is important. Mrs. Sidgwick records a number of cases in which one or more people have seen a "ghost" while others who were there at the same time saw nothing.

After publishing her careful report on 307 cases of "phantasms of the dead," Mrs. Sidgwick may well have felt that she had established her case once and for all. After her investigation, no cultured person could ever again dismiss ghosts as old wives' tales or delusions of credulous or over-excitable people. As another eminent investigator, Andrew Lang, pointed out, most people who have seen ghosts are not hysterics, but "steady, unimaginative, unexcitable people with just one odd experience." If Mrs. Sidgwick's 180-page report had appeared as a book—with a title like *Ghosts and Apparitions*—perhaps it might have achieved its intended effect of placing ghosts on the same scientific footing as radio or photography. But buried away in the pages of the *Proceedings* of the SPR, it never reached the general public. And anyone who bought that particular volume of the *Proceedings* would have been far more excited by Richard Hodgson's lengthy exposure of Madame Blavatsky as a fraud.

The same objection could hardly apply to the monumental *Phantasms of the Living* by Edmund Gurney, Frederick Myers and Frank Podmore, published in two large volumes in 1886. This dealt with one of the most puzzling yet most commonplace of psychic phenomena: the "appearance" of one living person to another at a considerable distance. One eminent witness of such an apparition was the poet Goethe, who was walking home one day after a heavy shower when he saw a friend named Friedrich walking in front of him; what intrigued Goethe was that Friedrich was wearing Goethe's dressing gown. He arrived home to find Friedrich in front of his fire, dressed in the dressing gown—he had been caught in a heavy shower on his way to see Goethe, and had removed some of his clothes for drying.

Another typical example can be found in a recent book on

telepathy by Joe Cooper. Cooper was staying on Jersey with the writer Jack Higgins (Harry Patterson) and borrowed the brake to drive into St. Helier to do some shopping. When he tried to find the car park, he realized he had forgotten where it was. It took him an hour of wandering around St. Helier to locate it. He arrived back late—most of the others had gone off to a friend's house for drinks, but Cooper's wife had stayed behind. She asked: "Why did you go away again?" Patterson had heard the brake drive through the gate. He had looked over and saw Joe Cooper get out of the brake and take a box out; by the time Patterson arrived, the brake had vanished and there was no one there. Cooper attributes this "apparition" of himself to his intense frustration as he searched around St. Helier for the car park.*

The 1,200 pages of *Phantasms of the Living* certainly establish such "apparitions" beyond all possible doubt, and recognize that they seem to be basically some form of "telepathic" phenomenon—one person thinking about another so intensely that some freak form of "thought transference" takes place. Yet the sheer size of the book, and its plodding repetitiousness, makes it virtually unreadable. Even a later abridgement by Eleanor Sidgwick is just as atrociously dull. So, like Mrs. Sidgwick's "Phantasms of the Dead," it simply failed in its intended effect—to establish the reality of such phenomena in the minds of educated people.

All this, then, helps to explain why the Society for Psychical Research failed to achieve the kind of breakthrough that its founders had hoped for. They believed that once the "facts" of telepathy, premonitions, ghosts, phantasms of the living, were established, science would begin to take them seriously, and they would become part of the intellectual inheritance of the next generation. But in spite of the impressive weight of evidence, scientists remained as bored and irritable as ever. Besides, the SPR itself provided its opponents with ammunition by being so prompt to denounce frauds; for in spite of Sidgwick's assertion that "it was not the practice of the Society to direct attention to the performance of any so-called 'medium' who had been proved guilty of systematic fraud," some of its members seemed to derive far more enjoyment from announcing disbelief than in admitting they were con-

The Mystery of Telepathy by Joe Cooper, 1983, p. 115.

vinced. Frank Podmore, the Oxford civil servant who wrote the first—and still perhaps the best—history of psychic phenomena,* became dogmatically convinced that all poltergeists were the result of trickery, and refused to budge from that position in the face of the most overwhelming evidence to the contrary; he evidently derived some sort of pleasure from seeing himself as a tough-minded sceptic. With friends like this, the Society had no need of enemies.

There were other setbacks. The Creery sister—the vicar's daughters whose skill at thought transference had led to the formation of the Society—were caught cheating; this was a severe blow, particularly as the authors of *Phantasms of the Living* declared that they owed their belief in thought transference to their experiments with the Creery sisters. The sisters insisted, probably quite truthfully, that they had only cheated once or twice; but this threw doubt on all their earlier performances. Then in 1880, Florence Cook—the medium who had convinced Crookes of her genuineness—was exposed at a seance when Sir George Sitwell—father of Edith, Osbert and Sacheverell—made a grab at the "spirit," and it turned out to be Florence Cook in her underwear. Crookes's other favourite medium, Rosino Showers, confessed that she had been cheating. In 1888, the two Fox sisters, whose rapping had started modern spiritualism forty years earlier, made a public confession of fraud, claiming that they had caused the raps by cracking their joints. Soon afterwards, it emerged that they had been involved in a bitter quarrel with their elder sister Leah, and that the confession had been made partly to embarrass her, and partly to make money; both sisters had fallen on hard times, and their well-publicized confession made them $1,500. The confession was the basis of a book called *The Death Blow to Spiritualism* by Reuben Davenport. It was not quite the death blow to spiritualism; but it *was* virtually the death blow to the Society's hopes of creating an intellectual revolution.

Then there was the baffling paradox of Eusapia Palladino, an Italian peasant woman who seemed to be the most remarkable psychical medium since Daniel Dunglas Home (who had died in 1886). In broad daylight she could cause articles of furniture to move, lie suspended in mid-air "as on a

Modern Spiritualism, 2 volumes, 1902.

couch," and cause musical instruments to sound on the other side of the room. Yet to the chagrin and bewilderment of her admirers, she would seize any opportunity to cheat. One investigator decided to give her total freedom to cheat, in order to learn her methods, and was puzzled to find that they were clumsy and obvious. Eusapia agreed that she cheated, but said that she did it in a semi-trance state, and that it was caused by malign influences she could not control. Eminent scientists —Lombroso, Ochorowitz, Richet, Lodge—studied her and concluded that the phenomena were beyond natural explanation. The stubborn Hodgson, who had failed to learn humility from his experiences with Mrs. Piper, produced all kinds of far-fetched theories of how the scientists might have been cheated, failing to convince anyone who had ever been in the same room with Eusapia Palladino. Yet the unfortunate fact remained: she cheated. And it was no good trying to explain to sceptical scientists that her genuine effects were beyond the skill of the most expert conjuror. If she cheated, she was a cheat. The logic was irrefutable.

It was also in 1888—the year of the Fox sisters' "confession"— that more gossip was aroused when Edmund Gurney died in mysterious circumstances in a Brighton hotel. He had been conducting experiments in telepathy with a stage hypnotist named George Albert Smith, and with a close friend of Smith's called Douglas Blackburn. Blackburn had to leave hastily for South Africa after a divorce scandal, and Smith then arranged another series of tests with various other youths in Brighton. Twenty years later, Blackburn, now a successful novelist, returned from South Africa and confessed in *John Bull* that the experiments in which he had taken part were faked, and that the Society's investigations had been as easy to deceive as children. It seems a fair inference that the later experiments with the Brighton youths were also faked by Smith, who had become Gurney's secretary.

On 21 June 1888, Gurney came home in the evening and found a letter with a Brighton postmark waiting for him. He did not tell his wife what it contained, but went off the next day to Brighton. Nothing is known about his presumed interview with the mysterious correspondent, but he wrote a letter to another member of the SPR asking him to come and help with certain "enquiries." The following day, a maid tried to get into Gurney's hotel room and was unable to get any reply; the door was forced, and Gurney was found dead in bed, a sponge bag over his face. By the side of the bed was a small bottle of chloroform. At the inquest, it was stated that Gurney often sniffed chloroform to relieve neuralgia, and a verdict of accidental death was recorded. But there was gossip at the SPR that this was no accident, and William James's sister Alice recorded in her diary: "They say there is little doubt that Mr. Edmund Gurney committed suicide." In 1964, Trevor Hall's book *The Strange Case of Edmund Gurney* suggested that Gurney had killed himself when he discovered that Smith had been hoaxing him for years, and that the brilliant theories of thought transference and telepathy that he had published in the *Proceedings* of the SPR had no solid foundation. (By this time, the Creery sisters had also been caught cheating.) What seems slightly more difficult to explain is why Gurney wrote a letter to ask someone to join him in Brighton if he intended to kill himself.

Whatever the truth behind the death, it was a serious blow to the Society. Gurney was one of the few members with a large enough fortune to devote his full time to its affairs. (The family's wealth was a by-word—W. S. Gilbert has a line in *Trial by Jury*: "At last I became as rich as the Gurneys.") He was also a man of immense enthusiasm and unimpeachable integrity. Myers and Podmore, who took over the editing of the *Proceedings* from Gurney, were not of the same quality. Podmore seems to have been a homosexual, and he has been suspected of intimate involvement with the Brighton youths he was supposed to be testing. Myers, a man of considerable intellect, was a womanizer who had come under a cloud at Cambridge when he "borrowed" twenty-five lines from somebody else's poem in his own Latin prize poem. Before Gurney's death, he had a passionate affair with his cousin's wife, who had committed suicide when she became pregnant, and had also done his best to seduce Gurney's future bride.

It was Myers's lack of critical acumen—to put it charitably —that was indirectly responsible for two of the scandals that shook the SPR in the 1890s. Some time before Gurney's death, Myers met an attractive young lady named Ada Goodrich-Freer, who claimed to come of upper-class Highland stock, and to have powers of second sight. There is some evidence that Myers and Miss Freer had a love affair,* and in view of Myers's known penchant for attractive girls, this seems highly probable. It was Myers who persuaded her to try crystal-gazing, and the result was a paper on the subject which was published under the pseudonym "Miss X" in the *Proceedings*. She claimed that she had been able to obtain from the crystal an address she had destroyed, and located a lost key and a missing medical prescription. Everyone at the Society agreed that such an attractive and refined young lady must be trustworthy, and no one seems to have bothered to point out that she made no attempt to provide any kind of verification for her stories. In fact, later investigation has shown that Miss Freer was an inveterate liar. She not only lied about her age, but about her antecedents. She was not the descendant of generations of Highland lairds, but the daughter of a vet from Uppingham, near Leicester; her family name was Freer, not Goodrich-Freer, as she liked to spell it. She was born in 1857, not 1870 (so she was about thirty when Myers met her). She was not—as she claimed—the first woman Fellow of the Royal Society; nor did she have "county connections"; nor did she walk twelve miles a day. Miss Freer was, in short, a female Walter Mitty. There seems to be no solid evidence that she actually possessed clairvoyant powers; the evidence that impressed Myers and the SPR seems to consist of her own unverified statements.

When, in the 1890s, the Society decided to undertake an investigation into second sight in the Highlands, Miss Goodrich-Freer (as she now called herself) seemed the ideal choice. Myers recommended her to Lord Bute, who had agreed to finance the expedition. Lord Bute was charmed by her and quickly became a total believer in her powers. Miss Freer's investigative trips to the Highlands were successful, and she collected a great deal of material which she used in her reports to the SPR and in lectures; it was only much later that it emerged that she had simply borrowed the manuscripts of a priest, Father Allan McDonald—a dedicated collector of folklore —and used them fully and without acknowledgement.

In 1895, Miss Freer heard rumours of the haunting of Clandon Park, near Guildford, and spent a night there in December, as the guest of its tenants, Captain and Mrs. Blaine, who

Strange Things by John Campbell and Trevor Hall, 1968.

had rented it from Lord Onslow. The Duke of Richmond also happened to be staying in the house that night, and he found Miss Freer an attractive and likeable young lady. He recorded in a letter the next day that Miss Freer claimed to have seen nothing.

Miss Freer herself seems to have taken a great liking to Captain Blaine, with whom she talked horses. "One knew his language." This may be the reason that Mrs. Blaine ignored a hint that Miss Freer would like to visit the house a second time. But in her report in the SPR *Journal*, Miss Freer declared that she had been dressing for dinner when she had seen a hooded female figure dressed in yellowish satin. This, she claimed, was the ghost that had been seen by many others. It vanished as she approached it.

Lord Onslow was infuriated—Clandon Park was obviously likely to remain untenanted so long as it was supposed to be haunted. In fact, Lord Onslow had to move in himself. He insisted that there was no ghost, and that the story had been started when some maidservants had tried to frighten the butler.

Clandon Park had been a let-down, but Miss Freer was not disheartened. When she heard of ghosts at Ballechin House, near Dunkeld, in Perthshire, she persuaded Lord Bute to rent it for her. Since its owner, a man called Steuart, would obviously dislike publicity about haunting, the tenancy was negotiated in the name of a Colonel le Mesurier Taylor, a member of the SPR, who claimed he wanted it for "a little winter shooting and some good spring fishing."

Miss Freer moved into Ballechin House in February 1897, together with Colonel Taylor, and her friend Constance Moore. The servants had been hired by Lord Bute. The previous tenants had been a Mr. Joseph Heaven and his family. The Heavens were Spaniards (their real name was Cielo), and the head of the family had made the mistake of allowing his wife and children to go there a few days before he arrived. During that time, they heard rumours that the place was haunted, and became nervous. They said they heard strange noises; Mr. Heaven himself heard noises, but was convinced that it was merely the hot water system. His family declined to be convinced, and they left the house with two months of the tenancy still to run.

The stories about the Ballechin ghost are of the type that

make any psychical investigator suspicious. Everyone agreed there were loud banging noises, such as Mr. Heaven heard. There were supposed to be unearthly shrieks, footsteps, and sudden drops in temperature; the ghost was also reputed to snatch bedclothes off the bed. In fact, bangings and the snatching of bedclothes are both familiar tricks of the poltergeist, the mischievous "spirit" that usually seems to be associated with disturbed teenagers. Screaming ghosts are seldom—if ever—found outside ghost stories; real ghosts are usually solid-looking apparitions that are quite silent. Poltergeists have occasionally been known to speak, but never—in my recollection—to scream. One guest, a lawyer named Cadell, who heard footsteps and banging noises in the night, states in his account that he does not believe in the screams, although the hooting of owls sometimes sounds like screams. (Significantly, he says that the footsteps he heard running down the stairs sounded like a "lightfooted person"; this was during Miss Freer's tenancy.)

The stories of snatched bedclothes also seem suspicious. The only documented account of this comes from a butler, who claims that, after his bedclothes had been thrown on the floor, his bed lifted three or four feet and, his hand held by some invisible power when he reached out for the matches, he then fell asleep. It would have sounded more truthful if he had described sprinting towards the nearest railway station in his nightshirt.

During Miss Freer's period in the house, about forty guests came and stayed; few of them seem to have experienced anything but the bangings—and one guest admits that there were hot water pipes outside both doors from which the noises seemed to come. Another spoke of waking in the night with a strong sense of some "presence" in the bedroom; but since Miss Freer usually spent the evening telling hair-raising stories about the ghost, this hardly seems surprising. An Oxford student named Balfour-Browne records that he and two companions slept in the three "haunted rooms" for several nights and heard nothing whatever. The next morning, Constance Moore remarked that the end of the house where she and Miss Freer slept had also been silent. But when Miss Freer came in to breakfast, she remarked that the ghost must have moved to their end of the house during the night.

Miss Freer and her companions made a habit of holding

seances with a Ouija board, and apparently received a message from someone called "Ishbel," who told them to go to a certain glen at dusk. They went, and Miss Freer claimed to see a black figure, like a nun, moving up the glen.

Miss Freer returned to London feeling highly satisfied. This time she had certainly managed to convince a number of people that *something* was going on, even if most of them had only heard the knocking noises. She began to prepare material for a book, cautiously entitled *The Alleged Haunting of Ballechin House*. At this point, she was enraged by an article that appeared in *The Times* by one of her guests, J. Callendar Ross, called "On the Trail of a Ghost." Mr. Ross was thoroughly sceptical about the whole thing, and concluded: "The only mystery in the matter seems to be the mode in which a prosaic and ordinary dwelling was endowed with so evil a reputation." He said that no one in the area of Ballechin House had ever heard of it being haunted, and this seems to be confirmed by the account of another guest, who asked the driver who was taking him to Ballechin about the ghosts "at which he laughed heartily and said 'Na, na! There are some Roman Catholics but nae ghosts there.'"

There followed a lively controversy about Ballechin House, in the course of which it became clear that Colonel le Mesurier Taylor had rented it under false pretenses—obviously knowing that its owner would be infuriated by reports of its "haunting." A violent storm broke in the columns of *The Times*, which further damaged the already battered reputation of the Society for Psychical Research. Mrs. Caroline Steuart, wife of the owner, wrote an indignant letter about the deception that had been practised on her. Myers did his best to back out of the limelight by claiming that he had decided that the Ballechin material was not worth publishing, and was promptly contradicted by a guest named Sir James Crichton-Browne, who declared that, on the contrary, Myers *had* been determined to publish the material. Miss Freer was enraged by Myers's desertion; she was already angry with him for arriving at Ballechin—in her absence—with a young lady who was certainly not his wife. Many correspondents took the opportunity to declare that they had known the house for years and had never heard that it was supposed to be haunted. Mr. Ross undoubtedly spoke for a large number of people when he referred to "the suspicion and disgust which close contact with the SPR always tends to excite." And when, in spite of all this, Miss Freer went ahead and published her book *The Alleged Haunting of Ballechin House*, it had the effect of rubbing salt into wounds, and the Society's attempt to disown it only spread the impression of incompetence and general disarray.

Myers became ill soon after the Ballechin scandal—Miss Freer remarked balefully in a letter that this often happened to people who crossed her, but it is more likely that the illness was to some extent a reaction to the stress of becoming an object of public ridicule. Miss Freer was not publicly condemned or disowned—that would only have increased the scandal— but there can be no doubt that she became *persona non grata* at the SPR. Her Scottish friends also became infuriated to learn that she had been publishing Father Allan McDonald's folklore material as if it was her own discovery, particularly when the news leaked out that she intended to publish a book called *The Outer Isles*. A folklore collector named Alexander Carmichael wrote to the priest in 1901: "We hear from various sources that Miss Freer is not genuine and some call her a clever impostor. I never got my wife to believe in her. In London it is said that one society after another, and one man after another, have thrown her off."

Trevor Hall presents evidence that there was some carefully suppressed scandal in which Miss Freer was caught cheating at table-rapping in 1901. In December of that year, she left England and went to live in Jerusalem. She married a German-American named Hans Spoer, an expert on the Middle East; he was sixteen years her junior, but she apparently managed to convince him that she was two years his junior. She died in America in 1931 at the age of seventy-four; her death certificate gives her age as fifty-six.

In retrospect, it is easy enough to see that Ada Freer was one of that peculiar breed of women, a mythomaniac, a person whose estimate of her own value is so high that she feels perfectly justified in inventing a story that moulds it "closer to the heart's desire." It was Myers's bad luck that she caught his roving eye and probably surrendered her virginity to him. (She had a nervous breakdown when he died in 1901.) By the time he realized she was not the upright and honest young woman he took her for—he must have realized after Ballechin that she was a virago as well as a pathological liar—it was too late. There is also an element of irony in the situation—of the biter bit. Myers had always had a streak of dishonesty—one contemporary recorded her impression that "he always rang a little false"—and it was this that made him the victim of a plausible confidence-woman.

Podmore also had an element of opportunism in his character. In 1894, he produced a book called *Apparitions and Thought Transference* that strikes a firm note of "toughmindedness" (an expression invented by William James). It was reviewed by a rising young novelist called H. G. Wells, who preached the gospel of pure science, and who accused Podmore of being too credulous. This and similar reviews seem to have pushed Podmore towards a position in which no one could accuse him of being gullible. From now on, his chief contribution to psychical research was simply to find reasons for disbelieving any piece of evidence, whether for apparitions, poltergeists or mediumship. With an increasing army of physicists, physiologists, anthropologists and psychologists all hurling abuse at the SPR, Podmore's attitude was hardly helpful. He was a senior clerk in the Post Office (at St. Martin le Grand), and in 1907 he resigned without a pension, and also separated from his wife. He encouraged the belief that he had resigned in order to be able to devote himself to psychical research; but since he seems to have been penniless, and since he had only a few years to run before retiring on full pension, it seems reasonable to assume that he was forced to resign, and that whatever forced his resignation may also have been the cause of his separation from his wife; that is, some homosexual scandal. He moved to a country rectory with his brother, and in 1910, was found drowned in a pond; the police evidence at the inquest indicates that they regarded his death as suicide. So died one more of that idealistic group who had hoped to find in psychical research the key to the riddle of the universe.

Oddly enough, the three founder members of the SPR—Sidgwick, Myers and Gurney—contributed more to psychical research after their deaths than during their lifetimes. Myers had often suggested that one of the most effective ways of establishing life after death would be a "group effort by the dead" to provide interlinked evidence through different mediums. Not long after his death, there were signs that this plan was being put into effect. Some years before his death, Myers had given Sir Oliver Lodge a sealed envelope containing a message about the place he would most like to visit after his death. In 1904, a friend of Myers, Mrs. Verrall, did a piece of automatic writing which included the words: "Myers sealed envelope left with Lodge . . . It has in it the words from the *Symposium* about love bridging the chasm." Plato's *Symposium* is, of course, a dialogue about love. When Lodge opened the envelope, it proved to contain a message that made no mention of Plato, but merely said: "If I can revisit any earthly scene, I should choose the Valley in the grounds of Hallsteads, Cumberland." This was the home of Annie Marshall, the wife of his cousin, with whom Myers had been in love. After her death, Myers wrote a booklet called *Fragments of an Inner Life* in which he speaks of Annie Marshall's home and goes on to talk about Plato's *Symposium* and the views on love it expresses. The connection is convincing.

Mrs. Verrall also received a script with the sentence: "Record the bits, and when fitted together they will make the whole." It was after this that no less than four mediums—Mrs. Verrall, her daughter Helen, Mrs. Fleming (Rudyard Kipling's sister) and Mrs. Coombe-Tennant—began receiving "bits" and fragments that fitted together like a jigsaw puzzle. It has often been said that these constitute the most convincing proof of "survival" that has ever been assembled. Yet from the point of view of the average reader, they have one tremendous drawback: the puzzle is so complex that it takes an enormous effort to make sense of it. But that it *does* make sense there can be no doubt whatever. The main "senders" claimed to be Myers, Sidgwick and Gurney.

A typical fragment of the puzzle is as follows. In 1906 Mrs. Fleming produced a message with the words "dawn," "evening" and "morning," a reference to bay leaves, and the name Laurence. Six weeks later Mrs. Verrall received a message referring to laurel and a library. Mrs. Piper came out of a trance saying the words "nigger" and what sounded like "more head." Mrs. Fleming produced more writing with references to night and day, evening and morning, as well as to "Alexander's tomb" with laurel leaves.

Eventually, the answer to the conundrum was discovered—the tomb of the Medicis in the church of San Lorenzo ("Laurence") in Florence, designed by Michelangelo, and containing sculptures of night and day, morning and evening. Lorenzo's emblem was the laurel, and near the tomb is the Laurentian Library. Alessandro de Medici ("Alexander's tomb") was half Negro, so "more head" should evidently have been "Moor head"—all Negroes being known as Moors in the Middle Ages.

The mediums themselves did not understand these strange clues, which only made sense when assembled together. There were literally dozens of similar examples. The most sceptical psychical researchers agree that it would be impossible to explain the "cross-correspondences" (as they were known) either by cheating or telepathy.

The logical conclusion is that the "survival" of Myers, Sidgwick and Gurney is proved beyond all reasonable doubt, and that, in spite of all setbacks and scandals, these founders of the Society of Psychical Research finally achieved the aim with which they set out.

The irony is that the very nature of the "proof" seems to support William James's remark that perhaps the creator intended the question of life after death to remain unproven. Few people have the patience to plod through hundreds of pages of cross-correspondences to make up their own minds.

And what of those pioneers of the paranormal, Joseph Rodes Buchanan and William Denton? Sadly, it must be recorded that neither of them achieved the place in intellectual history that they undoubtedly deserve. Denton, the younger of the two, died in 1883, at the age of sixty, and was thereafter virtually forgotten. Buchanan fared slightly better. His *Manual of Psychometry* came out in 1885, and gained him new readers and followers. But by that time, his original "nerve aura" theory of psychometry had been expanded to a point that most serious investigators found totally unacceptable.

The experiment that placed him beyond the limits of science was suggested by his interest in the new art of photography (for we are now retracing our steps to the 1850s). He tried handing photographs—suitably covered—to the psychometer, to see what impressions they produced. And with good psychometers like his wife he received convincing and accurate descriptions of the sitter. But this experiment ought *not* to have worked, since a photograph is mechanically produced, and therefore—unless its subject happened to have held it in his hands—should carry no personal "vibrations." Yet it *did* work. Buchanan concluded that "there was not, in such cases, any emanation from the person described, and the picture was merely the presentation of an idea to be grasped *by the intuitive perception which is independent of vision.*" [My italics.]

Clearly, this innocent-sounding statement either conceals a total breakdown of logic, or represents a revolutionary new theory of the nature of psychometry. According to Buchanan, it was a new theory. "Hence," he declares, "it became apparent that the object for psychometry was in such cases merely an index [he means an indication] leading the mind to the object represented, and need not be a picture, a relic, or anything associated in any way with the person or thing to be explored."

If this "intuitive perception which is independent of vision" could work on a photograph, it ought to work just as well on a mere name. Buchanan tried it. "I wrote the name of a friend and placed it in the hands of a good psychometer, who had no difficulty, notwithstanding her doubts of so novel a proceeding . . . in giving as good a description of Dr. N. as if he had made the description from an autograph."

Buchanan was carried away by wild enthusiasm. "Psychometry," he declared, "is the earthly IRRADIATION OF OMNISCIENCE and it will be known hereafter to penetrate all things." And he went on to ask his sensitives to psychometrize the names of all kinds of famous people: Homer, Shakespeare, Bacon, Jesus, Socrates, Confucius, the Buddha and St. Paul. A later volume called *Primitive Christianity* even contains a re-edited version of the Gospel of St. John.

And if a psychometrist can gather information from the past, then why not from the future? By 1884, the whole world was talking about the Moslem revolt in the Sudan, led by a religious fanatic called the Mahdi. General Gordon had been sent to try to subdue him. Buchanan wrote the name "Mahdi" on a sheet of paper, and asked a number of his students to try their powers on it. They produced impressions of a tropical country, a bloody war, men in Arab dress, and a leader of deep religious convictions—all of which might have been expected if they were unconsciously reading Buchanan's mind. What is rather more surprising is that many of their predictions for the future were accurate. Buchanan admired the Mahdi and disliked the British, so any predictions based on his subconscious hopes would involve victory for the Mahdi and defeat for the British. In fact, most of his students predicted that the Mahdi would ultimately be unsuccessful. When Buchanan asked "Is he about to capture a city?" (meaning Khartoum) the reply was: "He is preparing for an attack, but will be repulsed." In fact, the Mahdi *did* attack Khartoum, and was repulsed. Later, Buchanan again asked his wife about the war, and she predicted another attack with terrible bloodshed; within two days, the Mahdi had stormed Khartoum and murdered all the defenders, including Gordon. She went on to prophesy that the war would not continue in the summer, and that the British would withdraw their troops; both things happened as she had said. The prediction that "the war will be disastrous" for the Mahdi was also fulfilled; success made him fat and lazy; after the fall of Khartoum he withdrew into his harem for a prolonged debauch and died a few months later.

None of this surprised Buchanan; if, after all, psychometry was the "irradiation of omniscience," the future should present no more problems than the past. Buchanan pointed out, reasonably, that there have been many well-authenticated cases of precognition—he devotes a whole appendix of his *Manual* to the remarkable story of the French author Jacques Cazotte who, at a dinner party just before the French Revolution, accurately foretold the fate of almost everyone sitting at the table: Chamfort would open his veins with a razor, Condorcet would take poison to avoid the guillotine, and a notorious atheist named La Harpe would become a Christian. La Harpe was so derisive that he went home and wrote it all down. But in due course, it all happened exactly as Cazotte had said—even to La Harpe becoming a monk. The story is particularly well attested because it is referred to in other contemporary memoirs, as well as in La Harpe's own manuscript.

As far as contemporary science was concerned, all this was enough to place Buchanan beyond the pale. Even the American Society for Psychical Research—formed in the same year that the *Manual* was published—found nothing of interest in Buchanan's latest theories. Yet it is worth remarking, in passing, that some of Buchanan's own prophecies were surprisingly accurate. In 1859, he published in the *Louisville Journal* a prediction that America would experience six years of calamity; the Civil War lasted from 1861 to 1865. In 1885, he predicted a "period of calamity thirty years hence" —twenty-nine years before the Great War. He also remarked that there would probably be an "elemental convulsion" on the Pacific side of America, and that "I would prefer not to reside in San Francisco at that time." At the time Buchanan was writing, the only Californian earthquake in which there had been fatalities (forty dead) had occurred in 1868, and it involved six major cities. Buchanan had been dead six years when the San Francisco earthquake of 1906 destroyed twenty-eight thousand houses and killed seven hundred people.

He also had a prophecy concerning himself: that in the coming century he would be remembered as the "herald of the coming illumination," and that a statue would be erected to him. This prophecy has not so far been fulfilled; but there is still time.

4

The Akasic Records

IN THE LAST week of September 1877 there appeared in New York an enormous two-volume work entitled *Isis Unveiled* by Helena Petrovna Blavatsky. The mere sight of it seems to have induced mental exhaustion in the critics, and the reviews were scathing—the New York *Sun* dismissing it as "discarded rubbish." The publisher, J. W. Bouton, may have feared some such reception, for he had printed only a thousand copies, and priced it high—$7.50. To everyone's astonishment, including that of the author, these sold out within ten days, and it had to be reprinted.

Its forty-six-year-old author had only been in America for four years, most of which time she had spent in penury. Helena Petrovna Hahn had been born in Russia in 1831, daughter of a colonel and a well-known authoress. Even in childhood she had shown mediumistic powers; at nights she was visited by the spirit of a woman called Tekla Lebendorff. Her father's suspicion that this was pure invention turned to astonishment when he used his influential connections to check government archives, and discovered that the woman had really existed, and that all the facts she had given about herself were accurate.

At sixteen, to spite her governess, Helena became engaged to a man of forty; forced by her family to go through with the marriage, she promptly deserted her husband and ran away from home. The next twenty-six years were spent wandering around Europe and the East—according to her own account,

87

in search of esoteric knowledge, but more probably merely in an attempt to keep body and soul together. She worked as a travelling companion to various ladies, had a number of lovers, and learned about spiritualism at first hand from Daniel Dunglas Home. She claimed to have spent several years in Tibet, being instructed by "masters of wisdom," and said that it was under their instructions that she came to New York. It seems more probable that she had decided that her future lay in spiritualism, and that America was an ideal place to make a start.

After a period of near-starvation, she met a gentlemanly lawyer, Colonel Henry Steel Olcott, who also wrote about spiritualism for a New York newspaper. He was quickly convinced of her contact with the spirit realms—she could make raps resound from all over the room, and invisible bells tinkle in the air—and became her close friend and chief publicist. Together, they decided to form a society for the study of the "ancient wisdom," which they christened the Theosophical Society. Olcott deserted his family and moved into the same lodging house as Madame Blavatsky—although they were never lovers; there, at top speed, she wrote *Isis Unveiled*. Olcott sat opposite her for much of the time and described how her pen raced across the paper, and how, periodically, she would stare into space, as if listening to dictation. On one occasion she fell asleep, and woke up to find that her hand had added another thirty or so pages. She told her sister in a letter: "*Somebody* comes and envelopes me in a kind of misty cloud, and all at once pushes me out of myself, and then I am not 'I' anymore."

Madame Blavatsky's attitude to spiritualism was not entirely friendly. She had no doubt about the reality of spirits; her chief concern was that most of them are not what they pretend to be; they are "earthbound" spirits whose chief occupation is telling lies. So most seances are a waste of everybody's time. These manifestations, she says, have occurred in all ages, and many of the ancients understood them a great deal better than we do—particularly the ancient Egyptians and Indians. *Isis Unveiled* consists partly of a vigorous attack on modern science for its narrowness, partly of an attempt to outline the ancient occult wisdom.

According to her later doctrine—sketched only briefly in *Isis Unveiled*—man is not the first intelligent dweller on earth.

The first "root race" consisted of invisible beings made of fire mist. The second race was slightly more solid and lived in northern Asia. The third race lived on an island continent called Lemuria—or Mu—in the Indian Ocean, and consisted of ape-like giants who communicated telepathically and lacked the power of reason. The fourth race lived in Atlantis, and achieved a very high degree of civilization. They were destroyed by natural cataclysms; the last part of Atlantis, an island called Poseidonis, went down after a battle between selfish magicians and the people of an island called Shamballah. Our present race is the fifth root race, and—where matter is concerned—we are the most "solid" so far. This means that we find it far more difficult to express the power of the spirit; yet matter also enables us to be far more potentially creative than earlier root races. The root races—the sixth and seventh —that will follow ours will again be more ethereal.

How does she know this? According to Madame Blavatsky, the universe is permeated by a kind of psychic "ether" called *Akasa* (which, in Hindu philosophy, means simply space). This psychic ether explains, for example, the operations of telepathy and clairvoyance which are "waves" in the ether. It also *records* everything that has ever happened, and these "Akasic records" are available to clairvoyants and mystics. She goes on to praise the work of Buchanan and Denton, who have demonstrated the existence of these records of the past. She adds that anyone who can read the records of the past can also read the future, since it is already present in embryo.

Madame Blavatsky's praise of Buchanan and Denton was undoubtedly one more nail in their joint coffin. If scientists were already dubious about the design of their experiments, the approval of the author of *Isis Unveiled* must have been enough to convince them that the work of the pioneers of psychometry was beneath serious notice.

This is also the likeliest explanation for the otherwise baffling fact that the Society for Psychical Research behaved as if Buchanan and Denton had never existed. After all, William James was inclined to believe that psychometry was the explanation of "spirit manifestations," and the subliminal self theory of Myers and Gurney implied the same thing. And Buchanan and Denton *were* the first genuine experimenters in the field of psychometry—the true forerunners of the SPR. But Madame Blavatsky used them to buttress theosophy, and the SPR had decided that Madame Blavatsky was a fraud. It was guilt by association.

Madame Blavatsky's downfall came in 1884, two years after the founding of the SPR. The hostility that followed the success of *Isis Unveiled* had made her decide to abandon the undeserving western world and move to the country she admired so much, India. A new religious movement called the Arya Samaj indicated that it would be willing to amalgamate with theosophy. Madame Blavatsky and Colonel Olcott arrived in Bombay early in 1878, and immediately felt at home in this ancient culture. Theosophy was an immediate success. After more than a century of British rule, the Indians were delighted to be told that their culture was superior to that of the materialistic West. Olcott soon set up branches of the society throughout India and Ceylon—he became a Buddhist, to the disgust of the Arya Samaj, which decided to disaffiliate itself. But the Indians had no difficulty in swallowing the secret master in Tibet. A new disciple, Alfred Sinnett, asked if he might write to Master Koot Hoomi, and began to receive mysterious letters that appeared on his desk, or even fell out of the air. Then, just as Madame Blavatsky seemed to have achieved the security she had been seeking all her life, a disgruntled ex-housekeeper named Emma Coulomb began spreading stories that some of her most impressive psychic effects—like causing a shower of roses to fall from the air —had been achieved by fraud. The Society for Psychical Research sent Richard Hodgson to investigate. Madame Coulomb and her husband demonstrated how they had caused "Mahatma letters" to fall out of the air, and Hodgson tracked down the shop that had sold saucers and vases that had later appeared as "apports" from the Tibetan master. It became impossible to doubt that most of Madame Blavatsky's "miracles" were fraudulent. Hodgson's report to that effect appeared in an 1885 issue of the SPR *Proceedings*. As a result of all the scandal, Madame Blavatsky had to retreat ignominiously back to London. She was dying of Bright's disease, but still found the energy to write *The Secret Doctrine*, which is even longer than *Isis Unveiled*, and much of which takes the form of a commentary on an unknown mystical work called *The Book of Dzyan*. Psychometry and Elizabeth Denton come in for another favourable mention in a long footnote; under the circumstances, it would have been kinder to leave it out.

She died in 1891, at the age of sixty, leaving *The Secret Doctrine* still in manuscript.

The search was on for a scientifically respectable alternative to the word "psychometry." The most eminent of French investigators, Charles Richet, decided on "pragmatic cryptesthesia," cryptesthesia being another name for clairvoyance, or non-sensory ways of obtaining information. In a later work, Richet was to write censoriously: "The term 'psychometry' (soul-measurement) is so detestable that we cannot retain it in scientific language."*

The most eminent of Italian psychical investigators, Professor Ernesto Bozzano, preferred the term "metagnomy." Understandably, neither of these words caught on. Whether it was detestable or not, the word "psychometry" was easier to pronounce than these alternatives. So investigators like William James, Frederick Myers and Sir Oliver Lodge continued to speak about psychometry, while taking care never to mention Buchanan or Denton.

Theosophists had no such misgivings. They were inclined to cite Buchanan and Denton as far-seeing scientists who had proved the existence of the Akasic records. It was a theosophist, W. Scott-Elliot, who, in 1896, published a book whose revelations claimed to be derived from their methods. *The Story of Atlantis* achieved instant popularity, not only among theosophists but with the reading public, who seemed to have a boundless appetite for speculation about the lost continent. It has remained in print to this day.

Madame Blavatsky was not entirely responsible for the widespread interest in Atlantis. In 1882, an American politician named Ignatius Donnelly had caused a sensation with *Atlantis, The Antediluvian World*, in which he brought immense erudition to bear on the ancient problem, examining deluge legends of many races, and studying the geological and mythological evidence for the existence of the sunken continent first mentioned by Plato. Donnelly argued that the only remaining fragments of Atlantis are the Azores, which were the tops of its mountains. His book achieved the same impact that Immanuel Velikovsky was to achieve with *Worlds in Collision* in 1950. Again, Madame Blavatsky had achieved "respectable" support for one of her occult theories. In *The*

Thirty Years of Psychical Research, 1923, p. 177.

Secret Doctrine, she quotes some of her own words about Atlantis from *Isis Unveiled*, and remarks: "Since then, Donnelly's *Atlantis* has appeared, and soon its actual existence will have become a scientific fact." This forecast proved over-optimistic.

So it was perhaps to be expected that some devoted theosophist should attempt to study the Akasic records for a more precise account of the story of Atlantis. Scott-Elliot's book was introduced by Alfred Sinnett, now the leading member of the Theosophical Society in England. He explained the basic idea of psychometry in language that might have been borrowed from Buchanan or Denton:

> The memory of Nature is in reality a stupendous unity, just as in another way all mankind is found to constitute a spiritual unity . . . For ordinary humanity, however, at the early stage of its evolution . . . the interior spiritual capacities . . . are as yet too imperfectly developed to enable them to get in touch with any other records in the vast archives of Nature's memory, except those with which they have individually been in contact at their creation.

For, according to Sinnett, even ordinary human memory is not stored in the brain, but in some "superphysical matter" that lies outside the physical plane. So in theory, there is nothing to stop anybody from reaching beyond his own individual memory into Nature's "vast archives." Telepathy, for example, reveals that an individual is not restricted to his own memory, but can gain access to that of another person. Such a person, says Sinnett, "has begun . . . to exercise the faculty of astral clairvoyance. That term may be conveniently used to denote the kind of clairvoyance I am now endeavouring to elucidate, the kind which, in some of its more magnificent developments, has been employed to carry out the investigations on the basis of which the present account of Atlantis has been compiled."

Regrettably, Sinnett fails to explain in detail how Scott-Elliot went about "astral clairvoyance." But he does explain that "every fact stated in the present volume has been picked up bit by bit with watchful and attentive care, in the course of an investigation on which more than one qualified person has

been engaged . . . for some years past." And he hints that
these qualified persons have been allowed access to "maps and
other records physically preserved from the remote periods
concerned—though in safer keeping than in that of the tur-
bulent races occupied in Europe with the development of
civilization in brief intervals of leisure from warfare . . ."—in
other words, from the archives of the Mahatmas in Tibet. This
can hardly have been reassuring to anyone who had read
Hodgson's report on Madame Blavatsky's chicaneries. But
then, the theosophists remained convinced—as they are to this
day—that Madame Blavatsky was genuine, that Morya and
Koot Hoomi really existed, and that all the evidence against
Madame Blavatsky rested on the lies of her enemies.

According to Scott-Elliot, the Atlantean civilization was
flourishing as long ago as a million years. He was, of course,
aware that according to the geological records, *Homo sapiens*
has been on earth only about a hundred thousand years; but,
according to Madame Blavatsky, geology has grossly under-
estimated the length of historical epochs. Some 800,000 years
ago, the first of four great catastrophes took place. (This, according to Scott-Elliot, was in the Miocene era; here, his own
dating is faulty—the Miocene era ended about nine million
years ago.) There was a second catastrophe 200,000 years ago,
a third 80,000 years ago, and the fourth and last—the one
mentioned by Plato—in 9,564 B.C.

The theosophical view is that Atlantean civilization began
about five million years ago, in a vast continent that stretched
from present day Greenland into the middle of present
day South America. During the long period of its existence, it
was inhabited by seven sub-races. (They are called sub-races to
distinguish them from the seven root races, each of which is
sub-divided into seven.) One of these sub-races, the Toltecs,
ended by conquering the whole continent and building the
magnificent City of the Golden Gates, a vast circular city with
canals, described to Plato by an Egyptian priest.

There was a long golden age, then decay set in as kings and
priests began to use their psychic powers for their own selfish
ends. The connection with the "occult hierarchy" was broken.
The misuse of psychic faculties for selfish personal ends is
called sorcery. As more and more people practised the black
arts, Nature herself rose up against them; giant waves rolled
across huge parts of the continent.

In spite of this warning, black magic again slowly assumed its sway, and about four hundred thousand years ago, a "great lodge of initiates"—priests directly instructed by the "occult hierarchy"—moved to Egypt and founded a dynasty. It was they who built the pyramids more than eighty thousand years ago. (Another colony of "initiates" built Stonehenge, whose deliberate crudeness was intended as a rebuke to a civilization that had become effete.) Eventually, the remaining parts of Atlantis were also submerged.

In 1904, Scott-Elliot produced another book from the Akasic records, this time the story of *The Lost Lemuria*, the earlier continent that once extended from present day Africa to the Pacific Ocean. The existence of Lemuria had, in fact, been suggested by a zoologist named Sclater in the mid-nineteenth century, to explain why animals and plant life are so similar over a vast area of the southern hemisphere; the lemur, a small monkey, was the most typical form of this common animal life, hence the name of the continent. Scott-Elliot's study of the Akasic records convinced him that Lemuria had been in existence since the Permian period, and continued to exist well into the Cretaceous period—that is to say, from more than two hundred million years ago until around a hundred million years ago. Lemurians were about fifteen feet tall, with a yellowish-brown skin and flattened faces—a kind of fish-man. Unlike the Atlanteans, these Lemurians were not destroyed by sudden catastrophes; their continent was eaten away slowly by internal fires, until volcanic explosions filled the air with suffocating fumes and most of the inhabitants were asphyxiated. But a small colony of selected Lemurians settled in what is now Africa, and became the parents of the fourth root race, the Atlanteans. An adept from Venus undertook the role of Manu, or spiritual leader and instructor . . .

Scott-Elliot's books on Atlantis and Lemuria took their place beside *The Secret Doctrine* and Sinnett's *Esoteric Buddhism* as basic scriptures of the Theosophical Society. They deeply impressed a newcomer to the Society, Rudolf Steiner, who in due course undertook further investigation of the Akasic records relating to the lost continents.

To say that Steiner joined the Theosophical Society would hardly be accurate; by the time he decided to adopt its doctrines, he was already an influential writer and lecturer, and he simply made himself a spokesman for theosophy. He was the single most powerful influence on the movement after Madame Blavatsky. (A young Hindu boy, Jiddu Krishnamurti, who was chosen in 1908 by the leaders of the Society to become the true successor to Madame Blavatsky and the future World Leader, publicly renounced the role in 1929.)

Born in Hungary in 1861, Steiner was the son of a station master. As a child he was clairvoyant—at the age of eight he was sitting in the station waiting-room when a female relative came in and began making strange gestures; Steiner knew intuitively that she was a spirit; the woman had committed suicide at the moment Steiner saw her. In the countryside and woods near Wiener-Neustadt, Steiner was aware of nature spirits. He was a brilliant student—at the age of fifteen he taught himself Greek and Latin because his father would not allow him to learn them at school. He entered the Vienna Polytechnic and studied science. He became absorbed in the nineteenth-century German philosophers, and developed a passionate admiration for Goethe. He also met Nietzsche, who was already living in a mental twilight, and wrote a book about him. He became a tutor to a family of boys, and developed the ideas on education that were to become the basis of the Steiner Schools. His professor recommended him to the man who was editing Goethe's works, and Steiner was given the task of editing the scientific works—no doubt because the other scholars thought it a thankless task to edit such outdated nonsense. But Steiner, like Reichenbach before him, was excited and impressed by Goethe's scientific theories, and his edition of the works made him an academic reputation. He also wrote volumes on German philosophy and outlined his own ideas in a book called *The Philosophy of Freedom*. He spent seven years working on the Goethe-Schiller archive in Weimar, then went to Berlin and became a celebrated lecturer and the main figure in a circle of intellectuals. So when he delivered a series of lectures to the Theosophical Society in Berlin in 1900, he did so on his own terms, as one whose own theory of mysticism was already well developed. The Theosophical Society was delighted to welcome a man of his stature as an ally.

In spite of the warmth of his welcome, it was inevitable that Steiner should soon begin to feel uncomfortable among the theosophists. He had been trained as a scientist and as a scholar. He was an acute philosophical intellect. The theosophists must have struck him as hopelessly woolly-minded. Besides, Madame Blavatsky was, on the whole, rather hostile to Christianity. Steiner had been born a Catholic, and had studied the Christian mystics—Eckhart, Tauler, Suso, Boehme; he regarded the Incarnation as one of the most important spiritual events in the earth's history. In the long run, the only condition under which Steiner could have remained in the Theosophical Society was as its leader. And since by 1908 the "old guard"—Sinnett, Annie Besant, C. W. Leadbeater—had already selected their future leader—Krishnamurti—this was out of the question. So Steiner soon went his own way, calling his version of theosophy "anthroposophy." It is, in some ways, the most comprehensive of all occult systems.

Steiner's starting point is much the same as that of William Blake, or any of the other great mystics: the recognition that there is a world "beyond" the material world revealed by our senses. If we can accept their own accounts, both Blake and Steiner could actually see—or catch glimpses of—this "supersensual" world. If such a statement seems open to doubt—the "visions" of Blake and Steiner could have been pure imagination—then it might be more acceptable to say that, like Wordsworth, Steiner's childhood among mountains and lakes had imbued him with a deep awareness of "unknown modes of being." Yet, temperamentally, he was closer to the young H. G. Wells than to Wordsworth; he had a passion for science and for ideas. Like Madame Blavatsky, he was dismayed by the dogmatic materialism of contemporary science. Goethe provided Steiner with an alternative vision of science. Goethe started from the feeling that the world is a living, breathing whole, and that the scientist needs intuition as much as he needs reason to grasp it. It is pointless to try to understand the world by taking it to pieces and examining the parts, just as it would be pointless for a surgeon to try to understand the technique of a great actor by dissecting his body. Of course dissection can teach us something important; but we have to recognize that what we can learn from it is *limited*.

By the time Steiner came to theosophy, he took all this for granted. His bid to be accepted as a philosopher—with a book called *The Philosophy of Freedom*—had been ignored, so he had nothing to lose by stating his conviction that a "supersensual" world extends beyond the physical realm. This he did in a number of books that appeared while he was still a member of the Theosophical Society (with which he broke in 1912): *Theosophy, Knowledge of Higher Worlds* and *Occult Science*. An excellent summary of his ideas is provided in his short book *Rosicrucian Esoterica*, consisting of a series of lectures he delivered in Budapest in 1909.

According to anthroposophy, the human being is made up of four "bodies." The physical body is animated by the etheric body, which is visible to clairvoyants as the "aura." This is what Bergson called the *élan vital* and Shaw the "life force." Nowadays it might be called the "life field" or L-field. Next comes the "astral body" which, according to occultists, can leave the physical body under certain conditions. Above these is the ego, and principle of individuation. Man has slowly evolved these bodies after vast epochs of time, one by one. Plants only possess the first two. Man is the only creature on earth who possesses the ego body, which coordinates the other three. By working on these "lower" bodies with his ego, man can create three higher bodies: a spirit consciousness, a spiritual body, and an "ultimate soul," what the Hindus call *atman*, whose nature is identical with that of God.

It is in his book *Cosmic Memory* that Steiner gives his own account of human evolution, and of the story of Atlantis and Lemuria. Steiner, like Scott-Elliot, actually claims to have obtained his material at first hand from the Akasic records (or, as he calls them, the "Akasha chronicle"). "The person who has acquired the ability to perceive in the spiritual world comes to know past events in their eternal character. They do not stand before him like the dead testimony of history, but appear in full *life*. In a certain sense, what has happened takes place before him." To anyone who has read Denton's *Soul of Things*, these words present no difficulty. This is just as well, for Steiner goes on to say: *"Today* I am still obliged to remain silent about the sources of the information given here. One who knows anything at all about such sources will understand why this has to be so. But events can occur which will make a breaking of this silence possible very soon . . ." Steiner never seems to have kept this promise.

According to Steiner's account of human evolution, man began to evolve on some "primeval nebula" in the form of a mineral, and it was only long ages later, with the aid of certain "sublime spiritual beings," that he graduated to our earth, in the form of a being whose body was a cloud-like vapour.

As their bodies grew gradually denser, men lost their power to mould themselves, and started to become slaves of matter—just as we are. They became "dual"—the body subject to the laws of matter, and the inner being, subject to the laws of life itself. And since the "body" could die, death came into the world.

It was much later, when man evolved into the Lemurians, that he developed violent desires and passions, and became capable of behaving selfishly. This was because he was being entrapped in matter quicker than he could learn to control it. His evil desires created violent natural forces that eventually destroyed Lemuria. By the time Lemuria sank beneath the Pacific, Atlantis had already come into existence. The Atlanteans thought in images, and because they were closer to the earth, they could control the force of life. They could, for example, extract the life from a large heap of seeds, and somehow use it to propel their airships. It was during the mid-Atlantean period that man lost touch with his inner world, and became aware only of the external world of nature. Once man's senses were directed outward, towards nature, and he lost contact with his inner world, he became capable of believing that matter is the only reality. Once a man believes that, he becomes a pragmatist who feels that the end justifies the means. In other words, he becomes capable of crime.

The story of Atlantis is an alternative legend of the Fall. The Atlanteans were our ancestors. Since our race—the fifth root race—had lost natural powers of clairvoyance—the ability to see into the spirit world—we had to develop some alternative means of navigating our way through life. We developed the power of reason.

Steiner's account of the fifth root race deserves to be read as a perceptive sketch of human history. The first sub-race, the Indians, were too "spiritual"; they denied the reality of matter. The second sub-race, the Persians, accepted matter, but regarded life as a crude battle between matter and spirit, in which spirit is good and matter is evil. The next sub-race, the Egyptian-Chaldean-Babylonian, took a step nearer to "accepting" matter—they saw the world as an immense mystery, which is why they studied the heavens. Next came the Graeco-Roman sub-race, which went altogether too far in accepting the world of matter. In fact, the Romans went so far that they became virtually a nation of criminals. They had no "knowledge of higher worlds" to prevent them from becoming as selfish and brutal as the Atlanteans. The human race had reached a spiritual nadir. And at this point, says Steiner, Jesus Christ appeared, restoring to men a sense of the life of the spirit. So the task of modern man is to reconcile the opposite viewpoints of the Indians and the Romans—to treat matter as an ally without surrendering to it.

Steiner agrees with Madame Blavatsky that man is now slowly emerging from his total entrapment in matter, and that we can now anticipate a slow upswing back into spirituality. Ever since his earliest days on earth, man's evolution has been a series of swings, each of which has gone too far. But now at last, he understands his own history, and is capable of controlling his future. Steiner, like Madame Blavatsky, believed that philosophy will be the major religion of the new age.

Both were mistaken. The Theosophical Society had been badly shaken by the "unmasking" of Madame Blavatsky by Hodgson, and Krishnamurti's decision in 1929 to renounce his role as the new messiah finally destroyed all hope of a revival.

Steiner and theosophy began to go their separate ways in 1909. The occultist Edouard Schuré had attempted a re-creation of an Eleusinian mystery of ancient Greece; an actress named Marie von Sivers—whom Steiner married—translated it into German; Steiner presented this in 1907. In 1909, he presented another Schuré "play" as part of the Anthroposophical Congress at Munich. Like the Russian composer Scriabin, Steiner believed that drama, music and the visual arts somehow could be combined to present spiritual conceptions. The theosophists found all this a little too flamboyant, and Steiner finally broke with them in 1912. At this point, he decided to erect his own theatre, and when someone offered him a site near Dornach, in Switzerland, he accepted eagerly. He was fortunate that an earlier plan to build in Munich fell through, for Switzerland remained neutral during the Great War, and Steiner was able to continue his work uninterrupted. He proved to be a brilliant architect as well as a teacher, and the magnificent domed building called the Goetheanum rose steadily under his direction. He even carved statues for it. In 1920, he founded his own school, the Waldorf school, in Stuttgart. German education had always been based on rigid discipline; Steiner created a revolution by insisting that children should be treated as human individuals, and that the aim of education was to develop their personalities. He founded a hospital and clinic, whose method was based upon his recognition that mind and body are interdependent, and that the body can often be cured through the mind. He pioneered methods of educating psychopathic and handicapped children. He even turned his attention to agriculture, and developed the "bio-dynamic" method, emphasizing the importance of understanding nature's economy. He became deeply involved with the sacraments of Christianity, and founded a Christian community at Dornach. In spite of this crowded work schedule, he seemed inexhaustible.

But post-war Europe was no longer a safe world for religious idealists. Hitler was preaching antisemitism, and the Communists were denouncing religion as the "opium of the people." Steiner was hated by all kinds of religious and political groups. On New Year's Day 1923, the Goetheanum burned to the ground—almost certainly as a result of arson. For the sixty-one-year-old Steiner, this was a considerable blow. He had survived physical violence by political thugs and partial bankruptcy due to inflation; now he saw ten years' labours go up in smoke. A new Goetheanum began to rise on the site of the old one, this time of stone instead of wood. But Steiner himself was partly burned out. In spite of illness, he continued to give lectures at the rate of more than one a day, and also wrote his autobiography. He had just completed it when he died, in March 1925, at the age of sixty-four.

It is tempting to feel that Steiner's excursion into theosophy was an unfortunate aberration, and that he would have made just as powerful an impact as an anti-materialist philosopher. But this would be to ignore the depth of his commitment to occultism, and that he was as much a clairvoyant as a philosopher. In *Rosicrucian Esoterica*, he writes: "A clairvoyant sees how during the very first weeks and months after birth the child is surrounded by intensely active, powerful forces belonging to the etheric body . . . It is wonderful to see how certain forces surge up from the body below and then stream from the nape of the neck in all directions, wherever there is hair . . . ," and he is obviously speaking from personal experience. We feel this again when he writes: "The etheric body of an animal is quite different from its physical body. The etheric body of a horse, for example, extends far beyond its physical

form. If you could see the etheric body of an elephant clairvoyantly, you would be amazed at its gigantic proportions.''
And he goes on to add a comment that Jungians will find significant: that the etheric body of a man is female, and the
etheric body of a woman is male.

Non-clairvoyants—such as the author of this book—certainly find it hard to take this kind of remark seriously, and
sympathize with sceptics who dismiss it as pure fantasy. The
fact remains that clairvoyants throughout history have been
describing the same thing, and continue to do so to this day.
Reichenbach found that his sensitives all described the aura in
the same way. In 1911, a doctor from St. Thomas's Hospital
in London, Walter J. Kilner, invented a stained glass screen
which, he claimed, could make the aura visible to anybody
(and, since the colours of the aura vary with the health of the
patient, would provide an instrument of medical diagnosis).
For a few years, Kilner's experiments led the medical community to take the aura seriously; but after his death in 1920,
his work was quickly forgotten. But in the 1930s, two Yale researchers, Harold Burr and F. S. C. Northrop, discovered that
all living bodies have an electrical charge, which varies with
health. Burr and Northrop measured the electrostatic field of
trees by connecting a delicate voltmeter to the tree; but
nowadays, various devices—such as the toboscope, invented
by the Soviet scientist Viktor Adamenko—can register the
body's field as far away as eighteen inches. At about four
inches from the body, there is a sudden sharp increase, which
seems to support Kilner's observation that the aura has more
than one layer (he specified three). The strength of the signal
depends on the vitality of the subject. What is being measured
clearly corresponds very closely to what clairvoyants call the
aura, or etheric body.

The notion of the astral body has also gained a certain
respectability, at least in the field of parascience. When an
Oxford researcher, Dr. Celia Green, broadcast an appeal for
people who had had "out-of-body experiences" (usually
shortened to OOBs) in 1966, she received over four hundred
replies; her analysis of such cases revealed a fundamental
similarity in all such experiences. They occurred most often
under anaesthetic, and the patient usually found himself looking down on his body from above and slightly to the left. This,
according to Steiner, is the dissociation of the physical and

astral bodies, which always occurs during sleep, but which can also occur in waking states. An American, Sylvan Muldoon, experienced his first "astral projection" at the age of twelve, when he woke up in the middle of the night and found himself floating above his body, attached to it by a kind of cord; he assumed he was dead and went around the house trying to wake up the other sleepers; then he felt drawn back to his body. Muldoon later developed the power to leave his body at will (although it diminished as his health improved), and his experiences were investigated by Hereward Carrington, Hodgson's successor at the American Society for Psychical Research, who wrote a book in collaboration with Muldoon. So many cases are on record—literally thousands—that even if we dismiss them as some kind of illusion or psychological quirk, we have to admit that it is a curiously unvarying illusion.

So whether or not we can accept Steiner's occultism, we have to recognize that it was not merely some personal fantasy which can be dismissed in terms of megalomania. Most of his assertions about the "supersensual world" can be supported by testimony of the kind that the SPR found acceptable and convincing. If he is deceiving himself, then he is doing it in fairly respectable company.

But *Cosmic Memory* is more problematic. How is it possible to take Steiner's *History of Atlantis* seriously? It is difficult to believe that Steiner was deliberately setting out to deceive, or even that he was prepared to swallow the story of Atlantis because it suited his own purposes. The author of *The Philosophy of Freedom* and *Goethe as Scientist* is obviously no charlatan, while Steiner the educationalist, agriculturalist and medical theorist is a man who commands respect. It would help if we had some idea of how Steiner believed he obtained his information about Atlantis and Lemuria, but he refuses even to drop a hint.

One interesting clue is provided by a work called *Did Jesus Live 100 B.C.?* by G. R. S. Mead. Mead was an eminent scholar and historian, and although he was a theosophist and a friend of Madame Blavatsky, he was one of the few members of the Society who took a balanced and realistic view of that contradictory personality. *Did Jesus Live 100 B.C.?* examines the possibility that the New Testament stories of

Jesus may be mythical, concocted by the early Christians to support their views of Jesus as the Messiah foretold in the Old Testament. It considers the large body of documentary evidence, particularly a work called the *Todoth Jeschu*, also known as the Hostile Gospel, which suggests that the Rabbi Jeschu on whom the Jesus stories were based lived a century earlier than the gospel Jesus. The Rabbi Jeschu, according to these "hostile" sources, was a bastard, whose mother, Miriam, was betrothed to a certain Rabbi Jochanan, who was in the habit of visiting her at night. One night, a drunken neighbour named Joseph arrived first; when her lover arrived later, she asked him why he had returned, and both realized that she had been raped. When Miriam discovered she was pregnant, Jochanan deserted her. The child Jeschu was trained as a rabbi, learned magic in Egypt, proclaimed himself the messiah, and was eventually hanged.

Most biblical scholars accept that the *Toldoth Jeschu* is a Jewish satire on the gospels, perhaps written as late as the thirteenth century. Mead, bringing his considerable scholarship to bear on the problem, sets out to show that there is much historical evidence for the actual existence of the Rabbi Jeschu. And the introduction contains a curious passage in which Mead attempts to explain why he feels it worthwhile to consider a theory that is bound to give offence to many Christians. He has, he admits, a number of friends with clairvoyant faculties, "who have their subtler senses . . . more fully developed than is normally the case." These friends "are unanimous in declaring that 'Jeschu,' the historical Jesus, lived a century before the traditional date. They, one and all, claim that, if they turn their attention to the matter, they can see the events of those far-off days passing before their mind's eye, or rather, that for the time being they seem to be in the midst of them, even as we ordinarily observe events in actual life." He admits the possibility that this could be self-deception, or some type of contagious imagination, but feels this to be unlikely; the friends are of various nationalities, so unlikely to share some common religious prejudice, and some are convinced Christians who might be expected to lean over backwards to prefer the New Testament story.

Mead adds that he trusts the word of these friends because he has often had the opportunity to test their accuracy on more personal matters. Then he goes on to explain that this "method of investigation" does not involve going into a trance.

> As far as I can judge, my colleagues are to all outward seeming in quite their normal state. They go through no outward ceremonies, or internal ones for that matter, nor even any outward preparation but that of assuming a comfortable position; moreover, they not only describe . . . what is passing before their inner vision in precisely the same fashion as one would describe some objective scene, but they are frequently as surprised as their auditors that the scenes or events they are attempting to explain are not at all as they expected to see them, and remark on them as critically, and frequently as sceptically, as those who cannot "see" for themselves, but whose knowledge of the subject from objective study may be greater than theirs.

Mead is obviously speaking about himself.

He goes on to say that in many cases, he has been able to check their statements, and found them to be accurate. One colleague, whose knowledge of Greek was restricted to the alphabet, was able to dictate long passages in good Greek. Moreover, many of the facts and dates given in this way—facts and dates that could only have been available to a widely-read classical scholar—were later unearthed in ancient texts . . .

Regrettably, Mead has no more to say about his psychic friends and their methods. It is possible—in fact, highly probable—that some of them were among those who worked with Scott-Elliot on the search into the Akasic records of Atlantis and Lemuria. Scott-Elliot, of course, claims that some of his fellow researchers used ancient maps of Atlantis, preserved by occult masters—a claim that instantly arouses scepticism. Mead makes no such claim, any more than Steiner did. But in the final section of the book, Mead goes on to discuss some ancient "Hermetic" documents (he was to edit the works ascribed to the founder of magic, Hermes Trismegistos), and explains that certain secret knowledge about the origin of man and the universe "is not taught by ordinary means, not argued and demonstrated by the senses . . . It is a *memory* that God awakens in the soul . . . This state of consciousness is not a mediumistic state of trance; the master still has full contact with the physical world, but the centre or focus of his consciousness is, so to speak, transferred to the higher spiritual part of his nature.''

What are we to make of all these mysterious hints? If these theosophists had simply been using geological specimens, like Mrs. Denton, or even psychometrizing ancient documents we could at least understand what they thought they were trying to do. But Mead's account leaves us oddly up-in-the-air; it is hard to see why he decided to risk the derision of other scholars, then to make it worse by remaining silent about the details of the method.

Fortunately, there are other ways of gaining insight into what went on. To begin with, Mead's insistence that his colleagues made no use of hypnosis or trance mediumship suggests that he had in mind a curious work that had been published three years before his book on Jeschu (which appeared in 1903)—Theodore Flournoy's *From India to the Planet Mars*. Flournoy was a professor of psychology at Geneva, and a leading psychical investigator, and in 1894 he attended a seance with a pretty girl named Catherine Muller, who soon convinced him that she was genuine by telling him about events that occurred in his family before he was born. (This could, of course, have been simple telepathy.) Later, Hélène Smith (as Flournoy called her) went into deeper trances, and proceeded to ''remember'' a past incarnation as a Hindu princess. She seemed to have a considerable knowledge of the language and customs of India in the fifteenth century, although Flournoy felt that her husband's name—Prince Sivrouka Nakaya—sounded thoroughly un-Indian. Orientalists said they had never heard of him. Then, in a rare history of India by de Marlés, Flournoy discovered that Sivrouka Nakaya *was* a Jain prince who had lived at precisely the date Catherine said.

But if he was impressed by her Indian ''memories,'' Flournoy was thoroughly sceptical about her other ''incarnations'' —as Marie Antoinette, and as an observer of life on Mars. Mars had creatures exactly like earthmen, houses with fountains on the roofs, and horseless carriages without wheels that went past in a shower of sparks. Flournoy decided these visions were "puerile." He felt much the same about Catherine's incarnation as Marie Antoinette. Yet he had to admit that the Indian memories were highly convincing, and was not entirely happy about the theory that Catherine had read and then forgotten de Marlés. But in spite of his doubts, the general view was that Flournoy had demonstrated that Catherine Muller's "visions" were unconscious memories—or, as it was then called, "cryptomnesia." In insisting that his own colleagues were neither hypnotized nor in trance, Mead was almost certainly trying to rule out the possibility that this was another case of cryptomnesia.

Interest in this topic of "regression to past lives" revived again in 1956, with the publication of a book called *The Search for Bridey Murphy* by Morey Bernstein. Bernstein, a Colorado businessman and amateur hypnotist, placed a housewife named Virginia Tighe under hypnosis, and "regressed" her beyond her date of birth. Mrs. Tighe then began to describe a previous incarnation in Cork, Ireland, in the nineteenth century, when she had been a girl named Bridey Murphy. Bernstein's book became a bestseller, and was serialized in a Chicago newspaper—Mrs. Tighe had been brought up in Chicago. A rival newspaper sent out an investigator, who came back with the information that, far from knowing nothing whatever about Ireland, Virginia Tighe had an Irish aunt who had told her endless stories of the mother country when Virginia was a child. Moreover, Virginia had lived opposite an Irishwoman named Bridey Corkell, whose unmarried name had been Murphy, and with whose son, John, Virginia had been in love . . . All this ended the Bridey Murphy sensation as quickly as it had begun. Yet, as in the Flournoy case, the negative evidence is by no means as simple and clear-cut as the sceptics insist. A further investigation revealed that Virginia Tighe's Irish aunt was a New Yorker of Irish-Scots extraction, who had not even met her niece until Virginia was eighteen. Mrs. Corkell declined to be interviewed or to confirm that her maiden name had been Murphy, and the reason for this coyness emerged when it was revealed that her son John was the editor of the Sunday edition of the rival newspaper. Virginia Tighe insisted that she had never been in love with John Corkell, who was eight years her senior and married when they lived in the same street, and that she had never even spoken to Mrs. Corkell. Yet once again, the sceptical view prevailed.

But at least the Bridey Murphy case led to a renewed interest in hypnotic regression. In the year *Bridey Murphy* was published, 1956, a Cardiff hypnotherapist named Arnall Bloxham decided to try "regressing" some of his patients. One of the first of these was a girl called Ann Ockendon, who went back to a prehistoric incarnation in which everyone went naked and women wore decorative scars and animals' teeth. Another subject, a swimming instructor, became a naval gunner in the eighteenth century, showed an intimate knowledge of ships of the period, and screamed horribly as he was wounded in the leg. But the most impressive subject was a woman whom Bloxham calls Jane Evans, who recalled a whole series of past lives, including as a housewife in Roman Britain, a Jewess who died on a pogrom in twelfth-century York, a French courtesan of the fifteenth century, and a sixteenth-century Spanish maidservant. Unless Mrs. Evans was a passionate reader of history, the knowledge revealed under hypnosis was astonishing. (And in his book *More Lives than One?* Jeffrey Iverson reports that her only knowledge of history came from the usual elementary course at school.) She had no conscious knowledge that there had ever been an anti-Jewish pogrom in York; yet the tape recorded under hypnosis shows a detailed knowledge about the period. The Jewess, Rebecca, claimed that her family had taken refuge in the crypt of a church, and an expert on the massacre, Professor Barrie Dobson, identified this from her description of St. Mary's, Castlegate—the only problem being that St. Mary's had no crypt. Six months later, workmen renovating the church discovered the remains of a crypt under the chancel.

Bloxham's material is certainly far more impressive than Morey Bernstein's. Nevertheless, when someone discovered that the swimming instructor had read the Captain Hornblower books in childhood, this was generally regarded as proof that all Bloxham's cases could now be explained as "cryptomnesia."

In 1978, I became involved in a case of "regression" when our local independent television company, Westward, asked me to take part in a programme with a Liverpool hypnotist, Joe Keeton. Keeton had regressed a young nurse called Pauline McKay, who had begun to speak with a West Country accent, and claimed to be a girl called Kitty Jay, who had committed suicide near Chagford, Devon. Neither Keeton nor Pauline McKay had ever heard of Kitty Jay, so Keeton wrote off to Devon librarians to enquire whether she was known. He was startled to be told that "Jay's grave," on Dartmoor, is a noted tourist attraction, and that Kitty had been a milkmaid at Ford Farm, Manaton, some time in the late eighteenth century, who had hanged herself when she became pregnant.

Joe Keeton and Pauline McKay came down to the Westward studios in Plymouth, and I sat by her head as Joe placed her under hypnosis. Also present in the studio was Barney Camfield, a lay-psychiatrist and Unitarian minister, whom I had known for several years as the public relations officer for Westward TV. I had been fascinated, several years previously, when Barney had told me that he was convinced that his daughter had been killed by a kind of witchcraft—"ill-wishing"—and that he had had a horrifying precognition of her death by drowning.

Joe Keeton regressed Pauline—a pretty, dark-haired girl—back to her third birthday, and her voice changed to that of a child as she described it. Then he took her back further until she became Kitty Jay. She described how, at the age of ten, she had lived in the orphanage at "Chagiford" (as she pronounced Chagford). Then she described how she had gone to work at Ford Farm as a maid, and had become friendly with a man called Rob, who worked at nearby Canna Farm. She correctly named a bridge and the river where she and Rob went for walks. Rob apparently persuaded her to run away from the farm to live in an empty cottage, and forced her to have sex. She was half-starved there, and when it became clear that Rob had deserted her because she was pregnant, she went to look for him at Canna Farm, and hanged herself in the barn where he would return to do the milking. She choked and coughed in obvious distress as she spoke about this—in fact, the whole performance was painful to watch.

If Pauline McKay had, as she claimed, never visited the West Country and knew nothing about Kitty Jay, then it was certainly an astonishing performance. Joe Keeton explained that he was not convinced it was evidence of reincarnation. He had regressed many people—several cases are described in his book *Encounters With the Past* (co-authored with Peter

Moss)—and felt he might be plumbing some kind of racial memory encoded in the genes. Since Kitty Jay had died without passing her genes on to children, this hardly seemed to fit her case; but it was evidence of Keeton's freedom from dogmatism about his results.

Later, I listened with fascination to many tape recordings of his regressions. I even asked his cooperation in a case of "psychic detection"—the disappearance of the schoolgirl Genette Tate (which is discussed elsewhere in this book). More recently, he has concentrated his attention on the cure of various illnesses by deep hypnosis; his success in many cases—including cancer—suggesting that, as a medical tool, the importance of hypnosis is still thoroughly underrated.

It was in 1980 that Westward Television asked me if I would again attend a studio demonstration. This time it was to be presented by Barney Camfield, and what was being demonstrated was a technique known as "psycho-expansion." As described by the programme's producer, it sounded not unlike Joe Keeton's regression. But I quickly found out that there was one fundamental difference. Barney's subjects remained wide awake. They simply closed their eyes, "computed in" to some time and place suggested by Barney, then floated off into a kind of waking dream.

It emerged that Barney had been so excited by the possibilities revealed by Joe's regression of Pauline McKay, that he decided to try it out with his own patients. At this stage, his motives could have been described as more or less Freudian. The patient's problem was often buried deep in his past, and the task of the therapist was simply to probe until he found it. Barney's personal experience provided a case in point. Throughout his adult life he had felt nervous of policemen —indeed, of anyone in uniform. One day, he decided to try to get to the root of it. And eventually, by regressing himself, he found what he was looking for. As a very small boy, he had drawn pictures on a piece of newly-papered wall, and his father was furious. He told Barney sternly that if it ever happened again, he would have him taken away by a policeman. At that moment, there was a knock on the door, and his father said: "That must be the policeman I sent for. Go and wait in the other room." Barney spent twenty minutes or so in a state of terror. Then his father walked in, looked vaguely surprised to see him, and asked him what he was crying about. Scarcely able to speak, Barney reminded him about the policeman. "Oh that," said his father, who had evidently forgotten all about it since his conversation with the caller. "I've decided to let you off this time . . ." He was quite unaware of the psychological damage that could be inflicted on a child by making him "stew in his own juice." As he grew up, Barney forgot the incident, but the irrational fear of policemen remained—until he recalled what had caused it, whereupon it promptly vanished.

Another patient was a man who had been in trouble with the law for violence. Barney established that the man had a deep hatred of his mother—which seemed puzzling, since his mother had died when he was a child, and had never treated him badly. Probing finally revealed that when the mother had died, after a brief illness, the child was simply told she had "gone to heaven." He had no idea where heaven was, and assumed that it was a nearby town. His mother had deserted him, walked out without even saying goodbye. This was why he hated her—it was his defence against rejection. When he came to understand this, the patient's violent tendencies vanished.

This was why Barney found Joe Keeton's technique so interesting: it was a quick and easy way of getting at these buried memories. He quickly discovered that it was unnecessary to place the subject in a hypnotic trance. It was enough to induce deep relaxation, and ask the subject to recall, let us say, his fifth birthday.

A similar discovery had been made almost a century earlier by the French psychiatrist Hippolyte Bernheim, the founder of the Nancy school of psychotherapy. Bernheim was one of the great pioneering doctors who revived the use of hypnosis after it had been in a state of eclipse for half a century (Mesmer and his followers being regarded by the medical profession as charlatans). Bernheim recognized that the cures produced by hypnosis were due to suggestion, which led him to wonder whether this would not be just as effective if the patient was wide awake. In fact, it was—for, as we all know, the "subjective mind" is just as easy to influence when we are awake as when we are in trance. (Anyone, for example, can be made to scratch by a simple suggestion that he itches.)

But Barney Camfield, following Joe Keeton's lead, went on to more interesting discoveries. He found that his subjects became increasingly adept at entering a state of deep relaxation and exploring their own pasts, and that as they did so, the images became increasingly easy to focus—increasingly "real." And he also found that, like Joe Keeton, he could suggest that they regress to a period beyond their birth-date, and that they would then begin to describe "past lives."

In November 1979, Barney appeared on a local radio programme in Plymouth and talked about his discoveries. The result was a flood of enquiries—about three hundred—from people who wanted to try regression. Further programmes followed, in which his subjects—now no longer patients, but collaborators—demonstrated their power to float off into the past.

The Westward television programme that I was invited to watch in the summer of 1980 presented four of Barney's best subjects. It was interesting but, to be honest, not impressive. The interviewer had prepared cards, each one with a date on it, and Jim, Valerie, Sue and Hildegard were asked to close their eyes and take themselves back to these dates. Jim, asked to go back to June 1940, said that he was a German soldier on leave, and was having a picnic in the Black Forest. The interviewer had chosen this date because it was in the middle of the evacuation of Dunkirk, but "Kurt Wassmuller," understandably, knew nothing about it and cared even less; he was only interested in his girlfriend. Valerie was asked to go back to Holland on 17 April 1421. Barney had to explain that it was no good specifying a place, because she would go back to wherever *she* had been on that date (in her past life). In fact, Valerie said she was a kitchen maid in Warwick, working for "Lord John," and had no idea of any of the political events of the day—certainly not of the disastrous floods in Holland that the interviewer had in mind. Sue went back to her childhood in a Cornish village, and described the day with precision—friends from America were staying with them. She knew nothing about the first trans-Atlantic yacht race that the interviewer had in mind. And Hildegard was a child in Germany, so had no idea that it was the date of the coronation of Elizabeth the Second. As proof of reincarnation, or even of accurate regression into one's own past, it was a flop.

But when the programme was over, the interviewer suggested a few further experiments. One of these was that the team should try to "travel" clairvoyantly to his own home in

Plymouth—he gave the address. The results were startling. None of the four were familiar with the area, and some had never been there at all. Yet all four described a block of flats, facing the sea, and were able to add other details—such as which floor the interviewer lived on, and the fact that there was a boat on a trailer in the car park. (Since this part of the programme was not recorded, I do not have it on videotape, and have to rely on my memory; what I *can* remember clearly is that the interviewer was amazed at their accuracy, and said: "If only we'd transmitted *that*!")

The four were also asked to float off into the future. One was asked the result of a football match between Plymouth and Exeter that was to take place the following day, and how many people would be arrested—there had been a great deal of hooliganism at the previous match. Others were asked to go to the end of the present century, and beyond. The result of the football match was given confidently as a win for Plymouth by two goals to one. The forecasts about the immediate future were thoroughly depressing, involving widespread floods and earthquakes—I remember suspecting strongly that they were influenced by the gloomy prophecies of Nostradamus about the year 1999, and possibly those of Edgar Cayce. In fact, Plymouth *did* win, but by three goals to one. But when Barney listened to the football results, he was delighted when the announcer declared a two goals to one win for Plymouth. A few minutes later the announcer corrected himself. Barney's suggestion is that Valerie picked up the radio result rather than the actual score. She failed to discover how many people were arrested, which was not mentioned on radio.

The "hits" concerning the interviewer's home were impressive, but were quite irrelevant to the matter of regression. "Travelling clairvoyance" is a well-known phenomenon in psychical research—Ingo Swann demonstrated it under scientific test conditions at Stanford—and in the nineteenth century, many hypnotists demonstrated that their subjects could "float off" to specified locations and describe what they found there.*

Barney learned by experience, and the next time his team was interviewed on television—in 1982—he made sure that

---

*See *Abnormal Hypnotic Phenomena*, by E. J. Dingwall, 4 volumes.

they tried travelling clairvoyance at an early stage. The interviewer, Judy Spiers (of Television South West), gave the team the address of a house that had meant a great deal to her, and asked them to "go there." She was told that it was a semi-detached house, that the main entrance was at the side, that two steps led up to this door, that there were eaves, and a roof with a skylight in it. Members of the team described the hall with blue carpeted stairs opposite, and a bend half-way up the stairs. Several of them described a "black" feeling at the top of the stairs, and said they had problems getting further. They felt there had been trouble in the house, and someone seriously ill. A back bedroom was located as the source of this feeling of menace, and this was described with considerable detail—a bed in the corner, a large wardrobe facing it, a chest of drawers, and various other details. On the programme, Judy Spiers took the cameras to the house—her parents' home —and showed how accurate were all these descriptions. She then described how, one day in 1975, she had climbed out of bed in her sleep, and jumped out of the window on to the patio, breaking her back.

Again, it was highly convincing. Yet Thomas Jay Hudson would certainly have declined to believe that it proved even travelling clairvoyance. He would have said that the "subjective mind" of the team members read the mind of the interviewer. And it must be admitted that this explanation is just as convincing.

The regressions and "progressions" achieved by Barney Camfield's team are fascinating in themselves, but would certainly not convince a sceptic that this was anything more than pure fantasy. I have attended two of Barney's home sessions, and taped them. I found that being present in the same room was rather more impressive than watching it on television or being in the studio ambience. During the induction, he speaks slowly and softly, and the result is an atmosphere of deep peace in which time seems to be suspended. (During one session, someone rang the doorbell to ask if a car could be moved; the sound of the bell made me jump out of my skin, but I noticed that no one else in the room showed the faintest reaction. Asked afterwards, some said that they had not even heard the conversation that followed on the front doorstep.) Each member of the team is then told to go back, or forward, to a certain date. For five or ten minutes, there is total silence;

but everyone is fully awake—they occasionally open their eyes and write something down, then close them again. Then they are asked, one by one, to describe where they have been. They speak slowly and precisely, describing exactly what they can "see" at that moment; they can be asked to look around and describe further details. They may then be asked to "come back to the present," and give a resumé of everything they have experienced, and any background details they know.

What soon becomes clear is that they are, in some sense, actually present at the scene described. It has all the clarity of a waking dream. And this, it seems to me, is the only question worth raising. It is not particularly important whether the scenes from the past or the future are some form of imagination. What *is* interesting is that, if they are imagination, they are a form of *heightened* imagination. Valerie, describing her own experience of "psycho-expansion," says: "The first time I tried it I slipped straight into it, and had some fantastic experiences. That's why I came back a second time." Barney Camfield and most of his subjects would agree that *this* is the chief aim of psycho-expansion—to develop the ability to slip into a kind of mind-travel. Whether the experiences that take place in this state are "real" or not is, on the whole, irrelevant. For what Barney Camfield seems to have rediscovered is the "visionary" powers that we have already encountered in Swedenborg or in Elizabeth and Sherman Denton. It is the power of eidetic vision that was described by Thomson Jay Hudson. Jung preferred to call it active imagination.

And what is the psychological mechanism involved in "mental travel"? Jung himself found it impossible to be specific; he could only say that it was some kind of "descent into the unconscious." But the discoveries of split-brain physiology have made it possible to speculate with more precision. The essence of Roger Sperry's discoveries was that we seem to have two people living inside our heads, and that it is the left-brain self—what Hudson called the objective mind—that feels itself to be the rightful occupant of the head. This is what I call "me." Sperry's experiments also revealed some of the basic characteristics of this left-brain "me." To begin with, it is highly time conscious. More often than not, it is in a hurry. So when I am sitting in a dentist's waiting-room, the left-brain self begins to drum its fingers impatiently, and I experience boredom. I feel as if I am sitting in my car at a traffic light, with one foot on the clutch, one on the accelerator, waiting to start the moment the lights change. If I become very impatient, I may even develop a severe headache. It is actually in my power to cure this headache instantly, by simply relaxing. This would amount to taking my foot off the accelerator and putting the gearstick into neutral. But I do not do this because I am subject to my own suggestion that a dentist's waiting-room is not a place for relaxation; I want to get it over with and get out.

Sperry discovered that, by contrast, the right cerebral hemisphere has practically no sense of time. It is naturally relaxed. So when something deeply interests me, and I give myself the mental suggestion to concentrate my full attention on it, and forget everything else, I relax automatically; I switch off this vague feeling that I ought to be in a state of "general alert." This is why—as Hermann Hesse observes—total concentration on "small things" refreshes us and renews our powers.

Unfortunately, man has evolved at such a vertiginous pace in the past few thousand years that this left brain has acquired the habit of being on permanent alert. Cats and dogs curl up on the rug and seem to relax within seconds; human beings have to unwind with a dry martini or television or a hot bath. We have lost the natural power of "relaxing into the right brain."

But the right is also the visual hemisphere of the brain. It perceives shapes and colours and patterns. This is why, when I set out on holiday, everything looks so fresh and interesting. The left has accepted my suggestion that it can relax, and I am now, so to speak, looking at the world through the eyes of my right cerebral hemisphere. And the right enjoys observing the contrast of green fields and blue sky, and the patterns of trees and clouds and church spires. In the general rush of the working day it gets very little chance to exercise this faculty, for the left keeps muttering "Oh *do* get on . . ." Now it can relax, without any feeling of guilt, and simply enjoy patterns.

We have seen that a large percentage of young children possess eidetic vision—so they can look at one pattern of dots, then at another, and impose one on top of the other to form a picture. Children have not yet been caught up in the constant rush of the modern world. The powers of calculating prodigies are almost certainly a variant on this eidetic ability; they somehow instantly transform numbers into patterns, and *see* the answer; again, we observe the curious fact that most calculating prodigies lose their powers as they approach their teens. Child chess prodigies and musical prodigies are common, for both abilities involve patterns. Child literary prodigies are rare, for literature involves words, the other side of the brain.

In a book called *The Dance of Life*, the anthropologist Edward T. Hall speaks about the time sense of the Hopi Indians—or rather, their lack of it. And he underlines his point by describing a journey on horseback from Santa Fe and across the Jemez mountains. "I discovered it took a minimum of three days to adjust to the tempo and the more leisurely rhythm of the horse's walking gait. *Then I became part of the country again and my whole psyche changed*." [My italics.]

We can begin to see how civilization has suppressed—or condemned to underdevelopment—a whole range of powers of the right brain. It took Hall three days of the gentle rhythm of the horse to get rid of this obsessive, frantic left-brain awareness, and to relax into another kind of consciousness. But even a brief excursion into right-brain relaxation—due, let us say, to sudden relief after a crisis—can make us aware of the totally different quality of right-brain consciousness. To begin with, we *notice* more. Things that the left brain dismissed as uninteresting or repetitive are seen to have their own quality of existence. The left brain tends to see the world in terms of types or categories; the right brain sees everything as *individual*. To the left brain, a farm gate is just a farm gate; to the right brain, it is unlike every other gate in the world: those lichen stains, those white splashes left by the birds, that black damp in the cracks, give it an almost human individuality. Moreover, right-brain consciousness gives us access to vast stores of memory, so the smell of lichen or damp wood brings back glimpses of childhood. When Proust tasted a cake dipped in herb tea, floods of memory produced a curiously godlike feeling: "I had ceased to feel mediocre, accidental, mortal . . ." This recognition that we possess such vast stores of memory could be compared to a beggar suffering from amnesia, who suddenly remembers that he is actually a millionaire.

Left-brain consciousness makes us feel "mediocre" because it has stultified our natural ability to *renew* ourselves. When I am feeling tired or overworked, I ought to be able to revitalize myself within minutes by simply becoming "absorbed," by switching to right-brain consciousness. This is a faculty that our lopsided development has suppressed. There are obviously many others.

"Active imagination" seems to be among the most important of these. We can glimpse something of its power on the edge of sleep, when the left brain has switched itself off, and the right can give free rein to its image-making abilities. These pictures and visions that come on the edge of sleep are often so unexpected that they seem to be a product of someone else's mind, as if we were in a cinema watching a film. They are not; they are simply a product of the unknown half of our minds. If the female sex is suppressed—as the Women's Liberation movement claims—then the right brain is even more so, and we should give serious consideration to a Right Brain Lib movement. The experiments of Barney Camfield would make a useful starting point.

They certainly provide us with some insight into that otherwise baffling subject, the Akasic records. We can see, for example, why Mead's colleagues felt as though they were actually "in the midst" of the events they described. The right brain perceives the world in terms of images and patterns, so when it is allowed to "speak," it speaks in terms of images. Its discourse is a flood of pictures. In *A New Model of the Universe*, P. D. Ouspensky describes how he learned to induce "half-dream states" after he had woken up in the morning; he would fix his mind on some idea or image, and allow himself to doze again; what followed were "controlled dreams." Here is an example:

> I am falling asleep. Golden dots, sparks and tiny stars appear and disappear before my eyes. These sparks and stars gradually merge into a golden net with diagonal meshes which moves slowly and regularly in rhythm with the beating of my heart . . . The next moment the golden net is transformed into rows of brass helmets belonging to Roman soldiers marching along the street below. I hear their measured tread and watch them from the window of a high house in Galata, in Constantinople, in a

narrow lane, one end of which leads to the old wharf and the Golden Horn with its ships and steamers and the minarets of Stamboul behind them. The Roman soldiers march on and on in closed ranks along the lane. I hear their heavy measured tread, and see the sun shining on their helmets. Then suddenly I detach myself from the windowsill on which I am lying, and in the same reclining position fly slowly over the lane, over the houses, and then over the Golden Horn in the direction of Stamboul. I smell the sea, feel the wind, the warm sun. This flying gives me a wonderfully pleasant sensation, and I cannot help opening my eyes.*

Barney Camfield could have showed Ouspensky how to obtain similar "visions" without needing to be half-asleep. And we can also see how easily such a half dream of Roman soldiers could have been accepted as a genuine glimpse of the Akasic records.

But this is not to say that we can dismiss all such "glimpses of the past" as realistic daydreams. For the right brain—or "subliminal self"—is, as we have seen, the part of us that is responsible for genuine clairvoyance. Nellie Titus's right brain was able to tell her through a dream precisely where Bertha Huse's body was located, and how she had met her death. It was Mrs. Buchanan's right brain that enabled her to psychometrize letters so accurately, and that allowed Mrs. Denton to catch her glimpse of Sulla from a fragment of mosaic.

What happens in such cases is, almost certainly, what happened when Ouspensky dozed into a half dream, "keeping my mind on some definite image or some thought." The right brain will respond to the wishes of the left. So a letter or some other object is enough to nudge its images in a certain direction.

The problem here is that the right brain has access to such a vast reservoir of imagery that it is almost impossible to control. To ask it for some specific piece of information is rather like asking the Ancient Mariner to tell you the time. You are quite likely to get the information you want; the problem will be to sort it out from the flood of useless and irrelevant information.

*A New Model of the Universe, p. 282.

All this enables us to understand how Steiner came to write a book like *Cosmic Memory*. We do not know whether he sat in an armchair and went through some process of self-hypnosis, or whether he had some technique similar to Ouspensky's induction of "half dreams." He may even have taught himself Barney Camfield's technique of psycho-expansion. But what we can say, with a fair degree of certainty, is that he slipped into a state of which he literally *saw* everything he described.

In fact, the writings of his close friend Edouard Schuré provide us with an insight into what probably happened. Schuré was one of those Frenchmen who introduced the music of Wagner to his fellow countrymen; after this he moved to Italy and became closely involved in the occult group that had gathered around a Greek lady called Margherita Albana Mignaty. He later met Steiner, who presented his dramas in Munich, and went on to write a bestselling work called *The Great Initiates*, which quickly went through two dozen impressions, and was translated into many languages. *The Great Initiates* is still well worth reading. It begins with an impassioned diatribe against the narrowness of contemporary science—he is particularly indignant about the kind of positivism that insists that the universe is purely material and that man is no more than a machine.

Schuré is obsessed by a vision of history as a slow process of evolution. At some point in his career, he seems to have had some mystical vision in which he saw light flowing from one mystery centre to another, from the Himalayas to Iran, from Sinai to Mount Tabor, from Egypt to Eleusis. He presented a history of man's spiritual evolution in terms of the "great initiates"—Rama, Krishna, Hermes, Moses, Orpheus, Pythagoras, Plato and Jesus. What is so impressive about his book is the sheer imaginative vitality with which he presents their lives, and the realism with which he can conjure up the world they lived in.

This is even more apparent in his most "Steinerian" work: *Divine Evolution: From the Sphinx to Christ*. This bears all the signs of being another fragment from the Akasic records. We have the evolution of man and the solar system, and learn about the history of Lemuria and Atlantis, and about our own root race. Here the "imaginative" technique of *The Great Initiates* is taken even further. Each scene—the end of Babylon, the death of Cambyses, the ceremonies of Dionysus—is presented with a sharp clarity, as if Schuré had been there. The answer, almost certainly, is that Schuré *had.* We could say that he had learned to consult the Akasic records, or simply that he had learned the techniques of psycho-expansion. It makes no difference. What matters is that he had developed a faculty that every one of us possesses in embryo.

5

Spirits High and Low

IN THE WINTER of 1921, a number of people had come together in a room of the Metapsychic Institute—the French version of the Society for Psychical Research—in Paris, to test a clairvoyant, Madame De B-. Dr. Gustav Geley, a leading French investigator, and director of the Institute, asked someone to pass a letter to her. A painter and novelist called Pascal Forthuny grabbed it. "It can't be difficult to invent something that applies to anybody!" He began to improvise jokingly. "Ah yes, I see a crime . . . a murder . . ." When he had finished, Dr. Geley said: "That letter was from Henri Landru." Landru was at the time on trial for the murder of eleven women—crimes for which he was guillotined in the following year.

No one was very impressed by Forthuny's performance; after all, Landru's trial was the chief news-event of the day, so murder was an obvious topic to come into Forthuny's mind. Geley's wife picked up a fan from the table. "Let's see if that was just luck. Try this."

Still light-hearted, Forthuny ran his fingers over the fan in a professional manner and looked solemnly into space. "I have the impression of being suffocated. And I hear a name being called: Elisa!"

Madame Geley looked at him in stupefaction. The fan had belonged to an old lady who had died seven years earlier from congestion of the lungs; the companion of her last days had been called Elisa.

Now it was Forthuny's turn to suspect a joke. But Madame Geley insisted on another experiment. She handed him an officer's cane. This time Forthuny looked serious as he let his fingers stray over it. He began to describe army manoeuvres, somewhere in the Orient. He spoke of the young French officer who had owned the cane, of his return to France by sea, and of how the ship was torpedoed. He went on to say that the officer was rescued, but developed an illness and died two years later. Madame Geley verified that he was right in every particular.

For the novelist, it was one of the most bewildering moments of his life; he found himself thinking, "Do I possess a faculty I do not even suspect?" Madame Geley handed him a letter; Forthuny passed it between his hands, and said: "This letter was written in a beautiful city—the Orient. What a magnificent view, and what a blue sky!" It had, in fact, been written in Constantinople by her father.

In spite of his buffoonery, Forthuny was by no means a total sceptic about the paranormal. He was, it is true, an atheist and a materialist; but a few odd experiences had already planted seeds of doubt. In 1911—when he was thirty-nine—Forthuny had been on a journalistic assignment in Alsace, accompanied by a photographer. About to buy rail tickets to Mulhouse, he had suddenly turned to his companion and said: "Listen, I have to go back to Paris immediately." "But we have to go to Mulhouse!" "Don't laugh, but over there, in the corner, I had a vision of a coffin draped in black, with candles around it." It seemed absurd, for everyone in his family was in good health. He rushed to his parents' home in Neuilly, and found that his mother was ill with pneumonia; the next day, as he sat at the midday meal, he had another premonition and rushed to her bedside; she died as he approached.

He experienced no such premonition when his only son was killed in a plane crash in 1919. But in the following year, as he sat at his desk writing a novel, his hand suddenly refused to form the letters. Then, compelled by some unknown force, it began to scrawl crude letters like those of a child. Dumbfounded, Forthuny took a sheet of blank paper and rested the pen on it; his hand proceeded to write. He called in his wife and said: "This is funny. I've become a medium!" Although the writing went on for two hours, it made no sense. But during the following days, it began to improve. It seemed that two intelligences were guiding the pen. One was his dead son, Frederick, the other a being who signed himself simply "your guide." On one occasion, his hand began to write rapidly from right to left, and when it had finished, he had to hold it up to a mirror to read it. He himself tried writing from right to left, and found that he could only do it very slowly.

Ironically, the communications of his "guide" were all on such topics as the existence of God, the reality of the spirit, and the survival of the soul after death. The style was rather pretentious, and the guide seemed inclined to be irritable and touchy. One day Forthuny was told: "You are one of those whom God has designed to be a carrier of the flame of the astral world. Yes, you have been chosen to carry the word that Christ carried to his disciples . . ."

Worse was to follow. In August, his guide told him that he had to go Vanves, to the Maternity Hospital, and to enquire for a patient called Madame Lomonier in a ward named after a certain Dr. Vacquerie. This unfortunate lady, said the guide, was dying of Bright's disease; Forthuny was to tell her that she could be cured, and to take her to the house of a certain Madame Grand'homme . . . The next day, Forthuny went to Vanves and found the hospital; but there was no Vacquerie Ward, and although a patient called Lomonier had been in the hospital a few weeks ago, she was now dead. Forthuny took a sheet of paper and asked his guide what he was playing at. The guide explained that it had been a test of Forthuny's patience, and Forthuny passed it; the guide promised not to put him to further tests. But not long after this, he proposed that he should collaborate with Forthuny on a book about "Art as a Servant of the Spirit." Forthuny agreed, and the work proceeded swiftly as his hand flew across the page. But Forthuny found himself questioning some of the views of his guide, and began to raise cautious objections. The guide promptly lost his temper and became vituperative; the hand wrote so fast that it almost became incoherent, rebuking him for his "maladroit imagination inspired by human vanity . . ." Forthuny indignantly threw down his pen; but the next time he took it up, he received a roar of condemnation: "If you don't stop this arrogance I will abandon you. You just had the criminal thought of throwing the pen in my face. This would be your greatest sin since you were born. You must ask my pardon—but I can tell you that the rest of your life wouldn't be sufficient to gain my pardon . . ." It is impossible not to chuckle at this violent exchange between the sceptical materialist and the self-opinionated spirit guide.

Forthuny's son Frederick, on the other hand, was always affectionate and respectful; but he too bore witness to the "formidable truths of creation that have appeared to me in all their adorable splendour . . . ," and said he was accursed for having doubted the existence of God. Frederick predicted that his grandfather would die in a week's time—and proved to be mistaken; the old man was still alive in 1926, when the story of Pascal Forthuny was told by Dr. Geley's eminent assistant, Dr. Eugène Osty, in a book.* Like the guide, Frederick also told his father that he had an important mission to fulfil, but Forthuny remained dubious. But he was no longer sceptical about the reality of the spirit world. He had no doubt that the spirit of his dead son was speaking to him. So he began to read the works of France's most influential "spiritist," Allan Kardec.

Kardec, whose real name was Leon Denizard-Hypployte Rivail, had been an eminent educationalist and man of letters when, in the early 1850s, he became interested in the new sport of "table turning." Two daughters of a friend named Becquet were excellent mediums, and Rivail, inspired by the same scientific enthusiasm that led Myers and Sidgwick to create the SPR, started to ask the spirits all kinds of questions about the life hereafter. And the spirits explained at length that the universe is permeated by incorporeal intelligences and that human beings are simply spirits united with bodies. Their purpose is self-education—evolution—and when one body dies, they are reincarnated in another. In between times, they have no body, and may inhabit many different worlds. Higher spirits aid mankind's development. Lower ones may hang around the physical world and make a nuisance of themselves—for example, as poltergeists. Before returning to a physical body, a spirit can—to some extent—choose the trials and problems she will undergo in his new life.

Rivail published these teachings in 1856 under the title *The Spirit's Book*, choosing the pseudonym Allan Kardec, both of which names he had, according to the spirits, borne in a previ-

Pascal Forthuny, Une Faculté de Connaissance Supra-Normale by Eugène Osty, Directeur de l'Institute Metaphysique International, Paris 1926.

ous existence. The book was virtually responsible for the French spiritualist movement. But the teaching about reincarnation worried many spiritualists, and after Kardec's death—only thirteen years after *The Spirits' Book* appeared—there was a split between "Kardecists" and spiritualists which led to the gradual rejection of "Kardecism." (It nevertheless took root in South America, where it is still immensely influential.) Madame Blavatsky and Rudolf Steiner echoed many of the teachings of Kardec.

When Pascal Forthuny attended that critical meeting at the Metapsychical Institute in 1921, he was a more-or-less convinced Kardecist—even though the communications had now ceased; he even helped to edit the Kardecist *Revue Spirite*. The discovery of his psychometric powers seemed to be a fulfilment of the prophecies of his two spirit guides. Suddenly, Forthuny was a celebrity. Every time he was invited out to dinner, he was asked to demonstrate his powers, and they increased with use. Jean Meyer, who had started the Metapsychical Institute, persuaded him to give public demonstrations, and they were spectacular. At his first demonstration at the Institute, he stopped in front of a stranger and said: "Pierre . . . Petr . . . Peter?" The man replied: "My name is Petrov." And Forthuny proceeded to tell him in detail about his involvement in the Russian revolution and his movements since he left Russia. The demonstrations were recorded in detail, and published in Dr. Eugène Osty's book about Forthuny in the following year.

Osty was one of the great paranormal investigators of his time, and his book *Supernormal Faculties in Man* is a classic on the level of Myers's *Human Personality and Its Survival of Bodily Death*; he later became director of the Metapsychical Institute. Yet, oddly enough, he was disinclined to accept Forthuny's conviction that he had been in touch with the spirit of his dead son. Osty took the view that Frederick Forthuny and the guide were "subconscious elaborations of Forthuny's own artistic mental depths." The truth seems to have been simply that Osty felt it was hardly becoming to a scientist to accept life after death as an explanation of paranormal phenomena. But this meant that he was twice as dependent on the phenomena of psychometry. William James, we may recall, explained his experience of spirit communication with Hodgson as some kind of complicated tape recording, brought together by the mind of the medium. Psychometry is based on the notion that people leave their "vibrations" behind, like fingerprints. So, according to James, a medium is really a "super-psychometrist," gathering together a thousand fragments of information about a dead person, rather as a biographer may collect stories, photographs and even home-movies about his subject, and combine them into a living portrait. Osty was inclined to the same view: he explained spirit communication as a "crypto-psychism which lingers after bodily death."

So all Osty's interest came to focus upon this problem of the "supernormal faculties in man," and the book of that title is a treasure house of examples of psychometry. Yet the most interesting lesson to emerge from Osty's classic work is that, no matter how hard he tries, he cannot remain within the bounds of materialistic science (and all science is, by definition, materialistic). He finds himself in the same position as Buchanan: new phenomena continually destroy old theories. Buchanan took leave of conventional science when he discovered that a psychometrist could learn as much from a photograph as from a handwritten letter, even if the subject of the photograph had never had any kind of personal contact with it. Osty confirmed this puzzling observation. In 1921, an engineer who had just returned from Syria handed him a blurred photograph of some vaguely ovoid object. It was, in fact, of a tiny sealed capsule of nearly opaque glass, containing some liquid; this liquid had been sealed into a capsule when the glass was blown, so there was no way of getting it out except by breaking the glass. It had been found in a graveyard near the great temple at Baalbek. It was in a tomb that contained gold plate and coins (embossed with the arms of Alexander the Great).

One of Osty's best psychics, Madame Morel, was handed the photograph. It was so blurred that it might have been of anything. She immediately saw a "place with dead people," and one old man in particular. Asked about the old man's mode of life, Mme. Morel said she saw a vast place like an enormous church—obviously the temple of Baalbek: "The ground is cold, the roof is high . . . it is immense, immense. This man does not do manual work . . . I see his brain, far above the normal . . . a life entirely of the brain." Her description suggested the high priest of the temple. She then sensed a violent and sudden death, in which the man choked. She saw a gigantic funeral, and the body placed in a tomb. "I see other dead about him." Asked about the object in the photograph, she said it was an opaque globe half-full of a rusty coloured liquid. But this was not from the area of the temple. She saw a distant land with forests and mountains, and a scene in which a human being was sacrificed by a savage tribe. A man is thrown from some high point on a mountain, and it is his blood that is sealed in the glass capsule. Eventually, the capsule found its way to the tomb where it was discovered—placed there as a memento.

At the time of the experiment, Osty himself had no idea of what the photograph represented. He had to ask the engineer, who told him that it had been found in a rich tomb in the Bekaa valley, and that a well-known orientalist, M. Maspero, had dated it as some time before the Christian era. We may speculate that the sacrifice took place in some Roman province, probably Germany; the date and the description of human sacrifice and men in robes suggest that Druids may have been responsible, or some other non-Roman sect. The temple of Heliopolis, perhaps the greatest in the Roman world, would be a centre of pilgrimage. (The Romans were tolerant of other religions, provided they did not actively deny the Roman deities.)

The engineer was not present at the seance, so telepathy must be ruled out. The photograph may have been in direct contact with the glass capsule, but it seems unlikely. So it seems that Madame Morel picked up all the essential facts about the object from a photograph in which it was indistinguishable.

Surprisingly, Osty describes this experiment after speaking with approval of Denton's experiments with geological and archaeological specimens. We have already noted that British and American investigators took care never to mention either Buchanan or Denton—presumably because their views were regarded as too "far out." When they took over the psychometric hypothesis, Myers, Gurney, James and the rest abandoned the idea that everything that happens leaves its mark behind on the material world—it was too uncomfortably close to Madame Blavatsky's Akasic records. They narrowed it down to the apparently more sensible idea that only human events leave their traces behind, in the form of some kind of "mind vibration." But the moment we are willing to admit that a photograph might provide a clairvoyant with information, we have seriously weakened one of the main links in the scientific chain. If a photograph is going to carry any "vibration," it ought logically to be that of the photographer or the developer, not the person whose image has been mechanically recorded by light on silver nitrate. And if a mere photograph *can* carry information, then Buchanan's notion that "the past is entombed in the present" begins to seem less absurd. For we may recall that at the very beginning of his experiments, Buchanan compared psychometry to photography: Denton with approval suggests that, unlike the British and American researchers, he was willing to accept the notion that *all* events are somehow "photographed" on nature.

Other cases cited by Osty raise some equally awkward questions. He tells how a certain Madame R. missed an expensive brooch. The housemaid said she suspected the lady's maid, and the lady's maid said she suspected the housemaid. Madame R. decided to visit the Metapsychic Institute to ask Dr. Geley's advice. Geley recommended Madame Morel. Let us, before we proceed, ask: what would it be reasonable to expect Madame Morel to psychometrize in order to find the brooch? Possibly the jewel box in which the brooch was kept? Or some article belonging to the suspected thief? In fact, Madame R. sent a friend in to see Madame Morel, carrying a fur cape belonging to Madame R. Madame Morel handled the cape, and then said: "It is stolen . . . I see an article like a brooch" (the friend had only mentioned a missing jewel); she went on to describe the woman who had taken it—the younger housemaid—and said that if Madame R. behaved as if nothing had happened, the girl would become worried, would wrap the brooch in an old newspaper, and throw it under the table. Later the same evening, the brooch was found under the hall table wrapped in newspaper. The housemaid later confessed.

This seems preposterous. Madame R.'s fur cape could hardly "carry" any information about the thief; it would only have carried the "vibrations" of Madame R., who had no idea who stole it. What seems even more absurd is that Madame Morel could *foretell* that the thief would wrap it in newspaper and throw it under a table. Unless the maid was actively planning to do precisely that, and Madame Morel somehow read her mind, there is no way in which it could have been foretold. In fact, Osty makes no attempt to explain it in this way. For he had come to accept it as a fact that a psychometrist can often see the future as easily as the past.

This obviously raises a major question. Scientifically speaking, a "telescope into the past" is just conceivable; but a telescope into the future is an absurdity. Yet Madame Morel did it again and again—as Osty describes in *Supernormal Faculties in Man*. In the presence of a certain Count B., Madame Morel (who was under hypnosis) predicted that he would soon take action on some political matter, and that he would be addressing a large crowd of people. She added various details about men in uniform, open countryside and water in the landscape. All this meant absolutely nothing to the count. Later that day, the count happened to speak to a friend about an aerodrome which he was thinking of presenting to the local authorities in Savoy. The friend mentioned it to the war minister, and the count was urged to make the presentation as quickly as possible. (This was in 1913, and France sensed the rumbles of war.) In less than a month since the seance with Mme. Morel, the count was present at just such a scene as she had described. The aerodrome was at Challes-les-Eaux, which, as the name suggests, is on a lake. At a subsequent session, Mme. Morel foretold an aeroplane accident in which no one would be hurt, and that something was wrong with the construction of the hangars. An aeroplane over-turned on the opening day, and it was discovered just before the opening that some of the hangar doors were too low.

Osty goes on to describe a number of other examples, in some of which he was personally involved. Another clairvoyant, Mme. Jean Peyroutet, told Osty that he would soon be living in Paris. Osty (who was planning such a move) decided that it would make a simple and foolproof test to ask her to describe his future apartments there. Osty thought he knew what they would be like, for he was waiting for a certain lady to vacate a house at the end of her lease. But Mme. Peyroutet told him: "You will not get the house you are expecting." The lady would not vacate it as promised. At a subsequent session, she told him that "some people would look out on your account," and as a result, he would find a house with trees in front, and a statue; it would be in a square or small private garden. She went on to describe it in considerable detail, mentioning that it would be close to the Bois de Boulogne and to water.

The lady *did* let him down. Two days later, Osty happened

to mention to a friend that he was having difficulty finding a house in Paris. She mentioned it to her uncle, who wrote to various agents. Within three weeks of the seance with Jean Peyroutet, Osty was installed in a house near the Bois de Boulogne and the Seine; it stood in a small private garden with trees and a statue, and all Mme. Peyroutet's other comments applied precisely.

Osty was so fascinated by this power of precognition that when he encountered a remarkable German clairvoyant, Ludwig Kahn, in 1926, he devised a classic test: the "empty chair test." Kahn was taken into a room with chairs, in which a meeting of the Metapsychic Institute would later be held, and asked to describe the people who would be sitting in various chairs. Kahn's descriptions were astonishingly precise and accurate. And since, when the meeting was held, the audience was asked to select chairs at random, there was no possible way that Kahn could have picked up his information by telepathy—from Osty—or by psychometrizing a chair and "seeing" who usually sat in it. Osty had, for the first time in the history of psychical research, established precognition of the future beyond all possible doubt.

But how could a scientist fit precognition into any rational scheme of human existence? Osty tried to do it in two stages. The first was the proposition that "metagnomic sensitives" (psychometrists) "have the faculty . . . to connect themselves instantaneously with human individualities distant in space." In other words, the object held by the psychometrist serves exactly the same purpose as the article of clothing sniffed by the bloodhound: to establish a possible connection with the owner. The bloodhound picks up a scent; the psychometrist picks up a "vibration." This vibration enables him to home in on a subject, like some super television-detector van.

But even a television-detector van cannot home in on a TV set unless it is switched on. One of Mme. Morel's cases left Osty in no doubt whatever that the psychometrist can home in just as easily on a corpse.

On 2 March 1914, an old man went out for a walk in the woods, and disappeared. The woods covered more than two thousand acres, and all attempts to locate the body were unsuccessful. Osty was asked if he could help, and he asked for some article of clothing belonging to the old man. He was given a neckerchief, which he handed to Mme. Morel. She immediately described an old man lying dead in a wood, on damp ground. Nearby there was water. She went on to describe how the old man had left a house to go for a walk, had difficulty in breathing, and became confused; he had left the path and collapsed, then died. She described the old man with some precision—white hair above his ears, pendant lips, very old and wrinkled (he was eighty-two), a furrowed forehead, a long coat . . .

The manager of the estate on which the old man had died confirmed that the description was faultless. What bothered him was that Mme. Morel mentioned blocks of stone, and the district in which the old man died was chalky and had no rocks. So Mme. Morel was asked to try to provide some further clues. Under hypnosis, she described the route he had taken in detail, particularly a woodman's hut at a crossroads. Her description was again accurate; but the old man's son had been at the woodsman's hut all day, and had not seen his father; he insisted that his father could not walk that far. Mme. Morel gave yet more details of the spot where the old man was lying. Five men searched the area. One of them noticed what he thought was a rock, but what was actually a moss-covered tree stump, close to a stream. Within a few feet was the body. The tree stump was Mme. Morel's "rock."

The old man had not been wearing the neckerchief when he died. But Mme. Morel had picked up its "vibration," then homed in on the body of the old man. We have seen, in the first case in this book, how Nelson Palmer homed in on the body of Joy Aken by the same method. (Psychometrists seem to prefer something that has been in actual contact with the skin; another psychometrist, W. E. Butler, recommends that anyone trying to psychometrize gloves should turn them inside out.)* The inference is clearly that the object held by the psychometrist merely establishes a connection between the "bloodhound" and the person concerned. Osty concluded that, once it had been established, it would make no difference if the object was destroyed.

But the precognition cases are altogether more difficult to explain. And this is regrettable, since they are, in fact, extremely common. Nelson Palmer discovered his own psychometric powers accidentally when he was helping to unpack

*How to Develop Psychometry.

clothes of a relative who had come to stay with them; he had a sudden clear vision of the relative lying dead in the road, and a car nearby. A few days later, the relative was killed in a car accident; Palmer instantly recognized the police photograph of the body, with the car that had caused the accident nearby.

In his classic work on dream-precognition *An Experiment With Time*, J. W. Dunne noted that precognitions were often not of the event itself, but of the manner in which the subject learned about the event—through a newspaper headline, a photograph, a radio bulletin. *If* this is what happened in the Nelson Palmer case, then it can point to only one conclusion: that, in some paradoxical sense, our *own* future has "already happened," and we are able to catch a glimpse of it rather as we might turn to the end of a book to see what happens. But this obviously means that our freedom of choice is a delusion; the future is already "written." This is a view suggested by an astrophysicist, Dr. Michael Shallis, in a book *On Time**; he mentions, for example, an experience of *déjà* as a child:

> I remember coming in the back door of our house and calling out to my mother, who was upstairs, that I was back, and was then overwhelmed with the feeling that this moment had happened before. I knew instantly that my mother would call out that we had got salad for dinner and then, of course, she did so. Such an experience usually lasts for a few moments, but the intensity can be dramatic . . .

Understandably, since it turns upside down our most basic assumption about our own lives. Another personal example cited by Shallis is even more disturbing. Teaching a student in a lecture room, Shallis was again swamped with the *déjà vu* feeling. He knew he was going to suggest that he should show the student certain examples from a book in his office, then go and collect it. He decided to resist it. Yet just as he had firmly resolved not to go and fetch the book—as he had on a previous occasion—he heard his voice saying: "I'll just pop down to my office and get a book . . ."

This notion—that the future has already happened, and that there is nothing we can do to change it—is obviously irrecon-

*1982.

cilable with any rational view of human existence. Like William James, we *must* believe in free will if we are to get the best out of ourselves.

Aware of this problem, Osty tried another explanation of precognition—the second part of his two-stage explanation of psychometry. What he suggests is that there is "an immense mental world subjacent to appearances [i.e. behind the façade of this apparently "real" world] in which particular identities seem to be linked in an inconceivable psychic life. It is from this vast latent life of thoughts, of thought, that sensitives unconsciously draw the substance of their revelations, *being endowed with a sense that enables them to distinguish the evolving scheme of individual lines.*" [My italics.]

In this last phrase he goes to the heart of the matter. The clairvoyant, according to Osty, possesses an extra faculty—Richet coined the phrase "the sixth sense"—which enables him to see human minds and their interactions spread out like a web. He does not literally need to see *into* the future. He could be compared to a man on top of a high building who sees two cars speeding down streets at right angles to one another, and can see at a glance that, if they proceed at the same speed, there will be a collision. A modern psychic, Suzanne Padfield (of whom we shall speak later), has attempted to explain her own flashes of precognition by comparing the sixth sense to a computer that can instantly check out millions of possibilities and choose the likeliest. Hudson also believed that this is one of the powers of the subjective mind.

Osty's theory offers an alternative to the rigid determinism of the Dunne-Shallis theory of time. But it still leaves certain facts unexplained. He believes, basically, that psychometry works by contacting other people's minds, and that, because he can tune in to a kind of web of psychic life, the psychometrist may also be able to grasp what will happen in the future. But how does this explain Mme. Morel's vision of the old man leaving his house, and taking a certain route? His neckerchief should, according to Osty, merely supply the vibration that allows the "bloodhound" to home in on his body. But since he was not wearing the neckerchief on that final walk, how could it provide information about his exact route? We are forced to say that it was not the neckerchief that provided the information. But the old man himself was dead, and no living mind knew where he was lying. So tuning in to the "psychic web" would be of no use either. The only other view that explains it is the notion of Akasic records—Denton's theory that *everything* that has ever happened is somehow recorded, whether there is mind observing it or not.

Now although Osty quotes Denton with approval, his "web of minds" theory emphatically has no room for geological specimens that have somehow recorded past events—particularly when the events happened before man arrived on earth. It must be admitted that Osty's theory appeals to common sense and logic, and that Denton, by comparison, seems credulous and woolly-minded. Surely the simplest way to explain the visions of Denton's wife and sister is to assume—as Hudson did—that they were unconsciously reading his mind. This seems such a sensible explanation that it is hard to see how anyone can fail to accept it.

But the facts about the paranormal have a habit of refusing to conform to common sense. We have seen that, in some of Denton's experiments—notably, the one involving the fragment of tile from a Roman villa—the results cannot be explained away as telepathy: Mrs. Denton "saw" the dictator Sulla when Denton was expecting Cicero. And three decades after Denton's death, his "natural record" theory received unexpected support from a series of experiments impeccably conducted by Dr. Gustav Pagenstecher.

Pagenstecher became involved in psychometry by accident. A German physician who moved to Mexico City in the 1880s, he made frequent use of hypnosis in his practice. One of his patients was a Signora Maria Reyes de Zierold, the daughter of a former provincial governor. A long illness left her almost incapable of falling asleep, and even drugs failed to remedy her insomnia. Hypnosis proved more effective. Little by little, she began to recover.

One day, when Pagenstecher was treating her in her own home, she showed signs of anxiety as she lay in her hypnotic trance. Pagenstecher asked her what was troubling her, and she told him that her daughter was listening at the door. To humour her, Pagenstecher opened the door—and found the daughter standing there.

Now Pagenstecher was not in the least interested in the paranormal, and had never believed stories about patients who develop "clairvoyance" under hypnosis. But he was open-minded enough to check whether this could be coincidence. To his astonishment, she revealed unmistakable psychic abilities.

Maria de Zierold's descriptions confirmed the observations of Sir William Barrett, Pierre Janet and others who had claimed that the hypnotized person could somehow share the mind and senses of the hypnotist. Barrett, it will be remembered, could make a hypnotized girl wince by holding his own hand over a lighted flame, and make her smile by tasting sugar. Maria de Zierold affirmed: "While in deep hypnotic trance all my senses are blocked, and not only blocked, but transferred to the hypnotist to such an extent that I feel the pricking of *his* ears; I also feel the burning sensation whenever a match is brought near to *his* fingers."

Under hypnosis, with her eyes closed, she could, of course, see nothing. But when Pagenstecher ordered her to see him, she at first perceived a kind of shadow where he was standing. Later, she was able to see him quite normally—even if he stood behind her, or on the other side of a door. Again, many of the early experiments had described this phenomenon; but later psychical investigators chose to disbelieve them. Oddly enough, Maria's sense of his presence increased as he moved further away; she experienced it as a kind of magnetic attraction. This again seems to explain how Janet was able to summon his patient Leonie from the other side of Le Havre by a mental command. Maria also began to see Pagenstecher's "aura," and moreover, in precisely the colours that Reichenbach had described—a blue colour around his right side, and a red colour around his left.

Stranger still, she became aware of a "cord," luminous and with an "electric" quality, stretching from her body to his. We have seen that Sylvan Muldoon observed that he appeared to be attached to his physical body by the same kind of cord during his states of astral projection, and a majority (though not all) of those who have experienced astral projection mention it. The interesting inference would seem to be that, under hypnosis, Maria de Zierold's astral body became connected to Pagenstecher's.

Five years after the beginning of the experiments, Pagenstecher began to test her for psychometric abilities. Significantly, she recorded: "I absolutely live the events I visualize . . . All my senses are awake. I hear, I see, I taste, I smell . . . I

live through the scenes as if I were personally present." Like
so many clairvoyants, from Mrs. Denton to Rudolf Steiner,
she describes the sense of actually participating in the events.

This raises some interesting possibilities. Hypnotists have
always been able to induce hallucinations in the patient. I have
described elsewhere a television programme in which I took
part, when a hypnotist, by means of post-hypnotic suggestion,
made a woman "see" the ghost of an evil clergyman on Bristol
docks.* In 1982, a BBC 2 series on the brain included some
remarkable sequences concerning hypnotic hallucination: in
one, the patient—who was fully awake and normal—was
made to see two versions of the presenter of the programme,
and was unable to tell which was real. The hallucinated version even seemed quite solid when touched—the subject's
hand stopped abruptly as if encountering a real person. So it
seems that eidetic vision is easier to obtain under hypnosis. In
that case, we could regard genuine psychometry—as distinguished from Mrs. Denton's visions of Mars and Jupiter—as
hallucination *guided and shaped* by some kind of clairvoyant
perception of past events.

The powers displayed by Maria Reyes de Zierold in most of
these experiments resemble those we have already encountered
in Pascal Forthuny, Mme. Morel and other psychometrists—
the ability to hold an object and describe the person to whom
it had belonged. But she also revealed the ability displayed by
Elizabeth Denton and Mrs. Cridge: to psychometrize natural
objects. Handed a piece of meteoric stone, she seemed literally
to become a meteorite:

> I am floating high in the air. I see around me many lights
> which suddenly flash up and then subside again. I see the
> sun very near, immensely large . . . Now I feel as if an
> earthquake were coming on. (At this point she began to
> show signs of minor convulsions.) I am now being torn
> loose from where I stand; I begin to whirl, more and
> more rapidly, now I fall into an abyss. I close my eyes
> while I pass alternately through ice cold and hot regions.
> I am horrified. My God!

The stone had to be snatched hastily from her hand.

Mysteries, p. 302.

In this case, of course, it was possible that she was reading Pagenstecher's mind. In another case, Pagenstecher thought this less likely. His wife had picked up a seashell on Vera Cruz beach. When Pagenstecher handed it to Maria de Zierold, he expected a picture of the beach crowded with sunbathers. Instead, she saw an undersea panorama:

> I am under water and feel a great weight pressing on my body. I am surrounded by fishes of all kinds, colours, shapes and sizes. I also see different kinds of plants, some of them with large leaves. The water has a dark green transparent colour. I am among the creatures, but they do not seem to notice my presence . . .

This, again, is certainly not conclusive, since Pagenstecher knew it was a seashell, and she may simply have taken her cue from this knowledge. But an experiment carried out by Dr. Walter Franklin Prince, on behalf of the America SPR, is harder to explain away. On the Vera Cruz beach, Prince picked up a "sea bean." He had one like it at home, and believed it to be the seed of some marine plant. He handed this to Maria de Zierold when she was under hypnosis. She talked about tall tropical trees in a forest, with a river nearby. Prince was convinced she was mistaken, and told Pagenstecher so. Pagenstecher said he would prefer to believe Maria. They took the seed to be examined by two professional botanists. Both said it was a nut from a tree that grew in the tropical forest, and that when they were found on beaches, this was because they had been carried down by the river . . .

It is, of course, conceivable that Maria de Zierold already knew that the "sea bean" was actually a nut from a tree, but this seems doubtful when it took a professional botanist to identify it. In any case, when placed under hypnosis, she went into a completely trance-like state in which she became unaware of the material world; objects had to be placed in her fingers, and she felt them without looking at them. So while there is a slight chance that she recognized the "sea bean" through her sense of touch, this seems unlikely; Prince certainly thought so.

The most interesting clue to what actually happened comes from her description of what happened when she held an object. At the beginning of the experiment, she says, she was aware of the body of Dr. Pagenstecher. But as soon as she had "focused" the object, she ceased to identify with Pagenstecher, and identified instead with the object. If the object was pricked with a needle, she felt the prick. When it was moistened with alcohol, she tasted the alcohol in her mouth. When a lighted match was held close to it, she felt her fingers burn. If we can accept what she says, then it sounds as if the same process that connected her to Pagenstecher now connected her to the object—the seashell or sea bean or meteorite. And from that point on, she proceeded to experience the "life" of the object.

Now if, in fact, we can accept the testimony of Maria de Zierold, its implications are tremendous. To begin with, it would seem that two minds can, in a sense, share the same body. This in itself contradicts one of our most basic assumptions: that what goes on inside my head is private. "We each think of the key, each in his prison," says Eliot in *The Waste Land*, but if Maria de Zierold was telling the truth, there is no need for a key; we are not in prison.

What is even more startling is the notion that Maria de Zierold could just as easily share the identity of *objects*; somehow "become" a meteorite or sea bean. The philosopher Bergson said that there are two ways of knowing an object: through analysis or intuition. Analysis means knowing it from the outside, walking around it and seeing it from different points of view. Intuition means going *inside* it, and this knowledge is "absolute." Many philosophers have felt that Bergson was talking nonsense since we cannot enter "into" an object, even with intuition. If Maria de Zierold is correct, that is not true. The mind possesses a natural power of entering into things—or into people. And Bergson was right to call this power intuition, for it is a "right-brain" faculty, a power of the subjective mind.

The most important implication of the Zierold experiments is that this power can be released under deep hypnosis, when the left-brain ego has fallen asleep. This is not to suggest that we should all undergo hypnosis to release our psychic powers. The exciting implication is that the subjective mind has a natural power to join itself to other people or objects—perhaps by means of the "electric cord"—which is suppressed by the objective mind. Presumably this is the result of our human evolution which, dominated by the need for survival, has placed so much emphasis on left-brain development. But presumably there is nothing to prevent us from learning how to "unsuppress" the subjective mind when we feel so inclined, and so gain a whole new range of mental abilities. Plato once said that men and women are mere halves of some total being, and that our obsession with sex and love is the craving to be reunited with the "other half." But Pagenstecher's experiments suggest an even more interesting possibility: that we have suppressed an ability to "unite"—not only with other people, but with things—and that we all feel an instinctive longing to regain it. Such a philosophy would explain, in one single stroke, most of the riddles that the SPR was formed to investigate.

In fact, an idea closely related to this has been gaining ground in the field of psychical research since the end of the nineteenth century. I have described elsewhere how, in the 1890s, it became increasingly clear to psychical investigators that poltergeist phenomena were usually associated with adolescents who had just reached puberty. And when Freud popularized the notion of the unconscious mind, it was soon being suggested that the unconscious mind of the adolescent was somehow responsible for the phenomena. Most living authorities on the poltergeist—Dr. A. R. G. Owen, William Roll, Alan Gauld, Hans Bender—accept the view that poltergeist activities are actually cases of "recurrent spontaneous psychokinesis"—psychokinesis being another name for "mind over matter." A number of psychics—like Nina Kulagina, Uri Geller, Ingo Swann, Felicia Parise, Suzanna Padfield—have displayed an ability to move small objects—like pieces of paper or needles—by staring at them. This seems to imply that the strange activities of the poltergeist—objects hurtling across the room—could be explained as cases of powerful psychokinesis. The chief objection to this view is that psychics like Swann and Geller can only move very tiny objects in the laboratory; no psychic has, under test conditions, been able to generate even a thousandth of the energy needed to hurl an ashtray across a room, let alone turn a bed upside down with someone in it—one of the favourite tricks of the poltergeist.

Nevertheless, it could be said that the main trend of opinion since the foundation of the SPR has been to find the cause of all paranormal events in the unconscious minds of human beings. We have noted that this tendency was already present in Myers, Gurney and William James—not to mention Hudson; nowadays, it is held by almost every respectable psychical investigator in the world.

But there is an alternative view, and this is given its classic expression in the works of Allan Kardec. Kardec, as we have seen, affirms that most paranormal phenomena are caused by spirits. In *The Mediums' Book* (sequel to *The Spirits' Book*) the medium's "guide," who called himself Saint Louis, explains poltergeist manifestations are caused by the ill-will of a low-grade spirit towards someone in the house. Many spirits do not realize they are dead, and continue to live in the place they inhabited on earth. "He remains passive as long as there is no one fitted to be a medium." Such spirits can make use of a kind of "negative energy" which is leaked by certain people. Kardec asked if he could speak to the poltergeist that had recently caused violent disturbances in the Rue des Noyers, in Paris in June 1860. Saint Louis replied: "Evoke him if you will, but he is a spirit of low degree who will not be able to give you much information." When evoked, the spirit demanded disagreeably: "Why do you call me? Do you want to have some stones thrown at you?" This particularly violent spirit—it had broken every window in the house and finally driven the inhabitants out—identified itself as a rag and bone man who had died fifty years earlier; people used to make fun of him because he was always drunk, and this was why he was resentful. He explained that he had used the energies of a servant girl, who had been quite unaware that she was being used—in fact, she was the most terrified of all. These energies, said the spirit, were of "an electric nature."

Such views were regarded with derision by later psychical investigators, and still are. Yet there are a few who are willing to give serious consideration to the spirit hypothesis. One of these, Guy Lyon Playfair, spent many years in Brazil, first as a journalist, then as an employee of the American International Development Agency. In Brazil, Kardec's "spiritism" is still the religion of a large section of the population. After an experience with a "psychic surgeon" who performed an operation on his stomach with his bare hands, Playfair joined the Brazilian Institute for Psycho Biophysical Research, and investigated a number of poltergeist "hauntings." Playfair reached the unorthodox opinion that poltergeists *are* spirits, and that the Brazilians, with their tradition of voodoo (or *quimbanda*), are actually able to make certain use of such spirits to perform acts of black magic, just as witches have claimed throughout the ages. Playfair describes all this at length in such books as *The Flying Cow* and *The Indefinite Boundary*. In my own book *Poltergeist* I have explained how I came, with immense reluctance, to abandon my own conviction that poltergeists were due to "spontaneous psychokinesis" acting through the right brain, and to share Playfair's belief that they are spirits. It is certainly not a position that any investigator takes willingly; it is far more intellectually satisfying—as well as scientifically respectable—to believe that all paranormal phenomena can be explained in terms of the unconscious mind. The facts, unfortunately, point in another direction.

Even in the first decade of the twentieth century, the spirit view of psychic phenomena had become so unfashionable that few serious investigators would even concede its possibility. This probably explains why Professor George Henslow, of Christ's College, Cambridge—later President of the British Association for the Advancement of Science—decided not to reveal his authorship of a book called *Spirit-Psychometry* (with a sub-title "And Trance Communications by Unseen Agencies, Through a Welsh Woman and Dr. T. D'Aute-Cooper"). On the first page, he states: "The phenomena of psychometry do not seem to have been generally regarded as a phase of spiritualism, but as being purely psychical. The revelations herein recorded, therefore, throw a new and strong light upon the fact that the visions and impressions are largely, if not wholly, imparted to the seer by unseen agencies."

Henslow reached this conclusion as a result of his experiments with a Welsh medium whom he calls Olwen, and the Birmingham medium T. D'Aute-Cooper. The latter was best known as a psychometrist and healer.

From internal evidence, Olwen was a simple peasant woman, a thirty-nine-year-old cook in a farmer's family and a friend of Mr. Jaybee, who was high sheriff for his county in Wales in 1910-11. Olwen spoke only Welsh, but Mr. Jaybee took down all she said in English. To begin with, Olwen seems to have been a normal psychometrist, who could hold an object in her hand and receive impressions from it. In February 1909, she was handed a piece of earthenware found in a field in Cardiganshire. She received an impression of an ape-like man in a skin loincloth, standing in a field where peat was laid out to dry. The man seemed to be stacking peat; but after a moment, Olwen realized that he was actually building a small hut of peat. (This kind of "correction" is very common in psychometry, as well as in psycho-expansion; it is exactly as if the subject is looking at a film, and gradually begins to see what is happening.) Nearby, on the ground, lay an object that might have been the body of a man. A second man bent over this and seemed to do something to it. Then Olwen cried out in pain, clutching her chest, as if she had been stabbed, and had to drop the potsherd. After coaxing, she took it up again. Now she saw the man bending over the "body," and doing something with a long object, of a whiteish colour, which he placed across one end of the "body." At this, Olwen felt something cold on her own neck. A moment later she began to shout: "My knee! my knee!" and experienced a sensation as though the lower part of her leg was being severed and pulled off. Again, she had to drop the potsherd, and it took considerable persuasion to make her hold it again. She now saw a man making a crock from wet clay, and described its shape in some detail—particularly a kind of waist close to its top. After this she saw a bonfire, with smoke billowing upwards, and watched the two men feed it for a long time. She almost vomited at a smell of burning flesh. After a long time, the men raked something from the ashes, and placed it in the pot. The crock was then taken to a boggy area—Olwen felt her feet sinking into soft mud, and could see rushes. Then she began to clutch her throat and gasp as if she was being suffocated, complaining that she was sinking.

Olwen had no idea what this vision was all about; neither, at that stage, had Mr. Jaybee or his wife (who was also present). But a year later, the Cambrian Archaeological Association published an article that described a burial ground where the potsherd had been found; it had been on the edge of a lake (now dried up and replaced by a peat bog). A funeral urn containing partly burnt bones had been reconstructed from fragments found in the bog, and corresponded exactly with Olwen's description. What she had seen was apparently a cremation ceremony involving partial dismemberment of the body, probably with a stone knife. Mr. Jaybee claimed that Olwen knew nothing about cremation, or of threats made to local children that they would be seized by "little men who have been burned" if they didn't behave themselves.

In July 1909, Olwen was handed a piece of flint that had been found in a gravel pit at Kenilworth Castle; an expert on the Stone Age identified it as a chipping tool. Her visions included high mountains with glens, and a forest with animals. She saw a man dressed in skin, short of stature, with a "funny shaped head—he has no forehead."

Like Denton, Jaybee seems to have decided to try her with the same specimen at a much later date, to see whether she received the same impressions. This time she saw a large building with chimneys, which she described as "a large brown lump of a building . . . the largest I have ever seen." She described it as being "half built." Jaybee took this to be Kenilworth Castle, which is made of brown sandstone, and is now a ruin. She tried to describe a stone tablet set in the wall of the building—such tablets have now disappeared, but existed in the sixteenth century.

A stone from the ruined banqueting hall of the castle brought a vision of a scene with a lady kneeling on a cushion, surrounded by attentive males in cloaks. This was followed by a vision of crowds of people waiting as if expecting someone to arrive, and of a carriage being pulled by people, in which the same lady was seated. The lady was then escorted to a large throne-like chair. Olwen was, of course, unaware that Queen Elizabeth the First had made many visits to Kenilworth Castle, which was then owned by the Earl of Leicester. On a famous visit in 1575, Leicester (who was hoping to persuade her to marry him) spent £6,000 on her entertainment. On this occasion (according to a pamphlet describing the visit by Robert Leneham) she arrived on a white horse; but she was in the habit of travelling short distances by litter, which Olwen may have meant by a "carriage drawn by people." Olwen, who was illiterate, frequently failed to understand what she was seeing. She expressed puzzlement that the gentlemen should be lavishing so much attention on a lady who was plainly in the best of heatlh—illness being the only reason she could imagine for such concern. (At a later sitting, when describing an erupting volcano, she was frankly incredulous: "Oh good gracious! A mountain boiling over! . . . Here is nonsense for you, now!")

Henslow decided to hand the flint to another psychometrist, and chose T. D'Aute-Cooper of Birmingham who felt himself merging with the flint, and saw a whole series of visions of historical epochs, which sound similar to those of Mrs. Denton. In one of them, he described a bird with teeth in its beak and claws on its wing. According to Henslow, he knew nothing about the archaeopteryx, which fits this description. In a later vision, D'Aute-Cooper felt himself travelling in darkness until he arrived at a house—the flint was carted to Kenilworth in a load of gravel, which was spread on the paths. He felt himself being laid on a table in a well-furnished room to be examined by many people—the flint was sent to the Geological Society in London—then wrapped in soft material and once again sent somewhere (the flint was packed in cotton wool and sent to Wales). D'Aute-Cooper then clearly described Olwen—a buxom maid about five feet one inch in height, with brown hair; he described Kenilworth Castle. There were more geological visions, in one of which he felt himself to be a sponge at the bottom of the sea. Henslow states that the "flint" was actually a siliceous sponge.

In view of D'Aute-Cooper's insistence that he was totally uninterested in geology, and had only once attended a lecture on the subject, his geological descriptions, and further detailed accounts of the Carboniferous era—inspired by a piece of Cannock Chase Coal—are astonishingly accurate (although too long to quote). D'Aute-Cooper furnished another striking proof of his psychometric gift when he was holding some "prehistoric" flint implements. After descriptions that might have applied to various epochs in the life of the flint, he suddenly remarked: "I find that there is a man in London who is making them, and getting a good living out of them by putting them in the Thames and fishing them out as genuine." What no one knew at the time—including Professor Henslow—was that the implements were forgeries, made by a labourer out of Thames gravel.

Olwen, who continued to work with the Jaybees, frequently went into trance when she held an object. She believed she fell asleep, and always "woke up" with a start, apologizing for having dozed off. Jaybee decided not to tell her that she had been speaking in her trance state, convinced that she might be nervous about "talking in her sleep." It soon became clear that when she was in a trance, other intelligences helped her to psychometrize the objects. When they were trying to get her to read the inscription on the tablet in Kenilworth Casle, she complained that someone was speaking English in her ear, and was able to repeat the word "best." This was in October 1909. In January 1910, she suddenly became a "medium." Holding an American button-hook, she said in Welsh: "I do not feel as usual . . ." then fell asleep. Suddenly, a voice began to speak out of her mouth in English, saying: "I am sorry I am unable to oblige you; my medium is so prejudiced against all this . . ." and threatened that unless they could convince her of the reality of spirits, they would have to give her up. The spirit identified himself as Sam, and said he was a coloured man; he said he had a white friend called Dick with him. Jaybee suggested that if Sam could "show" Olwen some of her dead relations, she might be convinced that spirits were real. Sam agreed, and said that next time she practised psychometry, he would make sure that her uncle appeared to her.

Three days later, in her trance state, Olwen again held the button-hook, and described what sounds like an American dry-goods emporium with crowds of people walking around. Asked what the people were called, Olwen laughed and tried to "pick up" the name: "Moo, moon, moonkies or wi, wi, winkees . . ." Jaybee assumed she was trying to say "yankees." Olwen then dropped the button-hook in her lap, and said: "There is someone present . . . I can see some mist forming . . . In the middle of this cloud an outline of a man's head is coming to view . . . I know him! I know him!" Mr. Jaybee could guess who this was, for he had suggested to "Sam" that he should make Olwen see her recently deceased uncle Evan. "Shall I tell you who he is?" asked Jaybee. "He is your Uncle Evan." Olwen said excitedly: "Yes! How do you know? Can you see him?" Soon after this, her vision faded.

Soon after, Olwen again went into a mediumistic trance; this time, a child who identified herself as "Dora" spoke through her. Dora seems to have been a lively child; she not only spoke in Welsh and English, and an incomprehensible language which she identified as her own tongue, but also sang in Welsh and English. A week later, psychometrizing some object, Olwen suddenly saw the child standing beside her, and identified her as a black girl of about ten. The child leaned on her, and Olwen said she could feel her as clearly as she could feel the chair she was sitting in. Jaybee suggested that perhaps Dora wanted Olwen to go to sleep, and Olwen replied: "Yes, I know she does, but she shall *not* put me to sleep."

At the next session, Dora again took over. When Jaybee asked her if she could psychometrize the piece of wood in Olwen's hands, she explained she was no good at this. "To do what you require Sam must be present . . . He can assist and pass on the gift of seeing the surroundings of the articles to the medium." Jaybee asked: "Do you mean to say that any articles are receiving impressions in pictures of their respective surroundings?" (He obviously means to ask: "Do objects somehow record their surroundings?") Dora replied: "Yes, that is just what happens, and Sam can see these pictures, and he is also able to transfer his power of seeing them to the medium."

Here, then, we have a theory of psychometry that differs radically from the view of Buchanan and Denton. Or does it? Dora states that objects "record" impressions of their surroundings, then adds that spirits can see these impressions and pass them on to the psychometrist. In that case, it seems perfectly possible that good psychometrists can see the impressions without the aid of spirits.

To some extent, the development of Olwen's mediumship was a retrogressive step. In spite of her vision of her uncle Evan, Olwen was not sympathetic to spiritualism or occultism—probably having been brought up in a church that regarded such matters with distaste. So her own internal resistance made the sessions more difficult, and the information she gave was often worthless. When handed the forged flints, she described scenes that sounded vaguely prehistoric. Yet she later let slip that she had also seen some present-day visions, which she had ascribed to her own imagination, being convinced that she *ought* to be seeing the same kind of remote visions that had been conjured up by the Kenilworth flint. It seems clear that a psychometrist enters a realm of "active imagination" in which it is difficult to distinguish true perceptions from imaginings.

In spite of these problems, Olwen continued to demonstrate her clairvoyant powers convincingly. Jaybee trod on a needle one day and hurt his heel. He picked up the needle and found that its point was broken off. Assuming that the rest was in his heel, he went to see a doctor, who probed it; he was unable to discover the missing point. Searching the floor carefully, they found the point of a needle; but it did not fit the other part. Jaybee consulted Dora at the next seance. Dora replied that the point he had found was not the missing portion, and that if he searched the grate in his bedroom he would find the rest of it. They searched the grate, and found the "eye end" of the needle which actually fitted the point. Then where was the point from the original needle that Jaybee had trodden on? Dora explained that it had not had a point when Jaybee had trod on it; the point had broken off earlier and been thrown out when the mat was shaken. The blunt end of the needle had penetrated his heel, which was why it had become so inflamed.

Henslow adds to this an account of a lost ring recovered by a clairvoyant whom he knew; a man had lost the ring from his hotel room. The clairvoyant "saw" the servant dusting a table, and knocking the ring to the floor; then she picked it up and pocketed it. The owner questioned the servant, and recovered his ring.

After Olwen became a medium, the sittings became altogether less successful. Various undesirable "controls" tried to take over, including a suicide and a Welsh preacher who urged them to sing hymns. But Dora developed the ability to cause certain manifestations. The Jaybees' maid came in one day to say that something had been banging on the copper pans on the top shelf in the kitchen; at the next seance, Dora confessed that she had been responsible—trying to make the maid realize that two pans had been put in the wrong place. Later, a bell that had been disconnected rang furiously, although Jaybee himself could not make it ring even standing on a flight of steps. Dora was producing poltergeist manifestations. Soon after this, Dora became offended when Jaybee asked whether she could not get some other and more efficient spirit control, and told him she would never come again. She stayed away for two weeks, and returned one day in March 1911 when Olwen was psychometrizing a glove. Dora greeted Mrs. Jaybee, but refused to speak to Jaybee on the grounds that he had wanted to get rid of her. Jaybee finally coaxed her back into a good mood, and she promised to return. But she failed to keep her promise, and subsequent sittings were failures. So the Jaybees decided it was time to call a halt.

Henslow concluded *Spirit-Psychometry* with a chapter in which he summarizes the evidence. He is of the opinion that psychometry is probably a form of mediumship, and that it is spirits who communicate various impressions to the psychometrist. He does not explain why, if objects can somehow record events, a good psychometrist should not be able to pick up these impressions without the aid of spirits. He also assumes that the various "false visions" of Olwen were due to "undesirable controls." But if human beings possess the power of active imagination, then this assumption is also unnecessary.

In spite of this, *Spirit-Psychometry* is a work of central importance in the history of psychometry. Much of it again provides support for the theories of Denton and Buchanan. But the part of the book dealing with spiritualism is also impressive and convincing. Unless we assume that Jaybee or Henslow were liars, it seems impossible to explain how an illiterate Welsh cook could begin to speak fluently in English. The real importance of *Spirit-Psychometry* is that it again makes us aware that questions about the paranormal cannot be kept in neat compartments. Psychometry and clairvoyance and precognition and mediumship *tend to overlap*. Once we accept any one of them, it is almost impossible not to be drawn into accepting most of the others.

From the scientific point of view this is, of course, thoroughly unsatisfactory. The scientist does not wish to be drawn into a field that seems to have no proper limits. But if the scientist is honest, he finally has to admit that there are certain "facts" that seem to refuse to obey the laws of logic. And this is enough to throw most scientists into a panic, convinced that they are about to be swept away by what Freud called "the black tide of occultism." Their alarm is understandable; for there are few scientists who would want to commit themselves unreservedly to the beliefs of spiritualism. The spiritualist explanation of the world is somehow too crude and simple—that the problem of death is non-existent because we continue to live on another "plane." It is just as easy to imagine a philosopher on that other plane being puzzled by the mystery of the universe.

But it is hard to feel that Buchanan—an affirmed spiritualist—was any less scientific than Osty, who tried to explain clairvoyance without the aid of spiritualism—assuming, for example, that Pascal Forthuny's automatic writing was due to his "unconscious personalities." Osty was still unable to explain how Madame Morel could describe in detail the final walk of an old man, or how clairvoyants could describe something which has not yet happened. The success of his "empty chair test" proves beyond all doubt that precognition really takes place. Yet which is easier to believe: that some unconscious computer can guess who will sit in a certain chair in a month's time, or that the clairvoyant obtains his knowledge from spirits who are somehow outside time? In spite of his tough-minded attitude, Osty found himself obliged to swallow just as many "impossibilities" as Buchanan. *Spirit-Psychometry* is another case in point. Henslow is willing to submit highly convincing evidence for the reality of spirits and their connection with psychometry, yet he is apparently unwilling to put his name on the title page. No doubt the British Association for the Advancement of Science would have found *Spirit-Psychometry* very hard to swallow. But it is hard to believe that Henslow's reticence makes him a better scientist than Buchanan.

The problem is to find a theory that will embrace all the facts without becoming shapeless or useless. Scientific theories tend to be too narrow, while spiritualist (or occultist) theories tend to be too broad. This is largely because the scientists are seldom practitioners (mediums or clairvoyants), and the practitioners are seldom scientists.

One of the most comprehensive theories of psychometry was the creation of a man who succeeded, to a large extent, in being both; and this is reflected in the title of his best-known book, *The Secret Science Behind Miracles*. Max Freedom Long was born in 1890, majored in psychology, and in 1917 went to live in Hawaii because he was fascinated by the active volcano Kilauea. He became a schoolteacher in a remote valley, and made Hawaiian friends. He became intrigued by guarded references to native magicians called *kahunas*, or "keepers of the secret." Long proceeded to try to find out about the secret; but met a blank wall of silence. The *kahunas* had been outlawed since the islands became Christian. Long heard tales about ghosts, about fire-walking, about magical healing, and about a sinister practice called the "death prayer." The Huna religion, as it was called, was dismissed as black superstition by the few Christian writers who mentioned it. But there was one strange story of a Christian minister who had challenged a *kahuna* magician to a contest of prayers. Long later examined the minister's diary, which described how member after member of his congregation died mysteriously. Finally, the minister persuaded someone to teach him the death prayer, and the *kahuna* magician died within three days. But the minister seceded from the church and built his own small church.

Long was inclined to be sceptical until he met a young Hawaiian who had experienced the "magic"; he had walked into a forbidden temple enclosure to demonstrate that he could defile it with impunity; then his legs became useless, and he had to be carried home. The local doctor could do nothing, and he had to go to a *kahuna* to be cured.

After four years of trying unsuccessfully in the USA to find out about the Huna religion, Long returned to Hawaii, where he met Dr. William Tufts Brigham; Brigham was able to tell him a little about the *kahunas*. But it was not until he was back in America, eighteen years after landing on Hawaii, that Long woke up one night with an idea that helped him to solve the secret of the *kahunas*. It struck him that the Hawaiians must have had special words to describe their beliefs, and that these words must be in the dictionary. And since Hawaiian words are built up from shorter words, it ought to be possible to gather important clues from their sacred words. He looked up "spirit" and found there were two words: *unihipili* and *uhane*. He recalled that Christian missionaries had noted that the Hawaiians believe that man has two souls.

In fact, Long discovered eventually that the Hunas believed that man has three souls; besides the *unihipili* and *uhane* there is the *aumakua*. He discovered that the *unihipili* is what Freud called the unconscious—man's "lower self." The *uhane* is the conscious ego—the man's "middle self." The *aumakua* is man's "higher self," or superconscious mind.

We have seen that Myers, Gurney and other early psychical researchers believed that "psi" powers are due to man's "subliminal self"; Myer's remarkable book *Human Personality and Its Survival of Bodily Death* is largely a survey of unusual powers of the mind—clairvoyance, eidetic imagery, powers released by hypnosis, and so on—and an attempt to explain them in terms of the subliminal self, which corresponds roughly to Hudson's "subjective mind." But it is obviously difficult to grasp how the Freudian unconscious—with its guilts and repressions—could be the source of supernormal powers. In an introduction to a 1961 edition of Myers's book, Aldous Huxley tried to resolve the contradiction by suggesting that man has three minds: the Freudian unconscious—a kind of basement; the conscious ego; and a *superconscious* mind, a kind of attic, which is as much above ordinary consciousness as the unconscious is below it. This, Huxley suggested, comes closer to the Myers-Gurney concept of the subliminal self.

What Long discovered is that the three souls of the Hunas correspond to the unconscious, the conscious and the superconscious minds. And, according to the *kahunas*, man—the middle self—is as ignorant of the existence of the superconscious as of the unconscious.

But the reasons are slightly different. He is unaware of the existence of the low self because it seems, in practice, to be identical with the ego. It is the servant of the middle self, and resides in the solar plexus. Its purpose is the manufacture of vital force, *mana*. This life-force (created from food) is used by the two higher selves, but stepped up in vibratory rate. Although the low self is the servant of the middle self, it is often refractory and disobedient. It likes its own way. It is naturally violent and emotional; it behaves like a spoilt child. The middle self should attempt to discipline it and raise it to a higher level. In fact, many people give way to the demands of the lower self, and descend to its level. (This obviously applies to most criminals, particularly sex criminals.)

The high self or superconscious could be regarded as the guardian angel. It knows the future and can control it. Unfortunately, the middle self cannot make direct contact with the superconscious. The telephone line to the superconscious goes down through the low self. And since this telephone line is usually out of order, or made useless by static noises—the negative emotions of the low self—it can seldom be used.

According to the *kahunas*, magic is performed by means of low selves which have been detached from their two fellows. The unattached low selves are responsible for poltergeist disturbances. (Guy Playfair reports that Brazilian magicians can make use of poltergeists to do mischief.) They are earthbound spirits, stupid but not particularly malevolent, unless directed by a hostile *kahuna*.

Middle selves that have become detached after death are also earth-wanderers; but since memory is a function of the low self, they are devoid of memory; they are what would be called ghosts.

Each of the three selves has its own "astral body" or "shadow body"—the Hawaiian word for shadow is *aka*. One of the roots of the word *unihipili* is *pili*—which means sticky. The *aka* body of the low self sticks to things it contacts, and when it is removed, an *aka* thread is left behind, rather like the sticky thread that comes away from a flypaper when we touch it with a finger. The physical body is connected to the low self by such a cord—this is the "astral cord" described by Sylvan Muldoon.

The *aka* thread, according to Long, explains psychometry. Most objects have *aka* threads running from them, and a good psychometrist simply traces back this *aka* thread to its source. The source of such threads may be a dead person, or an inanimate object like a meteorite or a piece of volcanic lava—Long mentions the experiments of William Denton. Long also quotes Pagenstecher to the effect that the object acts "as a tuning fork, automatically [starting] in our brain the specific vibrations corresponding to the . . . events; furthermore, the vibrations of our brain once being set in tune with certain parts of the Cosmic Brain already stricken by the same events, call forth sympathetic vibrations between the human brain and the Cosmic Brain, giving birth to thought pictures . . ."

In his second book, *The Secret Science at Work*, Long tells how one of his Huna research groups collected various objects to be psychometrized, including a watch belonging to Long. The woman who held Long's watch reported a vision of an elderly gentlemen with a white beard and a kindly personality. Everyone laughed, since this description did not correspond to Long himself; but Long pointed out that she had accurately described the watch's original owner, who had died recently and left the watch to Long.

Since the superconscience can only be contacted through the low self, it is obviously important for the middle self to train the low self to act as a good intermediary instead of being obstructive. In the same book, Long describes the methods developed by the Huna Research Association to contact and influence the low self. They fell into the habit of referring to the low self as "George." Long explains their method of contact.

First, one must believe there is a low self, that it is really there to contact. Second, one sits down in a quiet place and invites the low self to make itself known. One may speak to it aloud, and one should then wait patiently and watch to see what impressions come into the mind centre which the two selves share . . . it often pays to hold a long one sided conversation with George on the first sitting. Tell him you have decided that the pair of you should get better acquainted, and you should have fun learning to play games together. This may seem childish—but the low self is something like a very precocious child. It can be whimsical, clever, obliging, wilful, stubborn or eager, according to its particular nature. No two low selves are alike . . .

One game one can play with George, says Long, is to invite him to bring back memories of things or events he liked best. The result can be a flood of deeply buried or forgotten memories of the past. In fact, Long is describing a simple form of "psycho-expansion," closely related to what psychiatrists call "abreactive therapy," or the release of long-repressed memories. According to Long's theory, it was Proust's "George" who was responsible for those flashes of "times past" that brought him such deep delight.

Long adds the important comment: "As a matter of fact, most of us have found that it is not George alone who needs to be trained—it is also the middle self. And often the realization has been rather a shock when we have been brought face to face with the fact that we have been sitting idly by most of our lives while we have let George run the show in any hit-or-miss way he might choose." An insight like this goes far beyond any question of how far we might find his "three souls" theory acceptable or not; it goes to the heart of the problem of how we waste our lives.

The next stage of the training is to try to communicate with George directly—to give him his own voice, so to speak. And the method Long suggests is the traditional one of making use of a pendulum—any small object, like a button or a glass bead on the end of a thread. The pendulum is held between the finger and thumb, with the elbow resting on some solid object like a chair-arm. Most people will find that if the pendulum is suspended over the right hand, it swings in a clockwise circle; over the left it usually swings anticlockwise. A convention of yes and no must also be established; Long says that his own convention is that a back-and-forth swing parallel to the body means yes, while a swing at right angles to the body means no;

a diagonal swing indicates "in doubt."

All this sounds absurd, yet it is a well-established method among dowsers—who, of course, also use the divining rod, usually a forked hazel twig. Sir William Barrett—the man responsible for founding the SPR—wrote a classic book on dowsing, *The Divining Rod*. Starting from the most obvious and convenient theory—that dowsing is simply some kind of physical response to the electrical field of underground water, he ended by admitting ruefully that "no physical theory can cover the facts." The fact remains that dowsing is used every day—to locate oil and minerals as well as water—and that of all the phenomena of cryptesthesia it is the easiest to demonstrate to sceptics.*

Split-brain theory offers a scientific explanation of why dowsing works. Roger Sperry performed an experiment in which red or green lights were flashed in the "blind eye" of a split-brain patient (i.e. the part of the visual field connected to the right brain). The patient was then asked: "What colour have you just seen?" Obviously, he was unable to answer the question because the person being addressed lives in the left hemisphere. But if he made the wrong guess, his muscles would convulse, as if the right brain had overheard the mistake, and was nudging him in the ribs. The point, of course, is that the right brain was "nudging" him by *tensing the muscles*.

Ordinary dowsing—for water—is almost certainly a response to the earth's magnetic field. We now know that birds migrate by means of a sensor in the brain that responds to the earth's field, and that animals use it for "homing." In human beings, this faculty has been partly repressed by the development of the conscious self, which perceives the world analytically. Yet it remains in us, with the result that nine out of ten people can dowse with a little practice. (Even I can dowse, and I am in every other way "ESP thick.")

So the explanation for the kind of dowsing that Barrett documents so exhaustively seems to be that the right brain *knows* about underground water because it has some kind of sensor. But it can only *tell* the left-brain self by causing the muscles to tense—hence the movement of the dowsing rod or the pendulum.

---

*For a fuller account see my book, *Mysteries*, pp. 51-5.

So what Long is suggesting is not so absurd. "George" knows the answer to certain questions, and he can communicate the answer through the pendulum. The sole difference between Long's theory of dowsing and the "split-brain theory" is that Long believes that "George" lives in the solar plexus, not the right brain. He could well be right. Most dowsers observe that if the hazel twig is held above the solar plexus, it twists upwards over water, while below the solar plexus it twists downwards. Certainly, the solar plexus seems to be involved. And another writer on Huna theory states without qualification that the middle self is located in the left brain, while the higher self is located in the right.*

According to Long, the pendulum is an admirable way of becoming acquainted with the personality of the low self; some low selves, he says, are as playful as kittens, others are sedate and sober. It is a good idea to test George with questions about people—"Do you like so and so?"—for, like a child, his response is often more penetrating than that of the adult middle self. Long also suggests that rewards are of use in training the low self—praise, or something it enjoys, like certain food. This seems to tie in with an interesting point made by Guy Playfair: that Brazilian magicians recognize that spirits enjoy the same simple pleasures as on earth—food, alcohol, a cigar, even sex, and that bargains can be struck with their aid.

We may or may not find the Huna theories—as expounded by Long—acceptable; yet one thing emerges very clearly: that compared with other theories of the paranormal that we have considered, they are satisfyingly comprehensive. There is almost no paranormal phenomenon that is not discussed and —to some extent—explained. In some cases, the explanation may seem naive or controversial; yet, more often than not, Long turns out to have sound evidence in his favour. One example is his account of hypnosis. According to Long, this is only partly a matter of "suggestion." The most important element in hypnosis, he says, is a transfer of vital force—*mana*—from the hypnotist to the subject.† (He even alleges that *kuhuna* magicians could transfer this vital force to a

Huna, a Beginner's Guide by Enid Hoffman, 1976

†Long: *Self Suggestion, and the New Huna Theory of Mesmerism and Hypnosis*, 1958.

throwing stick for use in battle, which would stun anyone it touched even lightly.) He asserts that when a serpent "hypnotizes" a bird, it projects its "vital force" towards it. Such a notion would be dismissed by most psychologists as an old wive's tale. Yet Ferenc Völgyesi's standard work *Hypnosis of Man and Animals* gives dozens of examples that make it abundantly clear that this describes accurately what occurs; he describes a hypnotic battle between two lizards, ending in the winner eating the other, and has many photographs of such battles between snakes and birds, snakes and toads and other creatures engaged in beating down one another's gaze.

Long's theory of psychometry—of *ake* threads running from all objects—seems to be supported by Maria de Zierold's observation that under hypnosis she could become "connected" to objects in precisely the same way that she was connected to Dr. Pagenstecher (and in the latter case she saw a cord running from herself to Pagenstecher). And the *aka* thread theory also provides an explanation for Hudson's observation that he could heal people who were hundreds of miles away. Healing, according to Long, is simply the transfer of vital force along the *aka* threads. This also explains the paradox that healers—for example, wart charmers—seem to be able to heal by merely speaking to the patient over the telephone, or through a letter.

Unfortunately, even Long's Huna theory has its limitations; it fails, for example, to explain the curious paradox known as map-dowsing. All good dowsers are aware that water can be located just as easily on a map as under the ground; yet this seems so preposterous that most "scientific" books on dowsing avoid mentioning it (Barrett's work being an example). "Professor" Joad once explained on a BBC Brains Trust programme that dowsing worked through some kind of static electricity—then added, as an afterthought, that he had once seen a dowser accurately replace all the streams on a map from which they had been removed. One of the most celebrated of twentieth-century dowsers, the Abbé Mermet, has a section in his book *Principles and Practice of Radiesthesia* entitled "Distance No Barrier," which states that with the aid of a map, the dowser can locate objects at the antipodes—Mermet himself located distant oilfields and sunken wrecks by this method. But Mermet's explanation—that thought travels as fast as light, and can encompass the globe in a fraction of a second, still fails to explain how "thought" *finds* its object. And Long's *aka* thread explanation is no more satisfactory, since there is no obvious connection between a map and the place it represents. It is true that Long accepts the reality of spirits, so the Huna theory could explain map-dowsing in the same way that George Henslow explains psychometry—through information received from spirits. If we find ourselves unable to accept anything so vague, then we are forced to include map-dowsing under the general heading of "clairvoyance," which is just as baffling. Once again we have to face the frustrating recognition that no theory of the paranormal seems to be able to accommodate *all* the facts.

6

The Mind Link

WHEN MAXIMILIEN LANGSNER set out for Fairbanks, Alaska, early in 1929, he had just solved one of the most puzzling murder cases in Canadian history. Langsner, who had studied under Freud in Vienna, had travelled to India after the First World War to study telepathy and mind control. In Alaska, he hoped to study the "psi" powers of Eskimos, who had not yet been corrupted by civilization. His researches were interrupted by death. A Canadian newspaper carried the following obituary:

> Maximilien Langsner, Ph.D. (University of Calcutta) was found dead yesterday in a small hut on the outskirts of Fairbanks, Alaska. Dr. Langsner was known for his theory of "brain waves" and for his ability, often demonstrated, in reading the thoughts of other people. He was engaged in research on this subject at the time of his death.
>
> Dr. Langsner was widely known, and his undoubted gifts had been made use of by Royalty. He had solved mysteries for the Shah of Persia, the King of Egypt, and had helped the British Government in Asia. He will be remembered, too, for the assistance he gave to many police departments faced with difficult cases.

Until Langsner appeared in Edmonton, Alberta, the Booher case seemed insoluble. On the evening of 9 July 1928, Vernon

159

Booher found his mother lying dead in the kitchen of their farmhouse near Mannville, eighty miles north of Edmonton; she had been shot in the back of the neck. In the next room he found his brother Fred, shot through the mouth. In a nearby bunkhouse was the body of a hired hand, Gabriel Cromby, also shot to death. Vernon Booher went to a neighbour's home to telephone the family doctor, and the police were summoned. Meanwhile, the owner of the farm, Henry Booher, had returned from the fields. He was in a state of shock when the police arrived, and could suggest no motive for the killings. Vernon Booher suggested that the culprit might be another hired hand named Rosyk. But he was found in one of the barns, also shot to death. All had been killed with a .303 rifle, which was nowhere to be found.

Medical examination established that Rose Booher, Fred Booher and Rosyk had all died at roughly the same time—about half past six that evening. Neighbours had heard the shots but thought nothing of it, since Mannville is hunting country. The puzzling thing was that the killer had apparently come back about two hours later to kill Cromby—Vernon Booher said he had heard two shots some time after eight o'clock, as he worked in the fields.

When a search failed to uncover the weapon, and questioning failed to uncover a suspect, or even a motive, the Edmonton chief of police, Mike Gier, decided that unusual measures were required. Dr. Maximilien Langsner had been something of a celebrity ever since he had solved a jewel robbery case in Vancouver by standing in the cell of the chief suspect and "reading his mind." After half an hour, he had been able to tell the police that the jewels were hidden behind a picture in a room with yellow walls; they recognized the description as the room of the suspect's girlfriend, and found the jewels behind a picture. Mike Gier telegraphed Dr. Langsner.

Langsner arrived in time for the inquest. He was a very small man with a heavy Viennese accent; he wore a neat dark suit and a black hat from under which his untidy white hair escaped. He sat quietly at the press table and listened to the evidence. A neighbour, Charles Stevenson, seemed the only likely suspect. He agreed that his rifle, a .303, had disappeared recently, and explained that he had called at the Booher farm on the evening of the murders to look at a farming catalogue.

Back in Gier's office after the inquest, Langsner said: "I

can tell you the name of the killer. Vernon Booher." Gier asked: "Have you any proof?" "No, but I can tell you where the murder weapon was hidden—in a clump of prairie grass at the back of the house."

The following day, Langsner accompanied the police to the farm. He led them around to the back of the house—Gier commented that Langsner reminded him of a water diviner using a hazel twig. He spent twenty minutes wandering around, apparently trying to get his bearings, then requested one of the policemen to take ten steps forward. At the ninth step, the policeman tripped over something. It was the missing rifle, hidden in thick grass. "It is no use looking for finger-prints, Vernon wiped it clean."

On Langsner's advice, Vernon Booher was placed in "pro-tective custody" as a major witness. Langsner went and sat on a chair outside his cell. At first Booher tried to make conversa-tion; he became angry as Langsner ignored him. Finally, they relapsed into silence. Then Langsner got up and left, saying goodbye to Vernon who ignored him.

Back in Gier's office, Langsner told the story of the mur-ders. For some reason, Vernon had come to hate his mother. He was her favourite son, but she ruled the house with rigid discipline. Vernon had deliberately shot her in the back with the stolen rifle, then realized that Fred was also in the house, and been forced to kill him. Going out to hide the gun, he saw Rosyk and became convinced that Rosyk had seen him; so he crept up and killed Rosyk. Two hours later, he decided that Cromby might also have seen him; so he shot Cromby.

One person could prove that Vernon had the opportunity to steal the weapon, said Langsner—a little woman with small eyes and a long jaw, who wore a poke bonnet. She had been seated at the back of the church on the previous Sunday when Vernon had slipped out to steal the rifle. Vernon knew she had seen him, and was worried about her.

The police soon located her; her name was Erma Higgins, and she was a spinster who paid attention to all the goings-on in the community. She confirmed that she had noticed Vernon Booher slipping out of church, and had watched to see when he came back. Since the gun's owner, Charles Stevenson, had already told the inquest that the gun was stolen while he was at church, the case against Vernon was now strong.

Vernon was brought face to face with Erma Higgins, who

told him: "Vernon, I saw you leave the church the day Charlie's rifle was stolen." "I know you did," said Vernon; then, after a long pause: "Let me confess. I killed them . . ."

His mother had tried to break up a romance with the daughter of a farm worker, and had even ordered the girl to leave the house. She enraged Vernon by telling him what she thought of the girl; his resentment built up until he determined to kill her.

By the time Vernon Booher was hanged on 26 April 1929, Langsner had already left for Alaska.

Telepathy was one of the first "occult" subjects investigated by the Society for Psychical Research—as we have seen, Myers invented the word; Myers, Gurney, Lodge and others soon came to the conclusion that, in spite of the possibility of cheating (the Creery sisters were a great disappointment) there could be no final doubt about the reality of telepathy.

But apart from the question of deliberate cheating, there was also the possibility of unconscious muscular signals. This became very clear after a spectacular exposure in 1905. A Prussian aristocrat named Wilhelm von Osten decided in 1888 to try to train a horse up to the human level of intelligence, and spent years training a Polish stallion called Clever Hans (Kluge Hans) to solve mathematical problems. He would hold up various figures on cards, and the horse would tap out the answer with its hoof. In 1904, a commission of Berlin scientists watched in amazement as Hans tapped out the answers to all kinds of arithmetical questions, and a circus animal trainer agreed that he could see no sign of trickery. But a brilliant student named Oskar Pfungst decided to test Hans until he had eliminated every possibility of natural signaling. He asked von Osten not to look at the cards before he held them up. And when von Osten had no idea of the answer, Clever Hans also failed. Pfungst got von Osten to stand outside the horse's line of vision, and again the horse was unable to give the correct answers. Studying von Osten's movements carefully, Pfungst finally concluded that he was quite unconsciously supplying the horse with visual clues about when to stop tapping—a slight movement of the eyebrows, a twitch of the nostril, a straightening of the body. Von Osten was absolved of all blame, but he became a laughing stock, and died an embittered man in 1909. This lesson about unconscious muscular signals was not lost on the investigators of the SPR.

Yet von Osten was, in a sense, vindicated. He sold Clever Hans to another enthusiastic horse trainer, Karl Krall, and Krall went on to train four more horses—they became known as the Elberfeld Calculating Horses—whose abilities could not be explained in terms of unconscious signals. Maurice Maeterlinck spent some time at Krall's stable at Elberfeld, and described his experiences in *The Unknown Guest*. In one experiment, Maeterlinck was left alone with one of the horses. He shuffled a pack of cards, then placed a number of cards in front of the horse without looking at them himself. The horse unhesitatingly tapped out the correct answer: the sum of all the cards.

But the incredible thing about the Elberfeld horses was that they showed the talent of mathematical prodigies. They could be asked to give the square foot—or cube root or fourth root —of an immense figure, like 7890481, and do it almost instantaneously. (The horse called Muhamed replied that the fourth root of this figure is 53.) Maeterlinck himself tested the horse by making up a huge number—written on a blackboard—and asking the horse for the square root. Muhamed stood with his hoof raised, unable to answer. Krall asked Maeterlinck: "Does it have an exact root?," and when Maeterlinck admitted his ignorance of mathematics, Krall worked it out and remarked that the problem was insoluble in round numbers, and Muhamed had been quite right not to answer.

The horses were also able to "speak"—in German—by tapping out letters with a code, and they could repeat someone's name, identify colours, and answer questions as "What is this picture?"—to which the answer was "A girl." "How do you know that?" brought the reply: "She has long hair." (*Weil lang Hr Hd.*). "And what does she lack?" "A moustache." (A modern stallion would probably give a cruder answer.) One day, Muhamed actually managed something like genuine speech; he whinnied something very like "The groom struck Hänschen."

Maeterlinck was obviously rather shaken by his experience of the horses. He performed tests with them when no one else was present, and they solved mathematical problems to which he himself did not know the answer, and answered verbal questions such as "What is that color?" Maeterlinck ruled out all question of trickery. But could he rule out telepathy?

One method of testing was to present the horse with problems which he himself could not see—problems taken at random from an envelope. The horses answered these as readily as any other. Yet Maeterlinck felt that *some* form of "subliminal faculty" could not be entirely excluded. He cites one authority who believes that animals probably live in a state of consciousness which in human beings would approximate sleepwalking. Their brains are in a permanent state of lethargy. But they can be galvanized into brief wakefulness—into "psychic flashes," so to speak. (He is here using "psychic" in the same sense as Hudson, meaning mental.) Human beings—Krall in particular—obviously played a large part in causing such psychic flashes in the Elberfeld horses. Maeterlinck goes on to point out that there is strong evidence for animal telepathy —he cites case studies by Bozzano. (Half a century later, he would have been able to cite experiments at Duke University with cats, dogs and pigeons that demonstrated telepathy.) The subliminal consciousness of animals (what Long calls the "low self") is stronger than in human beings, since it is less repressed by consciousness. So there could be a trigger effect from the trainer which helps to explain the intelligence of the Elberfeld horses. Yet Maeterlinck was not ruling out the possibility that all animals could be trained up to the same level. He points out that many mathematical prodigies have been children who otherwise showed no high degree of intellect; a "degenerate and near-idiot" named Fleury calculated in just over a minute the number of seconds in thirty-nine years, three months and twelve days, not forgetting leap years. On the other hand, the great mathematician Poincaré admitted he could not add up a column of figures without making a mistake . . .

If Maeterlinck had known about the pattern-perceiving powers of the right brain, he would have been able to formulate his theory far more precisely. For *this* is what he is saying: that perhaps intelligence is a pattern-perceiving faculty that is as natural to animals as to human beings: what animals lack is our human power to translate patterns into words or concepts. The really startling implication of this theory is that perhaps animals are not really so far behind human beings on the evolutionary scale after all (and the other side of this coin is the notion that if a horse can be "humanized" so easily, then perhaps we could be "superhumanized" just as easily) . . .

Telepathy is certainly a highly convenient starting point for any study of "psi" powers, since it is probably the easiest of all to establish. Naturalists have observed many examples of telepathy in animals and birds: for example, in his book *How Animals Talk*, William J. Long describes his own observation of the telepathic link between a she-wolf and her cubs. If a mother wolf cannot head off a cub that is vanishing into the distance, she raises her head and looks steadily after it; the cub abruptly halts and runs back.

Many animal trainers have demonstrated the telepathic link between animals and humans. In the 1920s and 30s, a Russian trainer, V. L. Durov, had a dog act in which he stood on stage, and the animals performed all kinds of tricks under his telepathic orders—Durov was studied by Professor V. M. Bekhterev at the Leningrad Institute for Brain Research. Bekhterev found that a terrier named Pikki could carry out fairly involved thought commands from himself, even when Durov was not present. In another typical experiment, Durov was in a room with Bekhterev while a terrier was in another room far away; Bekhterev would hand Durov a note with a number in it; Durov would concentrate, and in the distant room, the terrier would bark precisely the number of times indicated in the note.

The British newspaper editor Edward Campbell has described the relationship between a German lion tamer, Hans Brick, and his favourite lion, Habibi. Habibi was savage and unbroken, and Brick claimed that they had a tacit agreement that Habibi would never attack him so long as he kept his full attention on the lion. On the few occasions when he allowed his attention to lapse, attack followed instantly. During the Second World War, Brick was interned in England and Habibi was sent to a zoo. At the end of the war, a film company wanted to hire Brick and Habibi, but the zoo owner wanted paying before he released the lion. Brick could not pay unless he worked for the film company; so one morning, he slipped into the building and released Habibi. He made a mental pact with the lion, telling him telepathically: "You want to get out and I want to get you out. So no tricks." Then, with a whip looped around the lion's neck, he led him out—among rabbits and peacocks wandering around the floor—to a waiting cage parked outside.

In a pamphlet called "Some Unusual Aspects of Communication," Edward Campbell cites a personal experience. Shortly before the Second World War, he trained a lion, two lionesses, and a brown bear to perform in an indoor menagerie. He was on such good terms with the two lionesses that he would often go into the cage and play with them. Early in 1940, he went away on military service for about six months. Allowed home on leave, he hurried to the zoo to see the lions. It was on the first floor of a large building, and the approach was through a turnstile set in a wall across the entrance. There was a small spy hole in the wall for the use of the staff. Campbell peered through this, and saw his own lions pacing up and down their cages. Suddenly, they turned in his direction in an attitude of extreme alertness. As he continued looking, the two lionesses went into a frenzy, rushing from one end of the cage to the other. Campbell went and mingled in the dense crowd of visitors, and as soon as he did this, the lions stopped leaping, and went into an attitude of attention. As he walked towards the cage, they identified him and began leaping and bounding again. Campbell describes how he went through the safety cage and rolled around on the floor with the lions, who rolled on their backs and insisted on being scratched. Campbell discounts the possibility that they could have smelt him with about three hundred other people present in the room.

Insofar as any "psi" faculty can be described as "proven," the reality of telepathy has now been established on a solid basis of experiment. Even in the days before I became interested in the occult, I had no doubts about the existence of telepathy; for example, when my children were babies, I could awaken them by staring at them—it worked just as well through a closed window. During the course of writing this chapter, and by way of testing its basic assertion, I tried a telepathic experiment with my wife. On 21 April 1983, I had spent the morning in a local hospital having a routine check-up. The sister in charge of out-patients had told my wife to telephone at one o'clock to see if I was ready. In fact, I was back in the waiting area by midday. I decided to try to send my wife a telepathic message to say that I was ready to go. This was at about five past midday. Five minutes later, the sister came to tell me that my wife was on the telephone, asking when to come and fetch me.

When she arrived, I asked her what had happened. She said that she had felt a sudden impulse to check with the hospital in case I might be ready earlier than expected. The telephone boxes had been occupied, so she went into a chemist's shop to make a purchase; when she came out a few minutes later, a box was empty. This accounted for the five minute delay before she rang . . .

Most married couples could describe similar experiences. And many dog and cat owners are convinced that they have established a telepathic rapport with their pets. Although in most cases, this can be explained by signals, like putting on a hat, there are always the exception—the dog in another room leaping to its feet to go for a walk just as its master, in his study, has decided that he has done enough work for one day and that it is time for a breath of air . . .

In 1904, Sir Rider Haggard was so struck by a case of dream-telepathy that he wrote a long letter to *The Times* to place it on record. On Saturday 9 July, he woke from a "nightmare" some time after 12:30; he had a sense of oppression and of a struggle for life "such as the act of drowning would probably involve." Before his wife called to ask why he was gasping, he seemed to have another brief dream, in which his eldest daughter's black retriever Bob was lying on his side among brushwood, by the side of water. The dog's head was lifted at an unnatural angle, and seemed to be transmitting to him the knowledge that it was dying.

Assuming it was merely a nightmare, he made no enquiries about the dog. But on Sunday evening his daughter mentioned that Bob was missing. A few days later, the dog was found floating in the river, against the weir. Two railwaymen told Haggard that it had been killed by a train; they had found Bob's collar, with blood on it, on the bridge over the river. The dog had apparently been killed by the last train on Saturday night, when Haggard had his dream. This was some time after 11 o'clock. Evidence suggested that Bob had been knocked into the reeds, and had lain there, dying, at the time of the nightmare.

Scientists in general find it easier to accept telepathy than most other paranormal faculties, since it seems to depend on some form of wave transmission—Hereward Carrington suggested that there is some kind of "mentiferous ether." Yet, as with most paranormal theories, this one soon begins to show the usual inability to embrace all the facts. The case of the novelist Upton Sinclair is typical. His wife, Craig, had been telepathic in childhood—when her mother wanted her, she would usually be on her way before someone could go and find her. In adulthood, the faculty revived after the death of a number of intimate friends. Sinclair was not entirely happy about her gift, since it enabled her to follow his movements when he was away from her. He finally began a series of experiments involving the transmission of drawings, which left him in no doubt that his wife could pick up his own mental images. But some of her powers could not be explained in terms of telepathy. She could, for example, turn her back on a bookshelf, reach for a book "blind," and then describe its cover while holding it behind her. This could, of course, be explained as cryptomnesia or subconscious observation; but a further series of experiments ruled out that possibility. Sinclair would make a number of drawings, put them all in an envelope, then send his wife into a darkened room, where she would take out the drawings one at a time at random, and hold them against her stomach; she could then make a more-or-less accurate reproduction of the drawing. (In his book *Mental Radio* Sinclair reproduces many illustrations.) But by doing it in the dark she had not only eliminated cryptomnesia—she had never seen the drawings—but also telepathy, since Sinclair could have no idea of which drawing she would take out next. In short, she was demonstrating psychometry.

Sinclair soon observed a further complication. Having completed a drawing, his wife would sometimes continue to draw, adding something to the picture—for example, she added puffs of smoke to a drawing of a necktie. Then she took the next drawing from the envelope: it was of a burning match with puffs of smoke. The psychometry was being complicated by precognition. (In 1939, S. G. Soal discovered a similar effect when testing a housewife called Gloria Stewart for telepathy; her score was poor until Soal realized that she was frequently drawing the *next* picture.)

This tendency of the subject to blur into other paranormal phenomena was observed by other psychical investigators; it often seemed that the more they tried to make their experiments painstakingly precise, the more they were plagued by these intrusions. In 1912, a Munich ophthalmologist called Rudolf Tischner was intrigued by accounts of telepathy by his friend Professor L. Staudenmaier, and they asked Staudenmaier's best subject, Miss von B., to come and work with them. She showed an ability to make correct drawings of objects held behind her back. Then Tischner went into his study to a large box that contained miscellaneous letters and postcards, took out a postcard without looking at it, and sealed it in a thick envelope which was sealed with sealing wax. (As an extra precaution the postcard was first wrapped in black paper.) Miss von B. was then given the envelope, and lay on a couch with a pencil and paper. Within five minutes she had written down a number of words that were on the card, and described the picture on the other side—a house between trees. Telepathy was impossible, since Tischner had no idea of which of many cards he had taken out of the box. Moreover, Miss von B. had written the words on the paper in exactly the same positions that they occurred in on the postcard, as if she had somehow "traced" them through two thicknesses of heavy paper.

So this was not telepathy, but clairvoyance (or psychometry). Still Tischner *might* have glanced briefly at the card as he removed it from the box. To eliminate this possibility, he took a bundle of hundreds of cards, tied up with string, which had been lying around for years, and asked another experimenter to select one at random, wrap it in black paper, and seal it in an envelope. The psychometrist held it as before for five minutes—she was alone in the room, but Tischner was watching her through a crack in the door for signs of trickery—and then wrote some words on a sheet of paper. When Tischner came in she said: "The first word of the address is 'Family.'" This struck Tischner as highly unlikely, since he could not remember ever having received a card addressed to the Family Tischner. But Miss von B. was right—it was a card that had been sent to his father. And again, the words she had been able to "read" were placed accurately on the paper as if traced.

Aware now that he was dealing with more than telepathy, Tischner went on to conduct nearly two hundred similar experiments. Again and again his psychometrists accurately described the writers of letters he placed in their hands, or described the owners—and the history—of various objects. So Tischner's work on telepathy—which has become a standard textbook—had to be called *Telepathy and Clairvoyance.*

Two years after the book was published—in 1919—that arch enemy of occultism Sigmund Freud committed himself to a belief in telepathy. This may seem incredible, in view of his remarks to Jung about the "black tide of occultism." The explanation is that it was incidental to explaining his own views on repressed guilt and aggression.

Freud's paper "Psychoanalysis and Telepathy" begins with a blast of the paranoia to which he was subject. "We do not seem destined to work in peace on the development of our science. Barely did we victoriously repel two attacks (here he sketches the views of some renegade psychoanalysts, presumably Jung and Adler) . . . barely did we begin to feel safe from these foes, when a new danger arose; this time in the form of something tremendous and fundamental, which threatens not only us, but even more perhaps our opponents." The new danger is occultism; Freud explains that he objects to it because if human beings seek their answers in spirits or unknown powers, they may ignore the attempts of psychoanalysis to understand the unconscious. Yet in spite of this, he explains, he feels impelled to offer some observations he had made in recent years, observations he would like his close colleagues (to whom the paper would be privately circulated) to keep to themselves . . .

The first case he describes is of a young man who had incestuous feelings towards his own sister. She became engaged to an engineer. The brother and the engineer went mountain climbing and almost lost their lives—which Freud interprets as an attempt at murder and suicide. Later, the brother went to consult a Munich fortuneteller who required only his date of birth. (She was presumably an astrologer.) The brother gave her the birth date of his brother-in-law, whereupon the fortuneteller prophesied that in July or August, he would die of crab poisoning.

This prophecy did not come true. But it so happened that the brother-in-law *had* almost died of crab poisoning in the previous August. Freud concluded that the fortuneteller had picked this up telepathically from the young man, expressing his "death wish" towards his brother-in-law.

In the second case, a childless married woman went to see a fortuneteller, who told her that she would have two children by the time she was thirty-two. Again, the prophecy failed to materialize. But what Freud felt was significant was that the woman's mother had had two children by the time *she* was thirty-two. The woman had incestuous designs on her father, and identified herself with her mother. Again, the fortuneteller had picked this up telepathically . . .

Freud goes on to speak about a handwriting expert called Scherman, who could not only deduce a person's character from the handwriting (as most graphologists can), but could on occasion make predictions about the future. Freud adds indignantly that when a sample of his own handwriting was shown to Scherman, the graphologist said it was the writing of an insupportable domestic tyrant—which, says Freud, he is certainly not. But his behaviour towards many of his disciples was so vindictive and tyrannical that the handwriting expert was obviously not too unperceptive.

Freud goes on to discuss another case. One of his patients was involved with a kept woman, whom he treated so badly that the girl was often on the point of a nervous breakdown. In fact, the patient was in love with an upper class woman who made *him* suffer, and he was using the other mistress as a whipping boy. Finally, when he felt he had expressed all his resentment, he decided to break with the kept woman. At this time, he often took samples of her handwriting to Scherman, who assured him that she was on the verge of suicide. In fact, the woman did not kill herself. Freud infers that Scherman had been reading the young man's mind, and had picked up the fact that he wanted the girl to kill herself . . .

Freud concludes his paper by telling his disciples: "Perhaps the problem of thought transference will seem rather trifling to you in comparison with the great world of occult miracles. Yet consider: even this hypothesis already represents a great and momentous step beyond our present viewpoint."

It would certainly have been a great and momentous step if Freud had dared to state his convictions openly. Together with Einstein, he was probably the world's most famous scientist, and his admission of the reality of telepathy would have done more than a dozen books by Tischner to persuade science to take it seriously. As it was, the paper remained almost unknown until after Freud's death; and it would be almost another four decades before Jung would take his reputation in his hands and declare: "The authenticity of this phenomenon can no longer be disputed today. I have found by experience that telepathy does, in fact, influence dreams, as has been asserted since ancient times . . ."

Meanwhile, another painstaking experimenter, Dr. J. Hettinger, made the most comprehensive attempt since Buchanan to demonstrate the reality of psychometry. His book *Exploring the Ultra-Perceptive Faculty* is not as readable as Buchanan's *Psychometry*, being full of statistics and mathematical formulae, and singularly devoid of quotable anecdotes. Yet it is, in other ways, just as exciting.

Hettinger's method was simple. He asked various friends for objects or letters to be sent through the post, and these were then submitted to the psychometrist, a woman named F. Kingstone from Hounslow, often still in the sealed envelope. In writing up his results, Hettinger seems to go out of his way to be unsensational—he seldom even bothers to mention the nature of the objects that were psychometrized. Nevertheless, the results were strikingly accurate. The psychometrist had an impression of drowning; the person who submitted the article admitted that his father was drowned before his eyes. The psychometrist "saw" a thin woman's arm with a heavy gold bangle; the sender admitted that it was her arm and bangle. The psychometrist saw a classroom full of desks; the sender turned out to be a schoolteacher. With incredible persistence, Hettinger offers hundreds of similar examples—none very spectacular, yet impressive by reason of sheer volume. He also mentions a point that is seldom raised by writers on psychometry, but which is bound to bother anyone who has contact with a psychic—whether the psychic can "see" secrets of the person's sex life. Hettinger records that his psychometrists said they *could* pick up sexual details, but were too tactful to mention them.

He noticed that his clairvoyants often described events that had taken place *after* the article had been posted to him. For example, the psychometrist "saw" a small fire which caused little damage; the sender confirmed that after the article was sent, there had been a fall of hot soot down the chimney. With dozens of similar examples, Hettinger establishes what Osty had suspected: that the object merely serves to establish a contact between the psychometrist and another person, and that once this has been done, clairvoyance can take over. He also confirmed Buchanan's observation that a sheet of blank paper serves as well as a letter to provide the psychometrist with "vibrations." He would ask people to carry a sheet of paper around with them for a day or two, then hand it to the psychometrist. Holding one sheet of paper, the psychometrist said: "Owner distracted by a screeching bird." In fact, the owner had been annoyed by a screeching parrot, which prevented him from concentrating, while he was carrying the paper. Strong sensations—like anger and pain—seemed to come over particularly well. The psychometrist felt that the person who had carried the paper had recently burnt her finger by holding something hot; in fact, the sender had burnt her finger on a hot saucepan handle.

Perhaps his most significant result was the discovery that a few events occurred *after* the psychometrist had sensed them. On one occasion, the psychometrist saw bundles of buff-colored cotton fabric "undone and cut up"; four days later the subject bought buff-colored curtain material. So Hettinger had established one of Buchanan's most controversial claims: that psychometry can predict the future. It could, of course, have been coincidence; but the whole point of Hettinger's boring, painstaking method, with its hundreds of examples, is to accumulate so many cases that such an explanation looks absurd. Anyone who has the patience to plod through twenty pages of *Exploring the Ultra-Perceptive Faculty* will end with the feeling that it is definitive and conclusive, and that any sceptic who still insists that psychometry is "non-proven" is merely being perverse.

Yet this still takes us no closer to an explanation. Precisely a century after Buchanan invented the word psychometry, Hettinger has to acknowledge that no theory covers all the facts. He comments that his sensitives declared that they had to concentrate *and* make the mind a blank, which he finds incomprehensible. He suggests that the object held by the psychometrist establishes a connection between the psychometrist and the owner of the article, but then has to admit that this "mental radio" theory fails to explain how the psychometrist can sometimes pick up events in the history of the object which no one has actually witnessed—like Mrs. Denton's glimpse of the history of a glacial pebble, or Signora de Zierold's vision of the fall of a meteorite. As to the "ultra-perceptive cognition of future events," he can only suggest the existence of a "fourth dimension"—which, he admits, is just as puzzling as the facts themselves. In spite of which, he flatly refuses to accept the view that "spirits" might be responsible.

Yet, Hettinger has one very important comment to make: that "Man's potentialities of cognition extend beyond the normal sensory and intellectual perception, and this *ultra-perceptive* faculty is associated with a *state of consciousness* which is more or less different from the ordinary normal state." This in itself is a tremendous step forward: the recognition that we take normal consciousness for granted, as if it were the one thing of which we can be certain. Yet mystics have always insisted that normal consciousness *is actually sub-normal*—that the difference between "normal" consciousness and *real* consciousness is as great as the difference between night and day. So any attempt to describe the laws of nature from the point of view of normal consciousness could be compared to an attempt to describe a picture gallery in the middle of the night, when all the lights have been turned out.

Hettinger's observation that his sensitives need to concentrate *and* make the mind a blank affords another important clue. As soon as we know that man has two beings inside his head, the apparent contradiction vanishes. Most of us assume that "making the mind a blank" means making the left brain a blank, and that concentrating means concentrating with the left brain. Yet any artist is aware that he is at his best when he concentrates *and* makes his mind a blank. When a great pianist is playing at his best, he is concentrating, yet his mind is a blank—at least, as far as thoughts, ideas, perceptions are concerned. If he begins to wonder whether his wife remembered to meet the children out of school, the intensity will vanish. In short, the sensitive seems to be a person who has the knack of *concentrating with the right brain*. And the result of this unusual balance—right-brain concentration, left-brain blankness—is an intenser state of consciousness in which some of the normal laws of perception seem to be transcended.

As a crude working-model for psychometry and clairvoyance, Max Freedom Long's notion of *aka* threads is as satisfactory as any. The obvious objection is that there seems to be no evidence for the real existence of such "threads." Yet something very similar has been described repeatedly by visitors to the seance room. In his book *From the Unconscious to the Conscious,* Dr. Gustav Geley (whom we met at the beginning of the preceding chapter) has a number of photographs of the medium "Eva C" (Eva Carriere) "materializing" a face, and the materialization begins with a white substance flowing from her nostrils and finger-ends. Geley says: "I have been able to see, to touch and to photograph the materializations of which I am about to write." He goes on to describe how, after Eva Carriere had been put into a hypnotic state, she would begin to sigh and moan, like a woman in childbirth, then luminous liquid patches would appear on her smock, principally down the left side (i.e. the side connected to the right brain). Then the "ectoplasm" would appear. "The substance exudes especially from the natural orifices and the extremities, from the top of the head, from the nipples and from the ends of the fingers. The substance has variable aspects; sometimes, and most characteristically it appears as a plastic paste, a true protoplasmic mass; *sometimes as a number of fine threads* [my italics]; sometimes as strings of different thickness in narrow and rigid lines; sometimes as a wide hand; sometimes as a fine tissue of ill-defined and irregular shape." The photographs show Geley's hand holding that of the medium as she produces the threads, so trickery seems unlikely. He adds: "Sometimes it feels like a spider's web . . ." And he points out that it is mobile, and moves over the medium with a crawling, reptilian movement. The photographs show this substance moulding itself on the medium's breast (and while Geley holds her hands) into an image of the head of a pretty girl. But the possibility that it could be a cut-out or photograph is excluded in the following pictures in which it rises to the level of the medium's own head, on the end of an undulating column of the substance—producing the impression of a snake with a woman's face. Another photograph shows it dematerializing.

So unless we assume that Geley was party to some kind of fraud, it seems clear that Eva Carriere was able to materialize some "protoplasmic" substance, which then moulded itself into a face. If it could move with a "crawling, reptilian motion" we must assume that it was alive, or capable of transmitting life. All this certainly sounds very much like the *aka* threads of the Hunas, whose purpose is to act as transmitters of *mana*.

Freedom Long contradicts Upton Sinclair's belief that telepathy is a kind of mental radio, pointing out that radio waves diminish according to the inverse square law, while telepathy seems to function as well at a thousand miles as at a few feet.

He makes another comment that is relevant in the present context: that if the psychometrist can provide information about someone after death, then the *aka* threads must still be connected—evidence, says Long, of survival after death. The same comment seems to apply to telepathy, particularly "dream telepathy." As Jung says, the notion that telepathy influences dreams has been asserted since ancient times. In many cases, the explanation could be that telepathy occurred at the moment of death, but that the "receiver" was unaware of it until the right brain could transmit the information through a dream. This could, for example, explain one of the most famous of all cases of "dream telepathy," the Red Barn murder. In May 1827, a farmer's son named William Corder lured his pregnant mistress, Maria Marten, into a barn in Polstead, Suffolk, where he shot her. Maria was buried in a corner of the barn, and Corder soon afterwards left for London, where he married and became a schoolmaster. Maria's stepmother, who was known for her "second sight," began to have nightmares in which she was in the red barn, and saw the ground open up, to reveal Maria's corpse. She was even able to state the precise spot—underneath the right-hand bay of the further side of the barn. Maria's father managed to get into the barn, on the excuse of looking for some clothes his daughter might have left there. He went to the right-hand bay, moved some corn, and found some huge stones lying there. The handle of a rake showed that the earth was soft and yielding. Marten and a farm bailiff removed a few inches of earth, and found an iron spike. A few feet further down was the body of Maria Marten, tied up in a sack. Corder was arrested in London, and in August 1828, was publicly hanged in front of Bury St. Edmunds gaol.

To explain Anne Marten's dream of her stepdaughter's grave, we do not have to assume that Maria's spirit sent the dream. Maria was murdered in the barn. Corder had asked her to go to the barn dressed in men's clothes, so that she would not be recognized if anyone saw her. (He told her they were about to elope.) She seems to have been in the process of changing out of her men's clothes, back into a skirt, when Corder murdered her, so it is probable that she was in the bay where her body was later found—it is natural for anyone getting undressed to look for some concealment. Corder seems to have shot her, then used a knife—or the iron spike—to stab her. It follows that her death was not instantaneous. Anne Marten could have received the telepathic message about the place of the murder as Maria was dying; but it remained unconscious until it presented itself to her as a recurrent dream.

But there have been other cases where the "moment of death" theory fails to cover the facts. In April 1922, a young ex-army officer named Eric Tombe disappeared. He had been in business with a man named Ernest Dyer, running a racing stable at Kenley, in Surrey. The stable had not been very successful, but when it burned down, an insurance investigator found empty petrol cans in the ruins, and Dyer dropped his claim. He had been borrowing money from Eric Tombe, and the two men quarrelled. Then Tombe vanished, and Dyer went off to the north of England, where he used various aliases, and passed dud cheques. In November 1922, when police came to question him about suspected fraud, he pulled a revolver from his pocket and, in the ensuing struggle, shot himself. In his room, police found Eric Tombe's chequebook, with forged signatures, and Tombe's passport, with Dyer's photograph substituted.

Eric Tombe's father, the Rev. Gordon Tombe, was the vicar of a village in Oxfordshire, Little Tew. In April 1922, Mrs. Tombe began to dream that her son was dead, and that he was lying buried down a well, with a stone slab over its mouth. It seemed to be in the grounds of a farm. The vicar gave up his living and moved to Sydenham, in order to devote himself to finding his son. He called at Eric's Haymarket flat, and from neighbours learned about the stud farm—The Welcomes—at Kenley. The farm proved to be in ruins; but Ernest Dyer's wife was still living there. She told Tombe that her husband was dead—that he had been killed in a road crash that summer. She had no idea what had become of Eric. The vicar went to Scotland Yard; the police discovered that many cheques had been drawn on Eric Tombe's bank account since his disappearance in April.

Finally, to humour Mrs. Tombe—who continued to dream that her son was down a well—the police searched The Welcomes. There was no well, but on the edge of the paddock there were four cesspits, each covered with a heavy slab. The first three were empty, but the fourth was full of rubble. This was removed, and revealed an arched recess. In this was the corpse of Eric Tombe. He had been shot in the back of the head with a shotgun. At the inquest, the jury returned a verdict of murder by Ernest Dyer. It was only after the death of "Mr. Fitzsimmons" in Scarborough, two months later, that the police realized they had located Ernest Dyer.

Since Tombe had been shot in the back of the head—which blasted away his skull—he must have died instantly. In that case, it would have been impossible for him to have transmitted to his mother a telepathic message about being buried down a "well." (Mrs. Tombe, of course, saw the cesspit in her dreams and assumed it was a well.) The only other person from whose mind Mrs. Tombe might have picked up this information was Dyer himself, and since Mrs. Tombe did not know of his existence, this seems unlikely. It is difficult to resist the inference that Eric Tombe somehow communicated with his mother after his death.

This problem of "dream telepathy" is further complicated by certain cases in which there is also apparent precognition; such a case was described in the SPR *Journal* in 1960. The author of the account, Ian Stephens, had been Director of Public Information in India, and, after independence, became Director of the Historical Section of the Pakistan Army. In February 1960, Stephens dreamed that he heard screaming outside the window, and somehow knew a murder was being committed. Then he dreamed he saw a bed with a living person on it, the feet towards him but the rest of the body scarcely visible; he "knew" that the person on the bed was his best friend, and that this friend had committed murder. At this point, Stephens woke up. The next afternoon, he returned from a walk and saw a crowd gathered near his hotel. He learned that a man had been murdered by a close friend—who was also his cousin. To avoid the crowd, Stephens walked down a narrow alleyway—and saw a corpse lying on a string bed, the feet towards him, the rest of the body scarcely visible.

In his dream Stephens seems to have identified himself with the victim, since he felt that the murderer was "his best friend." (The confusion of murderer and victim on the bed is typical of dreams.) So the dream may be regarded as a case of dream telepathy emanating from the victim himself—except that the murder took place twelve hours later. If it was telepathy, then we must suppose that telepathy, like psychometry, can "scan" the future. And if we can accept this, then we have virtually accepted Long's belief that psychometry and telepathy are identical—telepathy being contact with another mind through the *aka* threads, psychometry being a similar contact via objects.

The Tombe case, with its implication that telepathy can involve "spirits," adds an unwelcome element of untidiness to the theory. Yet in the course of this book we have seen that, no matter what doubts we may have about spiritualism as a religion, its phenomena cannot be dismissed as trickery or imagination. And most mediums would agree with Professor George Henslow that there is a close connection between psychometry and spirit communication.

Yet a close connection does not imply that they are identical. An example of the distinction is provided by a widely discussed criminal case of 1937. On 5 January a ten-year-old girl named Mona Tinsley failed to return home from her school in Newark, Nottinghamshire. A neighbour of the Tinsley family reported seeing the ex-lodger, a man called Frederick Nodder, loitering near the school. Two other people said they had seen Mona with a middle-age man near the bus station. Nodder, who was living in the village of Hayton, some twenty miles from Newark, denied all knowledge of the child, but he was taken into custody on a bastardy warrant. Nodder had, in fact, been introduced to the Tinsleys by Mrs. Tinsley's sister, with whom he was having an affair. A few days after his arrest, Nodder changed his story, and admitted that he had met Mona in Newark and taken her home with him. But he insisted that he had put her on a bus to Sheffield, where his mistress lived. Nodder was charged with abducting Mona Tinsley—in the absence of a body he could not be charged with murder—and sentenced to seven years in gaol.

A few days after Mona's disappearance, Estelle Roberts,

one of the most celebrated mediums in England, offered to
help the police. Mona's parents agreed, and the police sent her
a pink silk dress that had belonged to Mona. In her
autobiography,* Estelle Roberts writes: "As . . . I held the
soft material in my hands, I knew that Mona was dead."

But having obtained this information through psychometry,
the medium then—according to her own account—addressed
Mona Tinsley directly, through the agency of her "control," a
Red Indian called Red Cloud. The child told her that she had
been taken to a house and strangled, and Estelle Roberts
"saw" a small house, with a water-filled ditch on one side, a
field behind, a graveyard nearby, and an inn not far away. She
seemed to travel across fields to a river.

When she described the house to the Newark police, they
were so impressed by her accuracy that they invited her to go
there, and sent a police car to fetch her from the railroad station. The house looked exactly as she had "seen" it. She was
allowed to wander around inside, and in the back bedroom,
sensed the child's presence, particularly near a water tank. She
was able to tell the police that Mona had slept in the back
bedroom, and learned that they had found a child's handker-
chief in the water tank. Mona was strangled in the back
bedroom. She had spent much of her time in the downstairs
front room, copying something out of a book. The police had
found scraps of paper with the child's writing on it. She added
that after killing her, Nodder had left the house with the body
by the side door. The police asked "Why not the front
door?," and she admitted she had no idea. They told her that
the front door had been permanently closed with screws.

She then led the police past the graveyard she had "seen,"
over a bridge and across the fields. She told them: "Beyond
these fields there is a river. You will find the child's body
there."

The police had already dragged the river without success.
But they now had good reason for supposing that the body
would be found in the river. In her introduction to the *Trial of
Frederick Nodder*, Winifred Duke states: "A clairvoyant insisted that Mona Tinsley was dead and had appeared to her.
The child declared that she had been strangled, her body
placed in a sack, and then conveyed on wheels to the water and

Fifty Years a Medium.

thrown in." Another medium told Mr. Tinsley that Mona would be found in the River Idle. The medium had tasted mud in her mouth. A third woman informed the Newark police that Mona's body would be recovered in water at a place thirty miles in a north-westerly direction from Newark, "close to an open meadow or pasture land, with tall trees lining the bank." It is not clear which of these three references is to Estelle Roberts.

In June 1937, a boating party on the River Idle noticed an object in the water, close to the bank; it proved to be Mona Tinsley's body, the head jammed in a drain below water level; the place corresponded closely to the medium's description. A sack with an odour of decaying flesh was found nearby. Nodder was tried a second time, and although he still strenuously denied killing Mona, he was sentenced to death.

Nodder's wife had left him because of his numerous infidelities. He was a heavy drinker, who had lost jobs through drunkenness. It seems probable that, while he had been a lodger in the Tinsleys' house (he had to leave after three weeks for non-payment of rent) he had developed a sexual obsession with Mona—there is some evidence that he was a paedophile. He may have been drinking heavily at the time he impulsively decided to meet her out of school and abduct her. What happened after that is uncertain; but at midday on the following day, a child was seen standing in the back doorway of Nodder's house. By the time it was dark, Mona was dead, and Nodder hurried across the fields towards the river, which was swollen with heavy rains. By nine o'clock he was in the local pub, drinking heavily. He returned home to find the police waiting.

In her account of psychometry, Estelle Roberts explains that she regards it as a form of intensified "intuition." Unlike many psychometrists, she apparently saw no "pictures" or events. "I can only say that as soon as I take the proffered object in my hand, I *know* its message. I can't tell you how I know, I can only say I know." She goes on: "An experienced medium handling a personal object can translate its vibrations into a detailed description of its owner, his character, idiosyncrasies and talents. Alternatively she may conjure up a scene or age far removed from the present time or place." And she goes on to tell of handling a small piece of flint, and feeling instantly that it had lain in the earth for a long time, and was probably a fragment of a stone axe. It had been handed to her by a mining engineer who had found it down a shaft. He afterwards submitted it to the British Museum, who were able to say that Estelle Roberts was probably correct. Another piece of stone conjured up an impression of a medieval castle and a battle. She felt that it had come from an arrow-slot in the wall of the castle. The man who handed it to her confirmed that she was correct, and said that it came from a castle in North Wales, reputed to be the birthplace of Prince Llyewellyn ap Gruffydd, who died fighting the English. She was able to identify a cannonball as having been used in the fight for Quebec, on the Heights of Abraham, in 1759.

One of the most interesting anecdotes is about a ring handed to her by Sir Hugo Cunliffe-Owen. She not only sensed a tragedy, but also that the ring bore a curse. Cunliffe-Owen told her that the tragedy was connected with his dead wife—to whom the ring had belonged—and that the stone set in it came from the tomb of Tutankhamun.

This raises one of the most interesting questions related to psychometry. Traditional magic has always asserted the magician's power to bless or curse objects, a notion we now dismiss as childish superstition. Yet clearly, if an object can carry some record of past events, and if the mind of the psychometrist can be affected by this record, then a "curse" could be defined as some form of negative vibration, and its effect be somehow related to telepathy. In *The Occult* I have described how, driving from the University of St. Andrews towards the Hebrides, I experienced a sudden and unaccountable depression. About an hour later, my wife told me that she had a raging toothache. The toothache persisted all that weekend, and so did my depression. When my wife had the tooth out on Monday morning, I knew the moment it happened, although I was walking around the town—the depression lifted quite abruptly. If I had had a car accident as a result of the depression, then it could reasonably have been called a "curse."

In his book *Design for Destiny*, Edward Russell discusses the findings of Dr. Harold Burr on the electrical "life fields" (L-fields) he has detected in all living creatures, and suggests that we need a parallel concept to explain the effects of telepathy. "It is up to us to coin a short title for a field originating with—or the result of—a thought, which can produce effects at a distance without any visible intervening means . . ." This pompous mouthful, it is suggested, can be reduced to "thought field" or "T-field" for short. He goes on to comment: "Though not recognized by science, this phenomenon has been known and used since early times. For it is the basis of the ancient customs of "blessing" material objects or of putting a "curse" on them . . ."

The career of the *Great Eastern*—which, when it was launched in 1859, was the world's largest ship—is often cited as an example of a curse. During its construction, a riveter and his boy apprentice disappeared. The man responsible for its construction, the great engineer Brunel, collapsed on its deck as it was launched and died soon after. From then on, the career of the ship was an unending series of disasters—fires, explosions, collisions. When it was broken up for scrap a mere thirty years later, the skeletons of the riveter and the boy were discovered trapped in the double hull. On the "psychometric hypothesis," such a "curse" would not be difficult to explain. The man and boy must have died horribly, starved to death, and trying for days to make themselves heard. The negative "T-field" could have been strong enough to unconsciously affect everyone on board, producing an atmosphere of depression, which in turn might lead to a failure to observe all kinds of small precautions, and result in accidents. . . .

The late Tom Lethbridge, a Cambridge don, devoted his retirement to studying dowsing and the use of the pendulum. He became convinced that a long pendulum—extending up to forty inches—could detect almost any given substance, each substance causing the pendulum to react at a certain length. (For example, at 12 inches, the pendulum would go into a circular swing over carbon, at 12-½, over mercury, at 22, over silver, at 30-½, over copper.) Then, to his astonishment, he discovered that it would also react to abstract ideas, such as evolution, life, death, sex, anger, even male and female. One of his experiments consisted in collecting a pile of stones from the beach, and then, together with his wife Mina, throwing them against a wall. The stones thrown by his wife reacted with a 29-inch pendulum, while those thrown by Lethbridge reacted at 24 inches—indicating that the "rate" for maleness was 24, and that for femaleness, 29. Stones collected from an Iron age fort reacted at 24 inches and also at 40. By various tests, Lethbridge established that 40 was the "rate" for anger;

so his experiment suggested that the stones had been (as he suspected) sling-stones that had been used in anger in an attack on the fort.

Max Freedom Long would have found nothing strange in this result; he would simply have said that "George," the "low self," was using the pendulum to transmit his findings about the *aka* threads of the stones. Whether Lethbridge was correct in believing that there is an objective "rate" for different substances—or ideas—or whether "George" was simply adopting Lethbridge's own "code," is a matter that must be left to further investigation.

Lethbridge also became convinced that the electrical field of water somehow records events, so that a sensitive is more likely to catch some glimpse of a past tragedy in a damp place than in a dry one. This conviction became established when he and his wife were collecting seaweed on a beach, and both experienced the same intense, unaccountable depression near a stream. On the clifftop, his wife experienced a feeling of depression and an urge to jump. Lethbridge later discovered that a man had committed suicide by jumping from the same spot, and concluded that his misery had somehow been imprinted on the place. If his wife had been of a suicidal disposition, and had decided to obey the urge to jump, then the recording would certainly have qualified as a curse. A curse, then, might be defined as a recording or imprintation of negative energy, which has a tendency to drain vitality and produce depression. A "blessing" is presumably the opposite—a recording of positive energy whose vibrations tend to produce a sense of heightened vitality. Certain houses associated with family happiness seem to produce this effect.*

Lethbridge himself had no interest in spiritualism, and believed that all ghosts are "tape recordings"—in spite of an odd experience when he was hurled on his face by some poltergeist type manifestation on the island of Skellig Michael. Yet in spite of this, his view of psychometry is not basically opposed to that of Estelle Roberts. Like Lethbridge, she believes it to be some direct form of intuition of the "vibrations" associated with an object. (For Lethbridge, the notion of vibrations was the key to the mystery of extra-sensory perception.) She simply goes a step further, and insists that the

---

*For a fuller description of Lethbridge—and the subject of "curses"—see my book *Mysteries* (1978).

same faculty is used by the medium to perceive spirits.

After so many facts that have failed to fit theories, and theories that have failed to fit facts, it is interesting to observe an outline of a broader explanation beginning to take shape at last. But past experience suggests that optimism should be tempered with caution. The paranormal can usually be relied upon to produce some new anomaly that forces everyone to think again.

7

Psychic Archaeology

THE NAME OF the greatest of all psychometrists is scarcely known outside Poland—perhaps because it looks so unpronounceable. Stefan Ossowiecki* was born in Moscow in 1877, the son of a factory owner. As a child he could see coloured auras flickering around people, so that his mother took him to an occulist; the drops that were prescribed fortunately made no difference to his ability to see auras. He later became a member of the Russian Cadet Corps, then studied chemical engineering at the St. Petersburg Technological Institute. At twenty, Ossowiecki was in most ways a perfectly normal young man. He possessed only one peculiar ability: the power to move heavy objects by concentrating on them. Once, as an after-dinner trick, he lay on a ballroom floor tied in a straitjacket, and moved a heavy marble statue several feet across the floor.

The direction of his life changed when he was twenty-one. On his way to visit a paper factory in Dobruz—where he was to study paper-making—Ossowiecki found himself on the station platform of a small town called Homel, with several hours to wait for the next train. He asked the stationmaster if there was anything worth seeing in Homel, and was told of an old Jewish mystic called Wrobel who lived in the suburbs. For want of anything better to do, Ossowiecki went to see him. The white-haired old man who lay on the bed looked at him

*Pronounced Ossovietsky.

187

and said: "Your name is Stefan." And he then proceeded to tell Ossowiecki about his past and his future. This was in 1898, and when the old man spoke of a revolution that would descend on Russia, and the blood that would be shed, Ossowiecki was both shaken and sceptical. But when he left—passing two distinguished visitors who had come to consult Wrobel—he was determined to return, and learn all he could.

Ossowiecki completed his training as a chemical engineer with a period in the paper factory in nearby Dobruz; he spent all his free time with the old Jew. Wrobel taught Ossowiecki that psychic powers came from superconscious mind, and that in order to release them, he had to learn to concentrate his will, and to still his body and his emotions. What Wrobel taught Ossowiecki differed very little from the teachings of the *kahunas*; that man possesses an unconscious mind, which is responsible for dreams, and a super-conscious mind, for which there are no barriers of space and time.

His training—both in occultism and paper-making—finished, Ossowiecki moved back to Moscow, where he worked in his father's business and moved in aristocratic circles. In due course came the revolution that his master had prophesied. The Ossowiecki family suddenly lost its wealth. Stefan was arrested, and spent six months in prison, expecting to be executed. The crisis brought him new depths of awareness and insight. When he was released in 1919, he returned to Poland, to pursue his profession as an engineer in Warsaw. There, as in Moscow, his psychic gifts made him a celebrity. But he made no money from them. For the remainder of his life, Ossowiecki was only moderately well-off. His years of affluence had made him indifferent to money. But he was studied by some of the most distinguished psychical researchers in Europe, including Gustav Geley, Charles Richet, Baron Shrenk-Notzing and the Englishman, E. J. Dingwall. In his book *Our Sixth Sense* Richet called him "the most positive of all psychics."

In 1935, Ossowiecki was involved in a remarkable experiment whose purpose was to determine whether psychometry is really some form of telepathy. A wealthy Hungarian named Jonky had left a sealed package, with instructions that clairvoyants should attempt to "sense" its contents eight years after his death. He specified an eight-year period because he felt that if the packet had "recorded" his own knowledge of its contents, then this recording would have evaporated in eight years—just as a bloodhound would receive little scent from an eight-year-old clue. It seemed a reasonable hypothesis. Ossowiecki, who knew nothing of all this, looked through fourteen photographs arranged on a table, and pointed to the one of Jonky as the man whose package he was about to psychometrize. Then, he says, "I stilled my consciousness and moved to the realm of the superconscious."* He proceeded to describe Jonky, and the professor who had taken charge of the parcel for eight years, then said: "There is something here that pulls me to other worlds . . . to another planet." He identified the content of the parcel as a small meteorite, and added that he also sensed sugar. The parcel was opened; it contained a meteorite wrapped in paper that had been round a piece of confectionery—it still had traces of powdered sugar. This feat was witnessed by a committee of fifty scientists. Ossowiecki had demonstrated clearly that the "psychometric aura" of an object is not dissipated by time.

As the news of this feat spread, Polish historians saw the implication: that Ossowiecki's powers might be used to solve some problems of history. In 1935, Polish scholars were intrigued by the problem of the true portrait of the greatest Polish scientist, Nicolas Copernicus. As with Shakespeare, there were several portraits that were alleged to be made from life; but no one knew which—if any—was genuine.

All available paintings and drawings were placed in front of Ossowiecki; he pointed out one which he said had been painted by Copernicus himself. How could the historians be certain that he was not simply guessing? Ossowiecki went on to describe Copernicus's life in detail, with many historical facts that would be known only to historians—and many that even they were unaware of. Every fact that *could* be checked proved to be correct.

A friend of Ossowiecki's, an engineer called Witold Balcer, told Ossowiecki about Rudolf Steiner and the Akasic records. If anyone could decipher the Akasic records, it should be Ossowiecki. Would he be willing to try? One evening, after a dinner with friends—Ossowiecki always worked best in a friendly casual environment—Ossowiecki held a sealed

---

*I am indebted to Stephan Schwartz's *The Secret Vaults of Time* for this material.

package, and spent about fifteen minutes going into a state of "superconscious trance" (he said that the room around him would fade and become unreal, as would his own body). Then he stated that the object originated several thousand years ago, before the birth of Christ. It was connected with a funeral. And, after some groping, he identified it as a petrified human foot. It was, in fact, a preserved mummy's foot. A month later, Ossowiecki again psychometrized it, and described the life of the woman whose foot he was holding—he said she was the daughter of some high Egyptian official—and how she had died in childbirth. The description of the funeral ceremonies was extremely precise. But, of course, it could not be checked.

If Ossowiecki's accuracy was to be checked, then it would have to be done by a scientist and historian who would know something of the background of the objects he submitted for psychometry, and who would have the means to investigate important statements. If Ossowiecki proved accurate, then it should be possible to use him to clear up some otherwise insoluble historical mysteries. In 1936, Ossowiecki was introduced to such a man—Stanislaw Poniatowski, professor of ethnology at the University of Warsaw. Poniatowski had access to some of Poland's most eminent scholars. He persuaded Ossowiecki to join him in an unprecedented programme of research, the kind of programme that Buchanan and Denton had dreamed about. A committee was formed which included scientists, mathematicians, philosophers, geologists and archaeologists. And a series of thirty-three carefully controlled, carefully recorded experiments took place at Ossowiecki's flat.

At the first session, Ossowiecki was handed a flint tool. He described huts made of twigs and clay in the midst of a forest. And for the next hour he answered questions from the experts on the culture of the men who had used the ten-thousand-year-old flint. The scientists knew their subject; Ossowiecki did not. But by the end of the hour, they had no doubt that what he was saying was not mere imaginative guesswork.

At a later session Ossowiecki held a skull dating back about three hundred thousand years. He appeared to enter a prehistoric scene, looking around him to left and right as if what was happening was in front of his eyes. When Poniatowski tried putting a screen in front of Ossowiecki's face, he complained that his view had been cut off. He described in detail the squat, hairy people with chocolate-coloured skin, broad noses and thick lips. He even made drawings. Most details were later confirmed by scientists.

Could this have been telepathy, with Ossowiecki merely gathering his details from the minds of those present? An artifact from Abbeville, in France, proved that it was not. Poniatowski's geography was weak, and he was convinced that Abbeville was in the interior of France. Ossowiecki said that he could "see" the Normandy peninsula. He went on to describe two prehistoric cultures in detail. After the session, Poniatowski told him he must be mistaken about the Normandy peninsula and his vision of the sea—he was certain it had been found inland in southern France. But when he checked the next day, Poniatowski found that Ossowiecki was right and he was wrong.

By February 1939, Ossowiecki had described eleven prehistoric cultures, and Poniatowski had made over four hundred pages of notes. Ossowiecki found the work exhausting and exacting, but his feeling that he was adding to scientific knowledge forced him to continue, in spite of severe headaches and fatigue. Sometimes his results could be confirmed—as when he drew and described a paleolithic hut made of skins stretched over saplings, and archaeologists later found identical remains of huts of this period; other insights were impossible to check—as when he described the way a Stone Age couple made love, with the woman sitting on the man and bouncing up and down, and then how she concluded by ritually covering his penis with green grass.

At this point there was a devastating interruption—the invasion of Poland in the autumn of 1939. The Warsaw ghetto was burned down and its inhabitants massacred; thousands of Poles were sent to concentration camps. Many eminent figures escaped via Italy; Ossowiecki felt that the Polish people needed him more than ever before, and decided to remain. Many people came to him to ask after the fate of loved ones; most went away comforted. On one occasion, he was approached by the brother of a missing cavalry officer, most of whose unit had been killed in a charge and buried in a mass grave. Ossowiecki was able to draw the graveyard and indicate where the body lay; then he accompanied the brother, walked up and down the site of the mass grave, and finally stopped and said, "Dig here." Several bodies were removed—none the correct one; then Ossowiecki said: "It will be the next." He was right.

In 1941, Poniatowski began a new series of seventeen experiments. Once again, Ossowiecki held prehistoric objects and described their background in detail, and the cultures from which they came. Again and again his insights have been confirmed. He said that the Sahara had once been a well-watered region of trees and grass; cave paintings found at Tassili N'Ajjer have since confirmed this. He said that Magdalenian man (about 15,000 years ago) had the bow and arrow; anthropologists of that time thought this unlikely, but we now know that the bow and arrow were invented by Neanderthal man—a culture called the Aterian—more than fifty thousand years ago. On the basis of a stone scraper, Ossowiecki said that Chancellade man—another Magdalenian—had a broad nose, a hydrocephalic head, and was about five feet tall; skeletons have confirmed his statement. Ossowiecki's description of Magdalenian funeral customs, with the ashes buried in an urn, contradicted what anthropologists of the time believed; Ossowiecki has been proven right by more recent finds. He described an oil lamp used by prehistoric man, and at the time, this seemed highly improbable; since then, a lamp like the one he drew has been excavated in the Dordogne.

Poniatowski began working on his book on Ossowiecki's "psychic archaeology" in the summer of 1942. Before he finished it, he was arrested by the Gestapo; then he vanished. Ossowiecki managed to get hold of the manuscript. But he was known as a patriot, and was also a marked man. In July 1944, he told his wife that he would soon be killed, and that his end would be horrible; he added: "But I have had a wonderful life." On 1 August 1944, the Poles of Warsaw rose against the Germans, hoping to hold the city until the Allies came. The rising was doomed; the Germans killed a quarter of a million Poles before the Russians took over the city in January 1945. By then, Ossowiecki's prophecy had been fulfilled. Trying to flee from Warsaw, he and his wife were arrested with crowds of other refugees. His wife Zofia was released; Ossowiecki was in a crowd of ten thousand Polish men that was mowed down by machine guns in a two-day massacre. Yet, incredibly, the Poniatowski manuscript—which Ossowiecki was carrying at the time of his death—survived. In 1952, it was handed to Zofia Ossowiecki by an unknown man who approached her in the street. It is still unpublished, but at least it has been studied by anthropologists and scientists. The most important work of the world's greatest psychometrist still survives.

Ossowiecki was the great pioneer of "psychic archaeology." In recent decades, many archaeologists have followed in Poniatowski's footsteps, and made use of psychics, including Stephan Schwartz, Jeffrey Goodman and David E. Jones, all of whom have written remarkable accounts of their explorations.

Yet the story of psychic archaeology began three decades before Poniatowski and Ossowiecki conducted their first experiment with a flint tool. The date was 7 November 1907, and the place the office of a Bristol architect named Frederick Bligh Bond. The ruins of Glastonbury Abbey had just been bought by the nation, and Bond, who was well known for his interest in historic buildings, had been appointed to take charge of archaeological excavations. Old records showed that two chapels had once existed; but the abbey had been destroyed in the time of Henry the Eighth, and no one knew where to start looking. The Church of England—who appointed Bond—might have had second thoughts if they had known that he was an enthusiastic student of the occult. Bond decided that the simplest way of locating the remains of the chapels was to ask "the spirits." He had a friend named John Allen Bartlett, who was able to produce automatic writing. And on that day in 1907, these two sat at a table, with Bartlett's hand holding a pencil, and Bond's hand resting lightly on Bartlett's, and asked aloud the question: "Can you tell us anything about Glastonbury?" The pencil immediately wrote: "All knowledge is eternal and is available to mental sympathy." And soon Bartlett's hand was drawing a plan of Glastonbury Abbey, with a long rectangle at its eastern end. It was signed "William the Monk." After many more communications—both in Latin and old English—Bond's workmen began to dig where the unknown communicators had indicated. They found the Edgar Chapel precisely where William the Monk had said it would be. It was even the length he said it would be, although Bond had believed this to be far too long. Later, by the same means, he found the St. Dunstan's Chapel and the Loretto Chapel. When he found the skeleton of a seven-foot man with another skull between his legs, Bond asked his "communicators" for an explanation, and they told him that the skeleton was of Radulphus Cancellarius, Ralph the Chancellor, and that the skull was that of Eawulf the Saxon, whom Ralph had slain in fair fight. This Eawulf, they said, was the Earl of Edgarley, a nearby village. Historical research finally revealed that there *had* been a "Eanwulf," Earl of Edgarley, and confirmed most of the story.

The full story of these astonishing communications has no place in a book on psychometry.* Bond himself finally decided to tell it in 1917, when he felt that the incredible success of his excavations had made his position quite secure. He was mistaken. *Gate of Remembrance* caused astonishment and outrage amongst his Church of England employers, and he soon found himself without a job. He went to America and spent more than twenty years in psychical research, receiving still more communications about treasure buried in secret passages at Glastonbury, as well as about King Arthur and the Holy Grail. But he was never allowed to renew his excavations at Glastonbury—at one point there was even an order forbidding him to enter the abbey grounds. The later communications still await investigation. Significantly, the spirit communicators—who mostly claimed to be connected with the abbey, and who called themselves the Watchers or the Company of Glastonbury—explained that they were able to draw upon a "Universal Memory," which sounds very much like Madame Blavatsky's Akasi records. Ossowiecki always said that the source of his knowledge was the "Consciousness of the One Spirit."

Another psychic archaeologist who claimed that his source was the Akasic records was the American seer and healer, Edgar Cayce.† The son of a Kentucky farmer, Cayce was born in 1877. His ambition to become a preacher was thwarted when he lost his voice at the age of twenty-one. Under hypnosis, it came back, but vanished when he woke up—indicating that it was a psychosomatic problem. The problem was that the newly-married Cayce felt he ought to be making

*It is told at greater length in my book *Poltergeist*.

†Pronounced Casey.

money, and some force inside him seemed opposed to the idea. The loss of his voice meant that he had to give up a job as a salesman. Finally, a hypnotist named Al Layne put Cayce into a trance and asked him to explain what was the trouble. In his normal voice, Cayce said that his vocal chords were partially paralysed due to nervous tension, and that his body needed to send more blood to the area. Layne ordered Cayce to send more blood to his vocal chords, and his throat immediately turned red. Cayce then told Layne to suggest that the circulation should return to normal and that he should wake up. When Cayce opened his eyes, his voice was normal again.

Layne decided to place Cayce under hypnosis and ask him about his own health problems. Cayce described his symptoms and explained how they should be treated. When Cayce read Layne's notes, he insisted that he had never heard most of the medical terms he had used in trance.

In the following year, Cayce placed himself in a trance, and diagnosed the problem of a five-year-old girl with a spinal injury. Cayce named which vertebrae needed readjusting, and within a short time the girl was well again. This was in 1902. From then on, Cayce began to devote his time to this form of "trance diagnosis." He found that it worked just as well if the patient was a thousand miles away. But he also discovered that he had another ability: to see into the remote past, and to foretell the future.

In August 1923, a student of occultism named Arthur Lammers asked Cayce to come to Ohio, all expenses paid, to see if he could answer some questions about the mystery of human existence; Cayce agreed to try. When he came out of his trance, he was shocked to be told that he had been preaching the doctrine of reincarnation. Cayce was a thoroughly orthodox Christian who read the Bible once a year (and very little else). But he gradually came to accept the idea of reincarnation, once he had convinced himself that the Bible nowhere condemns it. He also began to give "life readings" of patients that included insights into their past lives. Giving a "reading" on a fourteen-year-old boy, David Greenwood, in 1927, Cayce went on to describe his past lives under Louis the Fourteenth, Alexander the Great and in ancient Egypt; then he described his life in Atlantis about 10,000 B.C.

For the remainder of his life, Cayce continued to add

fragments to his story of Atlantis, and all have remarkable internal consistency—considering that they were produced over the course of decades. What he says bears a resemblance to the work of Scott-Elliot and Rudolf Steiner. (Cayce spells Akasic "Akashic" as Steiner did.) Like Scott-Elliot, Cayce claims that some of the survivors of Atlantis moved to Egypt; it was their technological skill that raised Egypt to the most advanced civilization in the ancient world. The records of Atlantis were buried, according to Cayce, in a Hall of Records between the Great Pyramid and the Sphinx.

Once again we confront the question: how far can all this be taken seriously? It has to be admitted that Cayce's accounts of Atlantis and ancient Egypt produce in the present writer much the same state of irritable confusion as the writings of Scott-Elliot and Steiner on the same subject. Yet there have been many individual points upon which his accuracy has been confirmed. Like Ossowiecki, Cayce stated that there had been a time when the Sahara had been well watered—a statement that, in 1925, seemed absurd. He said that in this remote time, the Nile ran westward and entered the Atlantic, instead of flowing north to the Mediterranean. But in the 1960s, geological studies revealed that the Nile *had* once flowed westward, to Lake Chad; and Lake Chad is about halfway between the present Nile and the Atlantic Ocean. Cayce talked about an obscure religious group called the Essenes in Palestine, whose main community he placed on the road from Emmaus to Jericho—that is, the road that runs along the Dead Sea. It was not until 1947, two years after Cayce's death, that the discovery of the Dead Sea Scrolls at Kirbet Qumran offered spectacular confirmation of Cayce's words. Cayce also stated that Jesus of Nazareth was at one time a member of the Essenes, a suggestion that has been made by many students of the sect, but which has never been confirmed. (The story of the Essenes, as it has begun to emerge, throws an interesting light on Mead's question, "Did Jesus live 100 B.C.?"; the sect was founded by a certain Teacher of Righteousness, who prophesied his own death, and was executed at the order of a "wicked priest." This Teacher of Righteousness—who was executed about 100 B.C.—also foretold his own resurrection. If Jesus was not alive a century before the usually accepted date, he certainly had an interesting forerunner whose story bears a remarkable resemblance to his own.) Cayce's detailed description of the community rules of the Essenes was dramatically confirmed by a text specifically devoted to them in the Dead Sea Scrolls.

Cayce's accuracy as a prophet of the future is still to be confirmed. Some of the prophecies credited to him are certainly impressive. In the 1920s, he is said to have predicted that two presidents would die in office, and that after the death of the second, there would be racial strife in America. In 1939 he repeated the prediction about two presidents. In 1945, Roosevelt died in office; in 1963, John F. Kennedy was assassinated. Racial riots followed. Joseph Millar's book *Edgar Cayce* opens with a section containing more than two dozen prophecies, including the Wall Street Crash, the New Deal, Hitler's invasion of the Rhineland, the Second World War, and the date the Second World War would end. But when we turn to actual transcripts of what Cayce said,* there is a disappointing lack of explicitness. Asked, for example, if 1939 and 1940 would usher in another business slump, his answer began: "Again, this depends on consideration of conditions throughout . . ." and goes on to say that if selfishness triumphs, there will be a depression. Asked specifically whether there would be a war "around 1942 to 1944," he missed a golden opportunity by replying that there would not be a war if "an attitude of peace and harmony is continuously kept." Asked about the Spanish situation, the Japanese and Chinese situation, the Russian situation, the German situation, his answers remain disappointingly vague and general, hinging on various "ifs." But on matters of wider import he is frighteningly specific. On 13 August 1941, he made a famous prediction about the period between 1941 and 1998, forecasting that there would be worldwide volcanic upheavals, heralded by the eruption of Mount Etna, and that these would include the destruction of California by earthquake, the emptying of the Great Lakes into the "gulf" (it is not clear which gulf he means), the destruction of New York City and large portions of the east coast of America, and the engulfing of Japan in the Pacific. He also foretold that Atlantis would "begin to rise again" in 1968 or 1969. When two airline pilots noticed formations that looked like undersea buildings in the "Bimini roads" off the Bahamas in 1968, there was wide-

---

See, for example, *Prophecy in Our Time* by Martin Ebon.

spread excitement, and much talk about the fulfillment of
Cayce's prophecy. But undersea exploration failed to confirm
that these are the remains of walls and buildings; the consen-
sus of opinion is that the pilots saw natural rock formations
split in such a way that they looked man-made. Since then,
there have been no further signs of the rising of Atlantis. We
may take this as a hopeful sign where more cataclysmic prophecies are concerned.

Whether or not Cayce's reading of the Akasic records is accurate, his example has had a decisive effect on the history of
"psychic archaeology." In the early 1960s, Ann Emerson, the
wife of one of Canada's most eminent archaeologists, J. Norman Emerson, read a biography of Edgar Cayce, and joined
the Edgar Cayce study group in Toronto. There she became
acquainted with Lottie McMullen, whose husband George had
been a bush guide. George McMullen had joined the group
because he apparently possessed "psychic abilities." Emerson
found the subject boring, and politely sidestepped his wife's
attempts to get him interested. Emerson's health was poor,
and one day, Ann Emerson asked George McMullen if he
could make any useful suggestions. McMullen not only made
suggestions; he described Norman Emerson's health with a
wealth of detail that suggested he had access to the professor's
medical records. Emerson was impressed. And when George
McMullen's recommendations caused a remarkable improvement in his health, he decided it was time to take the occult
seriously. He asked McMullen if he could psychometrize artifacts; McMullen soon revealed that his abilities in psychic archaeology were comparable with those of Ossowiecki.

At a meeting of the Canadian Archaeological Association in
1973, Emerson caused a mixture of astonishment and dismay
when he announced his newly-discovered faith in psychic archaeology. If he had not been the founding vice-president of
the Association, he might have been asked to resign. As it was,
his colleagues decided that Emerson's assertions were worth
testing.

An archaeologist named Jack Miller was the first to ask for
proof. He brought to the banquet of the Association a piece of
black stone—argillite—that looked as if it had been carved
into a crude, negroid head. It had been found on an Indian
site on the Queen Charlotte Islands, off British Columbia.
McMullen held the head, and then stated that it had been

carved by a Negro from Port-au-Prince in the Caribbean, who had been brought to Canada as a slave. Emerson was disappointed. Such a story sounded totally unlikely. He assumed that McMullen was making a mistake, and came close to apologizing to Jack Miller. But he held on to the head, and at a later date, asked McMullen to try again. McMullen repeated his story about the Negro slave, this time adding that he had been born in West Africa, taken to the Caribbean as a slave, then sold again and taken to Canada on an English ship. He had escaped and found an Indian tribe which accepted him. He had married and spent the rest of his life there.

Emerson decided to try another psychic. His daughter had recently returned from college with her room mate, who did Tarot readings. Emerson asked her if she could hold the head and see if she "saw" anything. The girl took the head, and told him immediately that it had been carved by a black from Africa who had been brought across the Atlantic as a slave.

Over the next few months, Emerson tried other psychics; again and again McMullen's findings were confirmed. The man had come from about thirty miles inland in West Africa, had been captured by another African tribe, and sold as a slave in the New World.

Emerson asked an expert from the Royal Ontario Museum what he thought of the head, and was told that it was carved by someone familiar with the art techniques of the Gold Coast of West Africa.

The most startling piece of evidence for the accuracy of McMullen's statements came two years later, when a team of anthropologists went to British Columbia to do a blood analysis of Indians; they reported that one tribe showed unmistakable signs of having had a black forebear.

Like Ossowiecki, McMullen was able to "see" the scenes he described. Walking around an archaeological site, he was able to describe houses, people, customs, ceremonies, as if he was an anthropologist walking through an Indian village. He claimed not only to be able to see the people, but to hear them and even smell them. Yet there was an important difference between Ossowiecki and McMullen: The latter claimed that he received his basic information from certain nonphysical entities who looked as if they were made of light. Like so many psychics, McMullen had begun to "see" things when he was a child. On one occasion, he had predicted that a youth who had gone off for the weekend on a motorbike would never return; in fact, the youth was killed in an accident. As a result, the local minister accused George McMullen of having relations with the devil. Fortunately, McMullen met an old man who also possessed psychic powers, and who taught him that we are surrounded by invisible entities with whom we can communicate. Soon, under the old man's guidance, George McMullen was able to develop his powers until he could see these entities, and ask them questions. Again and again, he found their information accurate.

The remarkable success of the Emerson-McMullen collaboration again raises this basic question of paranormal research: of how far it is necessary to accept the existence of "spirits," at least as a working hypothesis. When, in 1973, Emerson caused amazement at the meeting of the Canadian Archaeological Association by announcing his conversion to psychic archaeology, one of his ex-students, Charles Garrad, was encouraged to divulge an experience that he had so far kept secret. In the autumn of the previous year, Garrad had been digging at the site of an Indian village of the seventeenth century, in southern Ontario. After a week without a find, Garrad suddenly felt tired, cold and discouraged. He stood in the middle of the site, and shouted aloud: "Look here, you goddamned Indians . . . you'd better give me something in five minutes or I'll quit . . ." Then he went back to work. At first impact of his shovel, dust flew, and he saw a group of Indian pipes lying there. He began to dig again. But the ritual smoking pipes proved to be a foot underground; it was totally impossible that Garrad could have seen them by striking the surface. When he had excavated them out of the ground, Garrad went back to the centre of the site, waved a pipe in the air, and said aloud "Thank you." There was a sound of laughter, and Garrad saw a group of Indians—four adults and three boys—standing a few hundred feet away. As he looked, they vanished. So Garrad took no convincing about the value of psychic archaeology. With a sensitive named Sheila Conway, he went on to make some important discoveries in the field of Indian archaeology.*

Does it really matter whether psychometry is pure "intuition," or a kind of spirit communication? From the practical

*For further details, see Stephen Schwartz: *The Secret Vaults of Time*, Chapter 6.

point of view, no. Yet even the word "intuition" raises important questions. Anyone who has ever read a popular book on archaeology will know that many of the great archaeologists seem to have made their major discoveries out of a kind of serendipity. From Winckelmann's discoveries at Pompeii in the 1760s to Schliemann's excavations at Troy a century later, a whole series of important finds have been made by pure chance. In the 1870s a scholar named George Smith translated some ancient tablets found at Nineveh, and realized that it was a Babylonian epic about a hero called Gilgamesh. But seventeen lines were missing. The *Daily Telegraph* financed an expedition to search for them. It was a million-to-one chance; yet within a mere five days of digging, Smith found the missing tablets. In a case like this, "intuition" begins to sound more like clairvoyance.

The same may be said of the method by which Herman V. Hilprecht solved the problem of a cuneiform inscription in 1893. Hilprecht was writing a book about an inscription of King Nebuchadnezzar, and a colleague had sent him rough sketches of some small fragments of agate with characters traced on them. Two of these baffled him, and he spent weeks pondering over them, finally placing them in different parts of the book. One night, after trying vainly to decipher the characters, he went to bed and fell into an exhausted sleep. He dreamed that a priest of the temple of Bel, at Nippur, led him into a treasure chamber, on its southeast side; the floor was strewn with fragments of agate. The priest explained that Hilprecht was not, as he believed, studying fragments of finger rings, but of a votive cylinder, presented to the temple by King Kurigalzu. When the priests were suddenly ordered to make earrings for the god Ninib, they decided to carve the cylinder into three parts, two of which were used as ear-rings. So the two fragments Hilprecht had been studying belonged together—a fact that was not obvious from the rough sketches. The priest said that Hilprecht would never find the missing third part.

The next day, Hilprecht examined the sketches, and saw that the priest was right. They must have been fragments of a votive cylinder, for the inscription now read: "To the god Ninib, son of Bel, his lord, has Kurigalzu, pontifex of Bel, presented this (cylinder)." Later, in the museum of Constantinople, Hilprecht located the two original fragments of the

cylinder—in two separate cases—and found they fitted together perfectly. He could also see clearly that a third part of
the cylinder was missing.

It was verified that the fragments *had* come from the treasure room in the southeast of the temple, and that its floor was
covered with fragments of agate; but a colleague insisted that
he had imparted these facts to Hilprecht four years previously.
So a strong case can be made for cryptomnesia, and for Hilprecht's unconscious mind recognizing the relation between
the two fragments, and telling him about it through a dream.
But would his unconscious mind have also known that the
fragments came from a cylinder, not finger rings, and that a
third part of the cylinder was still missing? It is just conceivable; but similar cases cited in this volume make dream clairvoyance just as conceivable.

After Emerson's announcement in 1973, an increasing number
of archaeologists—particularly the younger ones—began to
realize that they could save themselves a great deal of discouraging work by making use of psychics. When Paul Emile
Botta began excavating Nineveh in the 1840s, he expended
enormous labour uncovering his finds; when Austen Henry
Layard began digging there a few years later, he began uncovering important finds with the first turn of the shovel.
(Legend has it that Layard also claimed to have been guided
by a dream.) But why rely on luck when a good psychic can
probably pinpoint the right place to dig by merely strolling
over the site, or even looking at a map?

Emerson was not, of course, the first to discover that psychics—or the unconscious mind—could save a great deal of
digging. In 1939, Clarence Wolsey Weiant was excavating one
of the vast stone heads—six feet in diameter—found near Vera
Cruz, in Mexico. He also decided to excavate a nearby mound,
one of about fifty in the area outside the village of Tres
Zapotes. It proved to be a bad choice. After days of fruitless
digging, an eighty-year-old man approached Weiant, and told
him that he could direct him to a better site. His name was
Emilio Tegoma, and he claimed to possess second sight. Weiant had been interested in parapsychology before he became
an archaeologist, so he decided to test the old man's powers.
The following day, they were led to a group of mounds about
two-thirds of a mile away. Weiant was doubtful—they looked

exactly like all the other mounds. But within minutes, his workmen had unearthed a beautiful "laughing figurine." The mound went on to yield all kinds of riches, and the doctoral thesis Weiant based on his researches was so impressive that it was published by the Smithsonian Institute. But Weiant did not tell the story of how he came to choose the right mound.

In 1956, a retired Major General, James Scott-Elliot (no doubt a relative of the author of the book on Atlantis and Lemuria), began to devote his time to dowsing. When, in 1961, a farmer near Scott-Elliot's home in Dumfriesshire reported turning up a large, flat stone with his plough, Scott-Elliot went over the field with his dowsing rod, marked off an area in which he sensed human artifacts, and then excavated a sixteenth-century drying kiln. Four years later, using the same technique, he unearthed a Bronze Age burial pit. But his most remarkable success came when an old lady told him she was convinced that archaeological finds would be made in her garden. The garden looked so unpromising that Scott-Elliot did not even bother to walk around it with his rods. Instead, he bought an ordnance survey map which showed the area, then carefully drew an even larger map. Then he went over his own map with a pendulum, mentally asking questions about human habitation. It began to rotate over the western part of the lawn. He asked the pendulum how many layers; it answered several. He asked the age, and was told the eleventh or twelfth centuries. (In a case like this, the dowser goes through the centuries one by one until the pendulum responds.) A trial cut at the site revealed animal bones, pottery and two post holes. The pottery was of the early twelfth century, and, just as the pendulum had said, there were several levels of habitation. In 1973, in Berkshire, he used the same method to predict an Iron ditch, a Roman road, and Saxon and Norman remains —all of which were duly uncovered.

Most historians of science have noticed how major discoveries are often made simultaneously by a number of totally independent workers—almost as if the discovery was "in the air," like a radio transmission waiting to be picked up. The differential calculus was discovered simultaneously by Newton and Leibniz, the theory of evolution by Darwin and Wallace, the planet Neptune by Adams and Leverrier, the telephone by Bell and Edison, the theory of relativity by Poincaré and Einstein . . . And while Norman Emerson was investigating

George McMullen's power of psychometry, two other young archaeologists had independently decided to test the use of psychics. On 30 April 1971, a student of archaeology at the University of Arizona, Geoffrey Goodman, woke up from a dream in which he had been standing on a large boulder, looking down on a dry creek bed. In his dream, he knew that there were many ancient skeletons buried in the ground, as well as jewels. He explained this to some scientists who were present, then cut into the earth at an angle, lifted up one bank like a trapdoor, and revealed bones and skeletons lying in black soil.

Goodman's main interest was oil exploration, but he felt that he ought to pay attention to his dream. He consulted friends who were interested in parapsychology, and they recommended a psychic named Aron Abrahamsen. Goodman asked Abrahamsen about the location of remains of earliest man in America, and soon received a cassette on which Abrahamsen, in a station of meditation or semi-trance, spoke of various mountain areas. Asked to be more specific, Abrahamsen mentioned Flagstaff, Arizona, Pueblo, Colorado, and Kino, Mexico. According to Abrahamsen, the earliest men in America were not Asians who crossed by the narrow bridge of land called the Bering Straits, but people from Atlantis who had landed about half a million years ago. For scientists, of course, such a dating is preposterous; half a million years ago, China was inhabited by the ape-like Peking man, and *Homo sapiens* lay more than four hundred thousand years in the future. Goodman *was* bothered by a number of curious anomalies; such as why the two hundred or so languages of American Indians bear no relation whatever to those of Asia, or why corn pollen over eighty thousand years old has been found in Mexico when agriculture is supposed to have begun in the Near East seventy thousand years later. But he was not willing to consider Atlantis as the solution of either of these riddles.

When Goodman visited the head archaeologist in the museum at Flagstaff, and said that he hoped to find remnants of early man in the area, he was told that there were no remnants of early man in the area. His admission that he intended to test information received from psychics was received with even less enthusiasm.

Studying maps of the Flagstaff area, Goodman found areas of sedimentary deposits, where such remains might be found.

One had a dried river bed, such as he had seen in his dream. The next day he drove out to the site. When he saw a huge boulder like the one in his dream, he began to shake with excitement. From the boulder, he looked down on the same river bed he had seen in the dream.

More tapes from Abrahamsen led Goodman to start—with the aid of a small team of enthusiasts—a 10 foot by 10 foot pit. First results were discouraging. Goodman telephoned Abrahamsen, and recorded his advice. Abrahamsen went into his semi-trance state, and Goodman found himself speaking to a spirit, who assured him that he had no need to worry; invisible entities were watching the progress of the dig, prepared to help. The spirit even told Goodman that it could see what was happening while he was away, and that a red marker had been moved. (When Goodman got back, this proved to be correct.) It advised him to dig a few feet due east of the present site. A number of flints were found there, but none looked promising. However, when Goodman got back to the university and showed them to his professor, he was delighted when one of them was definitely identified as man-made.

For two seasons, Goodman dug at the site, and discovered such artifacts as hand axes and scrapers. He describes the work in detail in his book *Psychic Archaeology*. Abrahamsen was wrong about some things; he predicted pottery, and they found no pottery; he predicted bones, and when Goodman wrote the book in 1977, there were still no bones. Yet Abrahamsen was remarkably accurate on predicting what geological layers they would encounter. And Goodman's dream had undoubtedly led to the finding of evidence of early man in an area where experts said there had been no human habitation. It was not a dramatic triumph for psychic archaeology; but it was undoubtedly a success.

David E. Jones, a teacher of anthropology in an American university, became interested in psychic archaeology in the late sixties, when he worked with a Comanche woman shaman. Sanapia, as she was called, held the same basic beliefs that have been held by all shamans, magicians and witch doctors in all cultures throughout history: that we are surrounded by invisible spirits who can be contacted by human beings, and that some people have the power to travel, in their spirit bodies, both in time and space.

When Jones was introduced to the community of

Cassadaga, Florida, a retirement centre for the Spiritualist Church, he began asking psychics for readings. One of them asked if he might hold a Navaho ring that had been presented to Jones by a friend. The psychic described the friend, and the circumstances under which the gift had been made. The same psychic described how he had psychometrized a number of figurines from South America, and an archaeologist later told Jones that the description of a burial vault seen by the psychic as he held the figurines was remarkably accurate. The result was that David Jones decided to conduct a series of experiments in psychic archaeology. Unlike Goodman, his aim was not to locate primitive artifacts or evidence of early man, but only to try to establish, on a scientific basis, whether psychic archaeology could be taken seriously. The book, *Visions of Time*,* in which these experiments are described, deserves to be classified with Tischner's *Telepathy and Clairvoyance* and Hettinger's *Exploring the Ultra-Perceptive Faculty* as one of the "scientific classics" of parapsychology.

Jones worked with four clairvoyants, Albert Bowes, Marjorie Niren, Diane Davis and Noreen Renier. All sessions were tape recorded, and these tapes are quoted extensively. Various objects were handed to the clairvoyant in boxes, and Jones took care to guard against telepathy by making sure that, on many occasions, he himself had no idea of which artifact was in which box. In a typical reading, Bowes was given a box containing bone combs, made in Boston about 1845; Bowes's impressions included prowed ships in the harbour, men in slicker raincoats with whaling harpoons, and fish as a main item of diet. One of the most interesting observations to arise from this first series of experiments was that if the articles had been kept together, one might "contaminate" another, so that, for example, Bowes related information about an Indian basket when he was reading an Eskimo knife with which it had been in contact. Bowes gave the explanation that Buchanan and many others have given: that objects have "vibrations," and that those with strong vibrations can somehow contaminate those with weaker vibrations. Bowes also explained that his psychic impressions came in the form of a developing picture, which gradually clarified and enlarged. In this respect, his experience seems akin to those of Barney Camfield's "time

*1979.

travellers'' described in an earlier chapter, rather than those of Estelle Roberts, whose psychometry was some kind of intuitive "knowing" process.

After establishing to his own satisfaction that his psychics could provide information about ordinary objects, Jones tested them with artifacts from archaeological sites, and asked for information about the people who had made them. He also discovered that the psychics could "read" photographs, and provide astonishingly accurate information about them— a confirmation of Buchanan's controversial claim. One of the most impressive experiments in the book concerned a photograph of the sacrificial well—or *cenote*—near the ancient Maya city of Chichen Itza. When Jones saw the photograph, he realized that it looked very much like a "sinkhole," a natural well that has crumbled into an underground water course. He decided to see whether Bowes would mistake it for a sinkhole. But Bowes quickly picked up a feeling of a "cliff" with water at the bottom, then almost immediately began to speak about sacrificial victims. Asked about the people who had used it, he said "they were like the Aztec people . . ." His dating of the site, "about the time the Vikings were in Great Britain," was again remarkably precise.

The chief problem with Jones's book is that he presents such an immense amount of material that it all becomes a little over-whelming. In the final experiment, for example, Jones presented three psychics with stones of whose origin he himself was unaware; in fact, they were all from Maya sites. The stones were pieces of debris from the sites. Yet all three psychics were able to give remarkably exact descriptions of the Mayas, their way of life, and the historical period concerned. There could be no question of telepathy, since Jones himself was unaware of the provenance of the stones. He himself underlines the point: "Remember . . . that those five nondescript stones could just as easily have come from an Eskimo site in Greenland, or a Bedouin site in Yemen, or a Papuan site in highland New Guinea." As a piece of psychometry, it is as impressive as anything in Denton's *Soul of Things*.

In spite of the persuasiveness of its advocates and the weight of their evidence, psychic archaeology has failed to establish itself as a respectable academic discipline; its critics are bitter and vociferous. Yet the hostility seems to be based on a misconception. Psychic archaeology is not a new way of doing archaeology, an attempt to replace rational, scientific principles with a form of occultism. It is merely one more possible tool among many. Most country doctors send patients with warts to wart charmers before they try more orthodox means to remove them; in the majority of cases, it works. This does not place doctors on a par with members of the Flat Earth Society; it merely demonstrates that they are pragmatists. Most good archaeologists, as we have seen, make use of an intuition that sometimes approximates to clairvoyance. There is probably not one among them who will reject a "hunch" because it flies in the face of reason.

In the 1950s, an anthropologist named Stiles passed on to Clarence Weiant an observation he had made while studying the Montagnais Indians of eastern Canada. The Montagnais could contact distant friends and relatives by telepathy. When they wished to make contact, the Montagnais would go into a hut in the woods, build up the correct psychic energy through meditation, then make contact through clairaudience —distance made no difference. Weiant had independent confirmation from two other witnesses who lived amongst the Montagnais. The method sounds highly convenient, but since most westerners can be contacted by telephone or telegram, it would not be of much use to the average businessman. But then, Stiles was not suggesting that we should replace the telephone with clairaudience. The knowledge that such things are possible adds an important dimension to our vision of reality.

And this is surely the central point. Most primitive people take such powers for granted, as many countrymen take dowsing and wart-charming for granted. *There can be no possible advantage in irritably declining to believe that such things are possible.* The person who does so is not really more "logical" than the pragmatic country farmer or vet; he is merely more narrow-minded, and such narrowmindedness usually has a disturbing touch of hysteria. In 1952, one of the father figures of American anthropology, John Reed Swanton, came out of retirement to state a conviction that all anthropologists should be willing to make use of psychics. He stated: "Adhesion to current orthodoxy is always more profitable than dissent, but the future belongs to dissenters. Prejudice and cowardice in the presence of the *status quo* are the twin enemies of progress . . ."

That is to say, if telepathy, psychometry, clairvoyance, can be shown to exist, this is not some kind of erosion of our scientific heritage. Rather, it is an extension of our knowledge of ourselves, and a recognition that consciousness has unexplored potentialities: in short, a recognition that human existence may be far stranger and more exciting than even the greatest scientists have given it credit for.

8

The Art of Psychic Detection

ON 10 JULY 1941, a thirty-year-old Dutch house painter was standing on a ladder high above the Hague. The ladder rested between two windows of a four-story building, and he had to lean a considerable distance either way to reach the whole area. Pieter van der Hurk cannot remember how he slipped; but he recalls that his whole life passed before him, exactly as it is supposed to with drowning people. He landed on his shoulder, which broke the impact of the fall. When he regained consciousness in the Zuidwal Hospital, he had a broken shoulder and brain concussion. He had been unconscious for four days, and his life had been saved by a brain operation.

When his wife came to see him, he was still blind. He asked about his son, Benny; his wife said she had left him with a neighbour. Suddenly, van der Hurk became hysterical. "Go now and get Benny! The whole room is burning!" She left hurriedly. In fact, their son was perfectly safe. But the vision came true five days later when the house caught fire; firemen broke down the door in time to rescue the child.

Van der Hurk's condition had improved greatly when, one morning, a new nurse came to his bedside. He suddenly took hold of her hand and said: "Be careful when you go on the train or you will lose your valise." The nurse asked: "How did you know?" She had already lost her valise on the train a few hours earlier.

He turned to the patient in the next bed, and said: "You are a bad man. Your father died recently and left you a gold watch. You have already sold it." Again, he was correct.

A few days later, a patient who was about to leave the hospital stopped by his bed to say goodbye. As they shook hands, van der Hurk suddenly knew with certainty that this man was a British agent, and that he would be killed shortly—he even knew the name of the street, Kalver Street. He held the man's hand so tightly that he had to be forced to release it. He told the nurse: "He is a British agent and he is going to be killed."

The man *was* murdered two days later. And his death almost cost van der Hurk his own life. A doctor and nurse came into his hospital room, together with a man in a leather jacket. They asked van der Hurk how he knew the man was going to be killed; they were certain that he was a traitor who had experienced a moment of remorse. One of them held his arms while the leather-jacketed man pressed a pillow over his face. As he struggled for life, van der Hurk gasped: *"Come aborrezo dar la muerte."* The pressure went away. He had spoken aloud the thought in the man's mind: How I hate killing. It convinced his would-be executioner that he was a genuine psychic.

When he came out of hospital four weeks after the accident, Pieter van der Hurk was still far from well. He heard noises in his head; he was unable to concentrate; he found the noise made by his family intolerable. He began to work again for the resistance—he had been an active member before his accident—and began to prefer the name by which he was known to other resistance fighters: Peter Hurkos. But he was unable to earn a living: the inability to concentrate made it impossible to return to house painting.

He discovered his vocation by accident. One day he was taken to a public performance given by a well-known psychic. Members of the audience wrote messages, which were folded and taken up to the stage by the psychic's wife. The psychic would then burn the paper in a brazier, and repeat the message aloud. Hurkos's friend sent up a message. When the psychic had burnt it, he said: "The message is from a Peter Hurkos. He says he is a far better psychic than I am!" He asked Hurkos to stand up, and invited him on to the stage. The audience tittered with amusement. Asked about his method, Hurkos replied: "I touch things." The psychic handed him his watch. "Will this do?" Hurkos held it for a moment; images rushed into his mind. He said: "This watch contains a lock of blonde hair from a woman who is not your wife." The psychic's amused expression vanished. "Her name is Greta, and you take her from town to town with you. She is in the audience now." At this point, the psychic interrupted hastily to ask him to return to his seat. As he walked back through the audience, Hurkos stopped by a young blonde girl, placed his hand on her shoulder, and said: "This is Greta." He had sensed that her "vibrations" were the same as those of the lock of hair. The girl blushed and ran outside. The audience began to chatter excitedly. Hurkos realized suddenly that he no longer had to worry about how to earn a living.

In fact, he was offered an engagement in a theatre, and was an immediate success. It was soon after this that he became involved in his first criminal case. The Limburg police were trying to solve the mystery of a fatal shooting; the victim was a young coal miner named van Tossing. Hurkos asked for some item of clothing belonging to the victim; the police brought him a coat. Holding this, Hurkos was able to tell them that van Tossing had been murdered by his stepfather, Bernard van Tossing, and that the stepfather was in love with the murdered man's wife. The gun, said Hurkos, was on the roof of the dead man's house.

The police found the pistol in the gutter of the roof; fingerprints on it led to the conviction of Bernard van Tossing.

In another case, Hurkos demonstrated Osty's contention that once a link has been established between psychometrist and the person he is concerned with, no further contact with the original article is necessary. When a Captain Folken came to ask about his son—who had fallen overboard from a ship in the harbour—Hurkos handled some of the missing man's clothing, and confirmed that he was drowned. The next day, Hurkos went to Rotterdam harbour, and as he approached the ship from which the man had fallen, suddenly had a flash of intuition. He was able to point to a certain spot and tell the father that his son lay there, under forty feet of water, caught in some refuse. The river police sent down a skindiver, and recovered the body where Hurkos had said it would be.

In the years immediately after the war, Hurkos performed in Belgium, Paris and Madrid—he impressed General Franco by his knowledge of certain obscure events in his past. He also helped the police in a number of criminal cases—these have been detailed in Hurkos's own autobiography, *Psychic*, and in the excellent biography by Norma Lee Browning: *The Psychic World of Peter Hurkos*. In 1948, he was invited to America by the scientist Andrija Puharich, who had decided to devote two years of his life to testing whether telepathy could be taken seriously. In his book *Beyond Telepathy*, Puharich tells a typical story about Hurkos. As they were watching the sunset, Hurkos suddenly burst out excitedly: "I see it . . . I see a hand. The wrist is cut and blood is coming from it." Puharich asked him if he knew what it referred to; after some thought, Hurkos said he thought it was to do with an acquaintance called Jim Middleton. As the impression clarified, he said that it seemed connected with Jim Middleton's brother Art. Puharich was sufficiently impressed to call Jim Middleton and warn him that his brother might attempt suicide. Middleton was astonished; he had just received a telephone call from his brother's psychiatrist, who wanted him to fly to Alburquerque—his brother was depressed. Middleton had been unwilling to go; now he changed his mind. As a result of the visit, the brother was hospitalized.

The next time Middleton spoke to Puharich on the telephone, Puharich told him in more detail about Hurkos's vision of cut wrists. Middleton was impressed enough to go to the hospital and begged the attending physician to place his brother under maximum security. In spite of this, his brother succeeded in breaking a pair of glasses and slashing his wrists. Fortunately, an attendant was nearby, and saved his life by prompt attention.

Hurkos's career in America was full of curious ups and downs. This was partly due to a certain innocent immodesty—most psychics seem to have a good conceit of themselves—which led journalists to publicize his moderate successes as outright failures. To some extent it was bad luck. The man who financed Puharich's research was a wealthy businessman, Henry Belk. Belk and Hurkos were close friends until, in June 1957, Belk's ten-year-old daughter vanished in the woods of North Carolina while playing. Belk rang Hurkos, who was unable to "see" anything. But soon after hanging up, Hurkos saw a clear picture of the child lying drowned in six feet of water, near a boathouse. The child's body was found precisely where Hurkos had said it would be. But Belk was bitter. "If he can see the future, why didn't he warn me?" The bitterness was unreasonable, but it served to alienate Belk and Hurkos.

One of Hurkos's undoubted successes was a murder that took place in Miami, where Hurkos was living in 1958. A naval commander was shot in his apartment. A cab driver was shot to death a few hours later, but at first the police did not connect the two murders. The Miami police approached Hurkos, who asked for a photograph of the cab driver, and asked to sit in the man's taxi. He immediately received an impression of a tall, skinny man with a tattoo on his right arm, and a slow, ambling gait "like a sailor." He was even able to tell them that the man was from Detroit, and that his nickname was Smitty. He added that he had been responsible for another murder in Key West, in the course of burglary. The police checked and discovered that the naval commander had been killed by the same .22 pistol.

A check with the Detroit police revealed that Smitty was the nickname of Charles Smith, who had been a member of a Detroit gang, and had been charged, among other things, with attempted murder. A waitress identified Smith's photograph as that of a man she had heard boasting that he had committed two murders. Smith was arrested a month later after a robbery in New Orleans, and was found guilty of both murders.

Less successful, from the criminological point of view, was Hurkos's involvement in one of the most horrifying murder cases of the late fifties. On 11 January 1959, Carrol and Mildred Jackson were out driving with their two children in eastern Virginia, when they vanished. Another couple stated that they had been forced off the road that Sunday afternoon by an old blue Chevrolet, and that as the driver had walked back towards their car, they had reversed and driven away.

Two months later, two men found the body of Carrol Jackson in a ditch; his hands were tied and he had been shot in the skull; underneath him was the body of his eighteen-month-old daughter Janet, who had suffocated under his body.

Later that month, boys playing in the woods came upon bodies of Mildred Jackson and her five-year-old daughter Susan; both females had been subjected to sexual violence before being killed.

The police investigation seemed to have come to a dead end. A Washington psychiatrist asked Hurkos to see if he could help. In Falls Church, Virginia, Hurkos handled some of the belongings of the Jackson family, and described a house where, he said, the murderer had lived. It was a broken down place on the edge of the woods, and the police were interested because one of their chief suspects—a trash collector—lived there. But Hurkos went on to describe two men: one was the trash collector, the other a tall, left-handed man with a tattoo on his arm and a walk like a duck.

Hurkos led the police further into the woods, to a cinder-block shack—it was within a few hundred yards of the place where Mildred Jackson's body had been found. Hurkos told them that the killer had been there. A search of the area revealed an ID bracelet belonging to the trash man. The police had no further doubts. They arrested the trash man, who soon confessed to the murders. The newspapers ran such headlines as "Psychic Solves Murder." But Hurkos had not solved the murder. Soon afterwards, the police received a tip from a salesman named Glenn Moser. Moser told them that he was the author of an anonymous letter they had received several months previously, stating that he believed the killer was a jazz musician named Melvin Rees; Rees had once stated that he did not consider murder to be a crime, and on another occasion, when Moser had asked him point blank if he had killed the Jacksons, had merely evaded the question. Now, said Moser, he had received a letter from Rees, who had become a piano salesman in a music store in West Memphis. In the home of Rees's parents, police found diaries in which he described the murders and the subsequent sexual violations. Rees was arrested in the music shop. He proved to be over six feet tall, with ape-like arms and a walk like a duck. Moreover, he had lived in the same house as the trash collector before the latter became a tenant. Rees was believed to have committed another sex murder in the area—a nurse called Margaret Harold—and to be responsible for four other sex killings in Maryland. He was found guilty of the murders of the Jacksons, and executed in 1961. Hurkos declared that his mistake had been due to unconsciously reading the minds of the police, who already suspected the trash collector; but psychometry had enabled him to identify the real murderer. In fact, Rees *had* been living in the cinder-block hut in the woods at the time of the murder of Margaret Harold.

Nevertheless, the same newspapers that had proclaimed that Hurkos had solved the murder now denounced Hurkos and the whole notion of "psychic detection." His later failure in the case of the Boston Strangler led to still harsher criticism.

Between June 1962 and January 1964, thirteen women were raped and strangled in the Boston area. The first six victims were old women—the eldest was 85—who were often left in obscene positions, with various objects inserted in the sexual organs. Then the strangler moved on to younger women. A businessman paid Hurkos's expenses to go to Boston, where his intervention in the case was widely publicized. Hurkos quickly convinced the police that he was a genuine psychic; they included among the photographs of the victims one woman who was unconnected with the case. Without even looking at the photographs, Hurkos snatched up the "fake" and said: "This one does not belong." Soon afterwards, a police officer came in half an hour late, complaining that his car had broken down. Hurkos told him: "You are lying. You are late because you stopped by your girlfriend's apartment for sex." The astonished policeman admitted that Hurkos was correct. Hurkos went on to describe the photographs—without turning them over—and precisely what had happened to each victim. The police were astounded at his accuracy.

Yet the following day, trying to psychometrize a map of the city, and to describe the killer, he produced a number of statements which, in retrospect, seem very wide of the mark. The killer, he said, dressed like a priest—he had been a trainee monk but had been "thrown out." He had a French accent, and was a homosexual. When the police handed Hurkos a rather odd letter, which had been sent to the head of the Boston College School of Nursing by a man who said he wanted to interview a nurse for a magazine article, and was on the lookout for a wife in the nursing profession, Hurkos instantly declared with great excitement that this man was the Boston Strangler. (The letter writer turned out to be a man with a history of mental illness.) According to Hurkos, this man was a homosexual woman-hater who was taking blood from the victims to wash his hands in . . .

In November 1964, a woman reported that she had been raped; her description of the rapist sounded very much like that of a man who had been in police custody some years before. He was known at the time as the "Measuring Man," because he told girls that he was looking for photographic models, and persuaded them to allow him to take their measurements. He never harmed the girls—never committed more than a few minor indecencies—and some of them reported him solely because they were indignant that the modeling jobs failed to materialize. Now the "Measuring Man" was arrested, and some of his rape victims identified him as their attacker. His name was Albert DeSalvo, and he was a thirty-four-year-old ex-soldier. DeSalvo was diagnosed a schizophrenic, and was committed to the Bridgewater mental institution. And it was in Bridgewater that DeSalvo confessed to another inmate that he was the Boston Strangler. At first, no one believed him. But his confession was so detailed, and he seemed to know so many undisclosed facts about the murders, that the police were finally convinced. DeSalvo never came to trial for the murders—since he was judged unfit to plead—but it was generally agreed that his confession closed the case. Hurkos vehemently disagreed, and apparently still disagrees. He remains convinced that the Strangler was the writer of the letter to the nurses' college. Could he possibly be right? There is only one piece of evidence in his favour. DeSalvo began as a minor sexual offender in 1960, and he ended as a multiple rapist in 1965. Most sex killers go on killing—either until they are caught, or until they commit suicide (which often happens). It is, to say the least, unusual for a man to become a multiple sex killer, then to go back to simple rape. It *is* conceivable that DeSalvo decided to confess out of some strange inner compulsion, like the garbage man in the Melvin Rees case, and that he had never killed anyone in his life. But in view of the intimate knowledge of the crimes shown in the confessions, this seems unlikely. Why Hurkos failed so hopelessly remains a mystery.

Yet Hurkos's success or failure in any particular case is hardly a matter of central importance. What makes him from our point of view one of the most significant figures in the history of psychical research is the accidental way he acquired his powers. The psychologist Stan Gooch is convinced that all our psychic abilities are derived from Neanderthal man, who died out about forty thousand years ago, probably exterminated by our own ancestor, Cro-Magnon man. Gooch believes that Cro-Magnons mated with Neanderthal women, and that our psychic strain is our Neanderthal heritage. Whether or not this is true (and as a theory, it has the advantage of placing things in simple perspective), it is clear that Cro-Magnon man then spent tens of thousands of years developing our ability to use the left brain like a microscope—to focus on problems "close up" and to stay focused on them for long periods. And "close up" focus is the opposite of that broad, intuitive state of consciousness in which we receive our psychic "flashes." (The nearest most of us approach to "Neanderthal consciousness" is probably when we are pleasantly drunk.)

In the past six or seven thousand years, since the foundation of the first cities, life has become steadily more complicated and dangerous; civilization has turned man into a ruthless despoiler of his own species. The problem of mere survival has forced us to get rid of that relaxed, intuitive awareness in favour of our present narrow, anxiety-ridden consciousness. We have deliberately suppressed our psychic faculties in favour of efficiency.

When Hurkos fell on his head, the concussion somehow destroyed the "suppressor" that man has developed, and he became "psychic." Inevitably, he also became "inefficient." He could not concentrate on any ordinary job. The accident restored to him the kind of intuitive consciousness that our ancestors needed to sense the presence of wild beasts lying in wait.

It also seems to have restored another curious ability: the power to heal himself. On 17 May 1958, Hurkos was in Henry Belk's New York apartment when he tripped, and twisted his leg so badly that one of the bones broke through the skin and he bled heavily. Belk has described how Hurkos bowed his head, as if in prayer, and "before our very eyes, the bone went back into place, and the torn skin healed and became smooth." Andrija Puharich has also noted that Hurkos seems to be immune to common infections. The implication seems to be that his psychic powers have created a deep accord between his body and his will—or spirit—which amounts to "mind over matter," and that this power is part of our common human inheritance.

Holland's other celebrated clairvoyant and psychic detective, Gerard Croiset, was also a gifted healer; in fact, he devoted most of his life to healing. In many ways, Croiset is a more typical psychic than Hurkos. Except for the accident that almost killed him, Hurkos would undoubtedly never have developed his psychic powers. Most psychics, as we have seen, develop their powers during childhood: for example, almost without exception they are able to see "auras." It is also observable that a large number of clairvoyants have had lonely and unhappy childhoods. They feel themselves to be misfits, outsiders. In this sense, Croiset was typical. His father was an actor who frequently went off with other women, returning home to Gerard's mother—his common law wife—when he felt inclined. Gerard and his younger brother had little home life. In 1917—when he was eight—his mother decided to give up the struggle to bring up her sons without a father, and placed them in foster homes. Gerard had six sets of foster parents over the years, and was unhappy with all of them. No doubt his unhappiness and insecurity made him a difficult child, and they reacted by treating him badly. One foster father chained him by the leg to a stake in the floor. He was frequently ill, and suffered from rickets.

Croiset revealed his paranormal abilities at the age of six; he was able to tell a schoolmaster who had been away for a day that he had been to see a blonde girl who wore a red rose; in fact, the schoolmaster had been to propose to her, and had been accepted.

At eleven, Gerard returned home to live with his mother and a new stepfather; but he was unhappy, and ran away again and again. Until he was twenty-five—when he married—he moved restlessly from job to job. His wife was a carpenter's daughter, and his in-laws lent him enough money to set up his own grocery store. It was a failure—due to his lack of business ability (the typical inefficiency of the clairvoyant)—and he had a nervous breakdown. After his recovery, he became a spiritualist, but found their beliefs unsatisfactory. Then, when visiting a watchmaker one day, he picked up a ruler, and found that images of the watchmaker's youth crowded into his head. All proved to be accurate, and the watchmaker told him: "You are a clairvoyant." Croiset, unlike Hurkos, never attempted to make a living from his psychic powers—he felt this would be wrong—but life began to improve steadily as his reputation as a clairvoyant spread. Again and again, Croiset had clear presentiments of the impending war; in one case, he was able to advise a woman who was thinking of going to live with her daughter in the Dutch East Indies that the war would also spread there, but not until two years after it would break out in Europe; he proved to be correct.

Croiset's mother—now dead—had been a Jewess; when the

Nazis invaded Holland, Croiset was arrested and sent to a German concentration camp. But he was released and allowed to return to Enschede, where his wife lived. He worked for the Dutch resistance, was arrested again and sent to a camp, then again allowed to return.

Croiset did not regard himself primarily as a clairvoyant—simply as a man who happened to possess clairvoyant powers. It was not until he was thirty-six years old that he realized suddenly that his clairvoyance could give his life direction and meaning. Croiset attended a lecture on parapsychology at an adult education class in Enschede; it was given by the eminent Professor W. H. C. Tenhaeff of Utrecht. It suddenly dawned on Croiset that he was not merely a man with psychic abilities; he was a psychic, and an unusually gifted one. Croiset approached Tenhaeff after the lecture and offered himself as a subject for investigation. Tenhaeff invited him to his laboratory in Utrecht. The collaboration between the two made Croiset the most celebrated clairvoyant (or, as he preferred to call it, "paragnost") in Europe.

In Holland, the attitude of the police toward psychics is altogether less prejudiced than in England or the United States. They often approached Tenhaeff to see whether any of his clairvoyants could provide essential clues to murder cases. Since Croiset soon became Tenhaeff's star subject, he also became Holland's chief psychic detective.

It was in March 1949 that the Dutch legal authorities recognized that Croiset might be a valuable ally. Tenhaeff was asked if he could bring a clairvoyant to the courtroom at Hertogenbosch; Tenhaeff deliberately asked very little about the crime, since he was aware that Croiset could pick up his own mental impressions and be confused by them. But on the way there, Croiset remarked: "I feel this case concerns the murder of two children—I saw their bodies lying across each other in the woods." Croiset's impressions always came in the form of sudden images—sometimes symbolic images which he had to interpret. In the courtroom he was shown two sealed cardboard boxes. He was able to sense that one of them contained a bloodstained shoe, and that two children had been murdered nine years previously in August 1940. (The case had now been reopened because the police thought they had some fresh evidence against their chief suspect.) He was able to describe how the children had been riding bicycles, and how they were followed by a poacher, who knocked them to the ground and strangled them—the motive was sexual. He was able to say that they were a boy and a girl, part of a family of seven children, and that tinfoil had been found near their bodies. He even stated that a "Stevens" was involved—the suspect's name was Stevenson. And although he was not able to provide any information that could lead to a prosecution, Croiset's accuracy so impressed the judges and the police that he was frequently consulted thereafter.

Distance made no difference to Croiset. In February 1961, he was consulted by the New York police about the disappearance of a four-year-old girl, Edith Kiecorius, who had last been seen playing on a street in Manhattan. The police suspected that she had been taken to Chicago by a woman—someone had reported seeing a child looking like Edith Kiecorius in Chicago. An airline offered to fly Croiset to New York, but he declined, saying that this might only confuse him. Instead, he asked for a photograph of the girl, and a map of New York. But he was able to state over the telephone that the girl was already dead, and to describe accurately the area in which she was last seen alive. He also described the killer—a small, sharp-faced man of about fifty-five.

Partly as a result of Croiset's information, police switched their investigation from Chicago, and renewed their search of the area from which the child had vanished. In a rooming house around the corner, there was a locked metal door. The police decided to force this. They found the child's naked body lying on the bed; she had been raped and beaten to death. The man who had rented the room was called Fred Thompson, and he corresponded to Croiset's description. A week later, Thompson was arrested, and confessed to the murder; he was found to be insane and placed in a mental institution.

In the mid-1970s, I had a chance to observe Croiset's powers in action when, with a BBC team, I went to interview him in Utrecht about a case of a missing girl. In February 1967, a girl named Pat McAdam had spent the night in Glasgow with a girlfriend; hitch-hiking back to her home in Dumfries, she accepted a lift from a lorry driver named Thomas Young. Her girlfriend was dropped off near her own home, and Pat drove off in the lorry; she was never seen again. The driver was questioned by the police, but insisted that he had dropped the girl near her home. A Scottish newspaper reporter consulted Croiset, who asked him to bring along some item belonging to the missing girl; he took her Bible with him to Utrecht (where Croiset had moved to be available to Tenhaeff). Croiset held the Bible for a moment, then said: "The girl is dead." He went on to say that she had been killed close to a bridge, and her body thrown into the river. Near the bridge, he said, was a house with an advertisement sign on it, and in the garden they would find a car with no wheels, with a wheelbarrow propped up against it. Now in fact, Young's lorry had been observed parked close to a bridge on the River Annan, and he had even admitted that he and Pat McAdam had made love there before he drove her home. Croiset told the reporter that the body was caught in the roots of trees, and that women's clothes would be found along the river bank.

In fact, there *was* a house with an advertisement sign close to the bridge, and in its garden there was a car without wheels, with a wheelbarrow propped against it. Nearby, along the river bank, women's clothing was found—but it proved to have no connection with Pat McAdam. And, regrettably, the body was never found—the river is subject to sudden flash floods when there is heavy rain, and it seems probable that a body would have been swept out into the Solway Firth.

It was ten years later that Thomas Young—the lorry driver —was arrested on a charge of holding a sixteen-year-old girl captive and raping her repeatedly over ten hours. When he was arrested the police found in his home evidence that connected him to the sex murder of a woman named Frances Barker, whose body had been found near Glasgow in June 1977. Young was sentenced to life imprisonment for her murder, and boasted of having had sex with more than two hundred women in the cab of his lorry. He was undoubtedly the multiple rapist who had been terrorizing Glasgow for many months.

Croiset reconstructed the case for the BBC team—we were making a series of programmes on the paranormal called "A Leap in the Dark." When I asked him if he could tell me how Pat McAdam was killed, he became very vehement, saying that he could *see* it, and that it was horrible. All he would say was that Pat and her killer had walked along a path by the side of the river, and that she had been battered to death with a heavy spanner. (Pat's girlfriend had already provided us with a motive for the murder when she told us that Pat was menstruating that weekend, and had refused to make love with a boyfriend in Glasgow on the previous night; no doubt she had refused her killer too.)

What surprised me most was that Croiset insisted that he *had* solved the McAdam case, and that Pat's body *had* been found because of his instructions. I assured him that this was untrue, and he assured me, very vehemently, that I was wrong. I decided not to press the point. But I was reminded of a passage in Jack Harrison Pollack's book *Croiset the Clairvoyant* in which, speaking of Tenhaeff's study of Croiset in his laboratory, he said: "Croiset was found to resemble most other paragnosts in being childlike, theatrical, insecure, tense, talkative, and suffering from a stomach disorder." Croiset *was* highly theatrical, and obviously derived immense satisfaction from his international fame. He also struck me as a good and generous man, who derived as much pleasure from his healing —his house was virtually a consulting room and hospital—as from exercising his powers as a paragnost. He wanted to take the whole BBC team out to dinner, to a restaurant owned by his brother, and was obviously deeply hurt when we explained this was impossible—even though we took care to make it clear that we would have loved to accept his invitation. In spite of a rather dramatic manner, and his obvious love of the limelight (which has made some other clairvoyants less than friendly towards him), there was something sincere and childlike about him that made it impossible to dislike him. I kept in touch with him, and was greatly saddened to hear of his death a few years later.

Croiset's insistence that he had solved the McAdam case focuses our attention on one of the main problems of psychic detection. With the single exception of Langsner's intervention in the Booher case, I can think of no murder case—or, for that matter, any other important criminal case—that was actually solved by a clairvoyant. All the cases cited by Pollack in his book on Croiset seem to end on the same note: "The police were impressed by Croiset's insights into the case, but his information was insufficient to lead to the arrest of the suspect . . ." The same applies to Hurkos's major cases; he failed to pinpoint the Boston Strangler or Melvin Rees, and although he provided the police with an important lead in the case of Charles Smith—the Florida killer—"Smitty" was arrested as a result of another crime. Even Nelson Palmer's intervention in the Joy Aken case was not conclusive; van Buuren was already the chief suspect, and was arrested without Palmer's help. Croiset obviously felt that the McAdam case *ought* to have ended with the finding of the body and the arrest of the killer, and convinced himself that this was what actually happened. But cases of psychic detection never seem to be as clear-cut as that. They seem to be subject to that frustrating law formulated by William James: that no case involving the paranormal should ever be *wholly* convincing.

The only case of psychic detection in which I was ever personally involved could be used as an illustration of "James's Law."

On Saturday, 19 August 1978, a thirteen-year-old schoolgirl named Genette Tate set out on her newspaper round in the village of Aylesbeare, Devon. She collected her newspapers and cycled along a narrow road called Within Lane, on her way back to the village. She passed two girlfriends who were walking along the lane, stopped to talk to them, then rode on. Five minutes later, the two girls rounded a bend in the lane, and saw Genette's bicycle lying on its side, with her newspapers scattered around it. They called her name, searched in the nearby field, then raised the alarm. In less than an hour, police were combing the area. But there was no sign of Genette and no clue to her disappearance.

It was two days later that I saw pictures of the search on television, and an interview with her father. Oddly enough, her family had lived in our village before they moved to Aylesbeare; Genette had even been in our house, at a party given by my daughter.

Now it so happened that I had recently been thinking a great deal about psychic detection, for I had been writing the introduction to the autobiography of a London psychic named Robert Cracknell. He had been recommended to me by a correspondent named Kevin McClure, who had been president of the University Society for Psychical Research at Oxford. McClure had been impressed by Cracknell's abilities at a spiritualist meeting, and had invited him to attempt the famous "empty chair test" devised by Eugène Osty—to predict who would be sitting in various chairs at a meeting to be held in the future. Cracknell's success had been spectacular. At Mc-

Clure's suggestion, I read Cracknell's autobiography, found it impressive, and tried to help him find a publisher.

A few days before Genette's disappearance, Bob Cracknell and his family had called to see me, on their way to a caravan site near Land's End. And now I found myself wishing that I had some method of contacting him there; for I suspected that his psychic abilities might help to locate Genette. And if he *could* solve the mystery, he would obviously have no difficulty in finding a publisher.

When he phoned me two days later, I asked Bob if he had any psychic impressions about the missing girl? "What missing girl?" The caravan site was not on the phone, and had no newspapers, and he had spent his days on the beach. I asked him if he was willing to try and help to trace Genette and he agreed. Next I rang a friend, Peggy Archer, at the BBC in Plymouth; she thought it might make an interesting story for the morning news programme. I put her in touch with Bob. Later that day, he rang me back. The interview had been a great success. He had told them that he thought Genette was dead, and that she had been abducted by someone driving a blue car.

The next day, Peggy Archer rang me again. The police at the Aylesbeare search headquarters had been so impressed by the interview—which had gone out that morning—that they wanted Bob to go to Aylesbeare and see if he could pick up any impressions that might help. This is how Bob and I came to be at Aylesbeare the following day, in the search headquarters. Chief Inspector Don Crabb, in charge of the case, showed us Genette's bicycle, which was new and unscratched. Bob asked suddenly if there was a place called Broad Oak in the area; one of the policemen said there was, and pointed it out on the map; Bob said it had suddenly come into his head. So had the name "John." There were two Johns in the case—Genette's father, and the boy whose newspaper round Genette had (temporarily) taken over.

Don Crabb also took us to the spot where Genette had vanished. Bob interrupted him when he started to tell us about the case; he said it might confuse his own impressions. He wandered off on his own, while the Chief Inspector and I stood and talked. When he came back, he said that he had the impression that Genette had been knocked off her bicycle by a man who had hit her on the right temple, after calling out her name. (This was embroidered on her shirt.) He then felt that the man had carried her over the hedge into the field, intended sexual assault; but rape had not been completed. He thought the man was a labouring type, with a record of mental illness.

Don Crabb offered to take us to see Genette's father and stepmother. I disliked the idea of intruding on them, but it was obviously necessary. We knocked on the back door of their cottage, and it was opened by John Tate, a small, bearded man with a serious, intellectual face. His wife, Vi, offered us a cup of tea; but Bob asked her to show him Genette's bedroom. They went off upstairs. Don Crabb and I sat talking to John Tate. I had half-expected him to be distraught, but he seemed quite calm; nevertheless, he became noticeably nervous when nearly half an hour went by, and Bob had still not reappeared. Finally, Bob came down alone, and said he was ready to leave.

In the street, he told us that he had immediately sensed that Violet Tate was under severe stress—and not simply on account of Genette's disappearance. In Genette's bedroom, he had asked her what was wrong; she had become extremely upset, and finally told him that John was having an affair with another woman . . . This was interesting, but it hardly helped to solve the mystery of Genette's disappearance. But it seemed to offer an explanation for another of Bob's impressions— that Genette had been in a state of emotional turmoil that day when she set out to collect the newspapers.

He also predicted that Genette's body would be found within ten days. In this he proved wrong. At the time I write this—four years later—Genette has still not been found.

That November, a television producer named Andrew Wilson asked me if I would be willing to join a team whose aim was to utilize the efforts of psychic detectives to find Genette, or solve the mystery of her disappearance. I agreed immediately, and gave him Bob Cracknell's telephone number. The result was that on 1 December 1978, a group of us met in the old search headquarters—the village hall—and gave a television interview in which we appealed for help in finding Genette, particularly from anyone who thought they might have psychic impressions. The team included Dick Lee, a retired detective, who had been in charge of one of England's most successful anti-drug operations. And it was from Dick Lee that I heard, a few days later, the story behind the domestic tension that Bob Cracknell had sensed as soon as he had walked into the Tate cottage. What had really been upsetting Vi Tate that afternoon was that John Tate had admitted to the police that he had engaged in an incestuous affair with Genette's step-sister Tanya (now a pretty, blonde teenager); the affair had started when Tanya was nine. In fact, in May 1980, a British Sunday newspaper published the full story under the headline "Shame of Lost Genette's Father." The police had decided not to prosecute because they felt the family already had enough problems.

But even this information brought us no nearer to solving the mystery of Genette's disappearance. There was certainly no question of John Tate being involved in it; he and Vi Tate had been in Exeter, shopping, at the time Genette had vanished, and this was confirmed by a number of sales girls.

All through that December, our team worked in the Aylesbeare area, following up clues and hints. The army provided men to drag all the ponds again. We checked various locations suggested by dowsers and psychics. Again and again we were told that Genette's body was under water. Gerard Croiset, consulted in Utrecht, said the same thing. Bob Crackness came down and tried to trace the route that, he felt, the killer had taken across the fields with Genette's body. A local firm lent us a helicopter, and we scanned the nearby common from the air, looking for any sign of a grave. It was all a waste of time. By Christmas, when the "psychic incident room" closed, and the team split up, we still knew no more about Genette's disappearance than on the first day of the search.

The sceptical view would be that the whole thing was a wild goose chase. To some extent, I am inclined to agree. We hoped to demonstrate that a case that has defied normal police work can be solved by psychic detection, and if we had succeeded, it would have been more than a landmark in the annals of psychical research; it would have been a spectacular violation of "James's Law."

Yet Bob Cracknell has demonstrated his powers in equally strange cases. In February 1977, a pretty blonde named Janie Shephard drove from her home in St. John's Wood, London, on her way to see her boyfriend; her Mini carried a For Sale notice in the back window. The car was found near Queensway, but Janie had vanished. More than two months later, her body was found on a common near St. Albans; she was fully clothed, but it was clear that she had been raped. A reporter who was writing an article about Cracknell asked him if he had any impressions about the murder. Suddenly, he had a flood of images; one of these was of a Mini car, with a contraceptive device on the back seat. His impression was that the man who had raped her had torn the device from inside her in the course of the attack.

The reporter checked with Scotland Yard; they denied that a contraceptive device had been found. Cracknell was baffled, certain that his impression was correct. The next day, a policeman who was working on the case called on the reporter, and admitted that the contraceptive device *had* been found on the back seat, but that it was being kept secret. Cases like this seem to inspire false confessions from the mentally sick, and it is essential for the police to keep back certain facts to check such confessions. Shortly afterwards, the police called on Bob Cracknell. It was obvious that he had suddenly become their chief suspect in the case. He managed to convince them that he was a psychic. They asked if he had any other impressions about the case; suddenly, it flashed into his mind that the man who had committed the murder was a West Indian with scars on his face, and that he was already in prison serving a sentence for another rape. The glance the policemen exchanged convinced Cracknell that he was correct, and that they entertained the same suspicion.

If the Genette Tate investigation raised doubts in my mind about Bob's powers, his performance in the case of the Yorkshire Ripper allayed them. Between 1975 and 1980, thirteen women were murdered and mutilated in northern England; the killer knocked them unconscious with a hammer before inflicting the injuries. Cracknell spent some time in Yorkshire, at the invitation of the police, and of a Sunday newspaper, wandering around the murder sites. In October 1980, he told a *Yorkshire Post* reporter that the Ripper would commit one more murder before he was caught. In December, the *Sunday Mirror* printed his description of the house the Ripper lived in, and his comment that the killer was a Bradford man.

In November 1980, Bob Cracknell and I were invited to lunch by the sales director of the publisher who had accepted his autobiography. During the lunch, I mentioned that Yorkshire Television had asked me to appear on a programme to mark the anniversary of the Ripper's last murder, and that I had refused because I felt that this amounted to encouraging him to commit another. In front of the sales director—Christopher Watkins—and his editor, Gail Rebuck, Bob commented that he had an intuition that the Ripper would kill again in two weeks' time. I suggested that he should place it on record with Kevin McClure, who would take steps to see that it was officially recorded; in fact, he had already done so.

Bob was mistaken only about the time factor. It was only six days later, on 17 November 1980, that the Ripper killed Jacqueline Hill on waste ground near Leeds University. Soon after that, the *Yorkshire Post* published Bob's prophecy that this would be the Ripper's last murder, and that he would soon be caught. On 4 January 1981, he happened to be in my home in Cornwall when there was a television news flash: a man had been arrested in the red light district of Sheffield, and serious charges would be preferred against him. A few days later, Peter Sutcliffe was charged with the Ripper murders. He lived, as Cracknell had said, in Bradford, and when photographs of his house appeared in the press, Bob pointed out delightedly that his own description had been accurate.

Unlike Croiset, Cracknell is not primarily a psychometrist; insights come to him suddenly, in the form of floods of images—as in the Janie Shephard case. He does not appear to have to establish contact with any particular object. Which raises again the interesting question of why psychics and clairvoyants should develop different sets of powers. In the case of Cracknell and Croiset, the point is underlined because their personal histories are in many ways similar. Cracknell was an unwanted child who was brought up for the first five years of his life by a foster mother. At the outbreak of the Second World War, he was evacuated to Nottingham, where he was kept half-starved and beaten for bed-wetting. A sympathetic school-mistress used to take him to chapel on Sundays, and he found in religion some outlet for his frustration and loneliness. The first thing that struck me when I met him—at a party in London—was that he is a highly dominant individual; he has a strong personality, and looks more like a boxer than a sensitive. Croiset was also highly dominant, but in a different way; I suspect that if he had not become a paragnost, he might have made a good actor. So here we have a common factor; naturally dominant individuals—what zoologists call "alphas"—placed in thoroughly frustrating life-situations. It is a combination that often produces criminals, as well as artists.

We have seen that Hurkos developed his powers after an accident, and his subsequent inability to concentrate suggests that the accident produced some kind of short-circuit or rupture in the channels that normally canalize our vital energies. In effect, the accident undid five thousand years of evolution. This suggests the notion that childhood frustration and misery produced a similar rupture in Gerard Croiset and Robert Cracknell, producing basically the same result. It is true that Croiset seemed to run his highly complicated life with remarkable efficiency—with the aid of a large filing system—while Cracknell was at one time a successful insurance investigator, using his psychic powers to detect frauds; but both struck me as examples of the "artistic temperament."

In his autobiography *Clues to the Unknown*, Cracknell throws out another suggestion that may be of use in classifying psychics; he points out that a large number of male mediums are homosexual. Statistically speaking, there seem to be far more women psychics than men, and few of these seem to have developed their powers as a result of childhood miseries or traumas. Psychic powers seem to be more natural to women than to men, and this is what we would expect if they are in some way dependent on the right cerebral hemisphere—Hudson's "subjective mind." We accept that women are more intuitive than men; the male role of breadwinner demands the development of left-brain qualities of aggression and concentration. The implication would seem to be that, while we all possess latent psychic powers, the development of civilization has suppressed these more fully in males.

Although we are still ignorant of why different psychics should possess different powers—mediumship, psychometry, clairvoyance, precognition, psychokinesis—it seems fairly clear that there is no basic difference in kind between these various abilities; anyone who possesses one can develop the others. In the mid-1970s, I spent some time studying Uri Geller, the Israeli psychic who had achieved sudden fame through his ability to bend spoons by merely stroking them gently. Apart from his spoon-bending, which I witnessed on several occasions, Geller's most impressive demonstrations were of telepathy—for example, he duplicated a drawing I had made under conditions where the most skilled magician would have found it impossible to cheat. (Geller's chief critic James Randi declined to attempt the same feat when we had a meal together—he said it would require preparation.) After his move to New York in the mid-seventies, Geller was asked by the police to see if he could help in a kidnapping case: Samuel Bronfman, the heir of the family who manufacture Seagram's Whiskey, had disappeared. Geller later sent me a tape describing the experience. He had been taken to the Bronfman apartment, near Central Park. In the middle of the room there was a large map of New York. "I looked at the map from a distance, and it was like a flash. I was drawn toward the map. I stood gazing at it for about two minutes, then raised my hand, and said 'Here.' I put my finger down in a place in Brooklyn." He adds: "It was as if someone was directing me to that point on the map." Later that day, he went to the kidnapped man's apartment and tried handling various objects belonging to him, without any further result; he even flew over Brooklyn in a helicopter. That first impression as he looked at the map had been the strongest. And it was, in fact, in this area of Brooklyn that Samuel Bronfman was eventually found.

I found that his most interesting comment was: "It was as if someone was directing me to that point on the map." Geller is not a medium or a spiritualist, and he was sceptical about the view of his friend—and "discoverer"—Andrija Puharich, who was inclined to believe that Geller's powers came from non-human entities from other worlds. But I had noted that in Geller's presence, poltergeist effects seem to occur with considerable frequency—small objects flying across the room, missing light bulbs, sudden "apports." If, as I later came to suspect, poltergeists are spirits, then it would seem logical that Geller is, whether he realizes it or not, a medium.

Another modern psychic, Matthew Manning, began as the focus for violent poltergeist activities when he was an adolescent—so much so that he was twice threatened with expulsion from his public school. Then he discovered that the phenomena could be kept under control if he practised automatic writing—resting his hand on a sheet of paper and holding a pencil; the result was not only writing, but drawings of remarkable talent in the style of artists such as Dürer, Picasso and Aubrey Beardsley. As soon as he began to channel his powers, the unwelcome manifestations ceased; Manning went on to develop powers of clairvoyance, psychokinesis, procognition, healing and mediumship. (One of his most remarkable books, *The Strangers*, describes his encounters with a ghost that haunted his family's eighteenth-century home.) Here again, it is practically impossible to draw a line between Manning's own psychic gifts, and powers for which he may act as a medium or channel. But his case seems to demonstrate again that most psychics can develop any particular gift that interests them, and "block out" those about which they feel doubtful.

This seems to account for one of the most striking changes in the field of psychical research in the past century. Some of the most gifted of modern psychics seem actively to dislike the seance room and to prefer the laboratory. Some, like the remarkable American Greta Woodrew, are firmly convinced that they are in touch with extra-terrestrial intelligences. But there seems to be a definite movement away from the beliefs of spiritualism as expressed in the books of Allan Kardec. The odd thing is that the basic phenomena remain much the same; it is only the interpretation that has changed.

A case in point is Suzanne Padfield, wife of the physicist Ted Bastin, and one of the most widely tested laboratory psychics of our time. Suzanne Padfield was discovered by a member of the staff of the Paraphysical Laboratory, Mervyn Hinge, and spent several years there being extensively tested by its founder, Benson Herbert, who has published many papers about her. Among members of the scientific community engaged in paranormal research, she is probably more highly regarded than any psychic since Leonore Piper. Yet her background and development have been fundamentally similar to those of most psychics since the days of Home and Eusapia Palladino.

For the first few years of her life, Suzanne Padfield lived in a house in Wells, Somerset, that had a reputation for being haunted. She first became aware of it at the age of three, when she woke up in the middle of the night, and heard footsteps walking towards her across her bedroom floor. Since she slept with the light on, she could see there was no one there. She hid under the bedclothes, and felt someone touching her. Then the footsteps went away across the room. Her parents told her that she had been dreaming; but years later they admitted that they had also been aware of the "haunting"; things vanished and turned up again weeks later—in one case, a large clothes-horse covered with clothes. The family moved to another house in Shepton Mallet, and there Suzanne was thrown out of bed almost every night—she would often wake up and find herself sleeping on the floor. She believed that this was due to "earthquake shocks" in the area. There were also the lights that moved around her room when the electric light was out; she and her sister used to sit in bed watching white and lilac and green lights hovering around the walls. This house, she later discovered, also had a reputation for being haunted. But what seems clear is that Suzanne was a natural medium who somehow amplified the effects.

She "saw pictures" that puzzled her; in a strange house, or sitting on a bus, images would come into her mind which had all the quality of memories from her own past; but they were *not* from her own past. They involved people she had never seen and places she had never been to. She might walk into a house and suddenly *know* that there had been a picture on a certain wall where there was now a mirror. Yet she never bothered to follow up these impressions. (One of the characteristics of right-brainers is that they take life as it comes, rather passively.) Then one day, when she was eighteen, she went on an archaeological dig at Cadbury Castle—a subject that had always fascinated her. The man in the next trench asked her if she was interested in the paranormal, and she admitted she was. When she told him about the "pictures," he asked if she would mind trying an experiment. He took a locket from round his neck, handed it to her, and asked if it gave her any impressions. She told him that she "saw" it lying under water and being dug up; she also said that her impression was that it was Viking. She was correct on all counts; the man—Mervyn Hinge—had dug it up in a tidal estuary; it had come from a long-ship. Hinge suggested that Suzanne should come along to the Paraphysical Laboratory at Downton to be tested.

She welcomed the idea. By this time she had left home and was living alone in a cottage at Stony Stratton. She worked during the winter at a full-time job (usually a switchboard operator) and then spent the summer writing poetry and children's stories, and living on bread and cheese. Anything that helped pay her expenses was welcome.

Benson Herbert had only just set up the Paraphysical Laboratory—in a farmhouse in the New Forest—in 1966, when Suzanne Padfield went there for the first time. Herbert had been a member of the SPR, and had worked with R. G. Medurst in experimental seances—on one occasion a flying table permanently scarred his jaw. Placed in a trance, he spoke with the voice of a Chinese guide who claimed to have died a thousand years ago. Herbert concluded that the guide was his own unconscious mind, and set up his laboratory to investigate the powers of the unconscious. Having taken part in seances, he was regarded by some of his eminent contemporaries with suspicion; they stuck to their laboratories and treated spiritualism as slightly unclean. But Herbert, a genuine enthusiast, was interested in plumbing the depths of the mysteries he had encountered.

At this point, Medhurst was still holding seances at Richmond. Suzanne attended many of these, but found spiritualism somehow repellent. So she disappointed Medhurst's hopes that she might become a medium. On the other hand, her performance in telepathy, psychometry, psychokinesis and psychic healing was so impressive that Herbert had no regrets, Besides, some of her phenomena came very close to mediumship. Unable to move her hands or feet, she could induce in sitters a feeling of being touched by some solid object pressing against them. She was able to move a heavy table—and this, as we have seen, is a feat associated with spiritualist seances rather than with psychokinesis in the laboratory. She could also move mobiles in sealed glass jars, even causing half a dozen of them to line up parallel to one another.

Some of the most interesting experiments in these early days were with clocks. Herbert had noticed that clocks sometimes make odd noises—clunks and clicks—that cannot be explained by anything in the works. He suspected that clocks can build up a "mini-psychic environment." He had the works of large clocks exposed through glass and projected on to a large screen, so every movement could be examined and filmed. Suzanne was soon able to influence the clunks and clicks to the extent of being able to say, "After I count three, you will make fifteen loud clonks." Herbert was convinced that this was another manifestation of the unconscious mind—to begin with, the noises increased in the presence of large numbers of people.

Although the dozen years she spent in Herbert's laboratory ended by boring her, it also seems to have developed her powers. One day, she and her sister stopped at a pub called The Pheasant near Winchester, and ordered sandwiches; her sister went to the toilet, and Suzanne suddenly had an impression of a man wearing a black cloak, looking at her across the table with an expression of hatred; she particularly noticed the teeth, which were so white that she described them as being "like a lightning flash." The impression had faded by the time her sister returned. Later, she went into the other bar, and saw a large portrait of the man; it was the writer William Hazlitt. She was told later that Hazlitt had been unhappily in love with the daughter of the publican, and that this had turned him into a lifelong misogynist. (The girl may have been an unidentified early love of Hazlitt's, Sally Shepherd; the girl who later caused him such anguish—and who is the subject of his paranoid *Liber Amoris*—was Sarah Walker, the daughter of his London landlord.) A book she consulted described Hazlitt as having a smile "that looked like a thunderstorm."

During her period at the Paraphysical Laboratory, she rented a large house—an old rectory—that belonged to the Deanery of Wells. This had a reputation of being haunted, and her presence there seemed to provide the ghost—or poltergeist—with all the energy it needed to produce violent manifestations. The rent was minimal, because she was there as unofficial caretaker, and this was the main reason that she stayed. Soon after she moved in, the manifestations started: ghostly hands were placed on her shoulders, electric fires switched on, bathroom taps turned on, the lavatory flushing all night long, footsteps across her bedroom, doors sounding as if they were bursting into flames. On one occasion, a ten-pound sack of brown rice shot along the corridor from the kitchen, and on another, her bed shook so violently that she called in several friends (who were staying) to ask them to sit on it to see how many of them were needed to keep it still. With all of them sitting on it, it still shook.

After one of her early experiences with the "ghost," she ceased to be nervous. One night the light in her bedroom went out and the door creaked open; she saw a black shape in the dim light. A tremendous racket came from the landing. She was tempted to climb out of the window, but decided that her fear of heights was greater than her fear of ghosts. She cowered under the blanket most of the night; at dawn, the noises stopped. She discovered that the power had been turned off at the master switch. She was shaken, but the experience convinced her that she would come to no harm. (In fact, there is no case on record of a ghost ever harming anyone.) After that, she often wandered around the house at night without even bothering to switch on the lights.

In 1975, she married the physicist Ted Bastin, whom she had met in a television studio; at the time, Bastin was one of the physicists investigating Uri Geller. By that time, she had already had her first experience of psychic detection. In June 1974, a ten-year-old girl named Alison Chadwick left her home near Shepperton, Middlesex, and vanished. A man working on the case asked Suzanne Padfield if she could help. He told her nothing about the case—psychometrists prefer to know as little as possible—but handed her a pencil case and a teddy bear that had belonged to Alison. The vision she experienced was so harrowing that it made her physically ill. She saw the child being attacked and killed, then saw the attacker conceal the body under leaves and shrubbery; she was able to draw a map of the area, which was passed on to the police. Eight months later, the child's body was found in a sack near a disused gravel pit in Shepperton. A man was later sentenced to prison for manslaughter of Alison Chadwick. The case cannot be counted one of her major successes, since she "saw" neither the water in the pit (where the body was probably dumped) nor the fact that the body was placed in a sack.

But a case in which she became involved in 1980 undoubtedly rates as a striking success. In December 1979, nine-year-old Inessa Tchurina went skating at a rink near her home in Fryazino, near Moscow, and failed to return home. When the police failed to find any clue to her disappearance, her father asked one of Russia's leading parapsychologists, Viktor Adamenko, if he could help. Adamenko wrote to Benson Herbert, and Herbert sent a sample of the girl's schoolwork, and a photograph, to Suzanne Padfield. She was eating breakfast when it arrived, and visions came so fast that she had to leave the table. She saw the girl in the skating rink, speaking to a thick-set, burly man. They became friendly; he talked to her outside and she walked along the street with him. The man invited her into his home to look at some new skates. Suzanne's impression was that the man was not actually intending rape; he merely found her attractive, and wanted to make a pass. When he placed his hand on her shoulder, she panicked and she tried to scream. He placed his hand over her mouth and then, as she tried to break loose, hit her on the left side of the head. The child fell, unconscious, and the man, now terrified, strangled her.

Perhaps the oddest part of Suzanne Padfield's vision is what followed. The man wrapped the body in "something blue," then, carrying the bundle, caught a bus out of town. He later dumped the body in a river.

Her picture of the man was particularly clear and detailed: about thirty, with a round face, brown hair and beard, and prominent eyebrows. She also "knew" that he had since shaved off his beard and left town. All this information was sent to Viktor Adamenko. Soon afterwards, he wrote to say that the murderer had confessed. The police had interviewed many suspects, including a labourer who corresponded exactly to Suzanne's description. Now they questioned him again. Faced with what seemed an eye-witness description of his actions, he broke down and confessed to the murder. He had wrapped the child's body in a blue blanket, and left town on an electric commuter train (not a bus). The body had, in fact, been found, but was so badly decomposed that the parents had been unable to identify it. The murderer had subsequently shaved off his beard and moved elsewhere. Since the Soviet Union still has capital punishment, he was sentenced to death and executed.

Here, then, it seems, is the exception that proves the rule: a criminal case that *was* decisively solved by a psychic. Yet the circumstances tend to reinforce our general conclusion. Suzanne Padfield was not approached by police officers in urgent need of a "lead," or by press men looking for a story. The letter containing the photograph and the schoolwork arrived when she was relaxed at the breakfast table; it was a case from a distant country, so there was not the slightest personal pressure on her to solve it. The result was that that strange faculty which seems able to perceive distant events felt free to provide her with an exceptionally detailed picture of the crime, even to the colour of the blanket in which the child's body had been wrapped.

Why does this faculty work so erratically? Thomson Jay Hudson provided the basic explanation when he pointed out that the powers of the subjective mind are easily blocked by an attitude of scepticism or hostility. And our knowledge of split-brain physiology provides us with a more precise explanation. The "you," the ego, lives in the left cerebral hemisphere; the non-you, which seems to be responsible for psychic perceptions, lives in the right. It operates best when the left is totally relaxed. As soon as the left becomes anxious and begins to interfere, it is a case of too many cooks spoiling the broth; the right becomes self-conscious, and its powers are blocked. Since it is highly suggestible, the merest hint that it will fail is enough to cause it to do so.

Another reason is suggested by certain "brain radiation" experiments of Dr. Oscar Brunler, which throw an interesting light on the whole subject of psychometry. Brunler, who died in 1952, was a chemical engineer who invented the "Brunler flame," a flame capable of burning underwater, which was used to undermine the German defences in the Allied invasion of Normandy in 1944. Brunler made the same discovery that Tom Lethbridge made two decades later, that the pendulum was "absurdly accurate," and could be used as a precision instrument.

In France, Brunler came across an interesting device invented by a certain Antoine Bovis, who worked as a food inspector for the French government. Bovis has achieved a belated celebrity in recent years as the man who, in the 1930s, noticed that small animals which had died in the King's Chamber of the Great Pyramid had become mummified, instead of decomposing; Bovis tried constructing smaller pyramids on the same scale and—allegedly—discovered that they also had curious properties, such as the power to mummify animals and cause seeds to grow much faster than usual. (It is only fair to add that the claims of the pyramid enthusiasts have been widely disputed.) Bovis had also discovered that a pendulum could be used to determine the state of preservation of food or wine. If he placed his left hand on a sample of the thing to be tested, then moved his right hand—holding the pendulum—along a metre rule, the pendulum would begin to swing back and forth at a certain point. If the food or wine was in perfect condition, the pendulum would begin to swing at 100 centimetres. Bovis's grading of food and wine was so swift and accurate that others began to use his methods; Bovis invented a simple device which he called a "biometer," with a metal plate mounted on a slotted board, which provided support for the hand holding the pendulum. Oscar Brunler saw a biometer in France, and proceeded to improve it by using a longer scale, allowing him to measure up to a thousand. Bovis had already discovered that the biometer could be used to diagnose health problems. With his extended scale, Brunler concluded that it could pick up a whole range of higher radiations connected with the workings of vital energies.

Brunler was a scientist, and wanted to know exactly what the biometer was measuring. The answer had already been provided by the researches—in the early years of the century —of a highly unorthodox San Francisco doctor named Albert Abrams, who had concluded that healthy tissue can be distinguished from diseased tissue by the radiations it gives off. Abrams measured the radiations of the nervous system with a simple device involving a piece of electric wire, two electrodes and a variable resistance. What he was doing, in fact, was measuring the "fields of life," the L-fields, later discovered at Yale by Harold Burr, and measured by a fine voltmeter. Abrams's discovery was called "radionics."*

Brunler discovered that the best place to measure a patient's "radiations" was through the thumbs. As he took hundreds of readings, he observed that 95 per cent of his patients had readings between 220 and 260; but a small number were as high as 500. What did it mean? These readings seemed constant, so had nothing to do with health.

The answer came one day when he was testing an imbecile girl. Her reading was only 118. He also noticed that her reaction time was unusually slow—it took her precisely two minutes and eighteen seconds to answer even the simplest question. So the biometer seemed to be measuring "mental speed." Brunler explained it by saying that when we are presented with a problem, the answer is provided by intuition, or the unconscious mind; so the speed of the answer indicates

*See *Report on Radionics* by Edward W. Russell, 1973.

how good is the connection between the conscious and the unconscious. In the case of the girl, the connection was obviously very poor indeed.

A very good connection is obviously another name for genius—an observation made, we may recall, by Thomson Jay Hudson, who called the conscious and unconscious the objective and subjective minds.

It seemed, then, that when Brunler measured his patients' thumbs, he was actually measuring their "brain power." He tried testing this by running a silk thread from the patient's head to the biometer, and found that he obtained exactly the same readings as from the thumbs. (He used silk because he became convinced—for reasons too complex to explain here —that the radiation involved is a "di-electric"—non-electric—current.)

Max Freedom Long would have said that what Brunler was doing was to use "George"—the low self—to measure brain power. (In fact, Brunler later went to California and worked with Long, who writes about him in *The Secret Science at Work*.) Long could also have told him that "George" could also be used to psychometrize objects. But this seems to be a discovery that Brunler was to make himself. His biometer, he found, worked just as well on handwriting as attached to the patient's head—he was repeating the discoveries made by Buchanan nearly a century earlier. This meant that if he could get a sample of the handwriting of some famous man, he could assess his brain power. It worked just as well with paintings and sculptures; and here Brunler made the interesting discovery that ordinary household salt would absorb the "radiations" from a painting, and that he could then use the biometer to measure the painter's brain radiation through the salt.

He also records his discovery that with creative—or constructively thinking—people, there is a clockwise reaction of the pendulum, while in criminals, it swings anticlockwise. In the case of people of strong will, the pendulum moves in a straight back-and-forth. In the majority of people, the pendulum moves 45 degrees to the left then 45 degrees to the right, in a V shape—indicating a fluctuating will.

Brunler set out to measure every person he could persuade to sit still for five minutes, and every letter, manuscript and painting he could lay his hands on. The resulting table of figures was highly revealing.

Brunler discovered that most people—95 per cent—had readings below 260. Above that, he moved into the range of such people as successful hotel managers, highly skilled workmen, and so on. Just below 310, physical skills reached a high point of development—as in champion athletes and sportsmen. Beyond that figure, there was a steady development of mind. He discovered that mind readers and hypnotists were between 320 and 330. (Brunler says that mindreading is the lowest form of psychic ability.) People between 330 and 370 were highly intuitive—the higher the figure, the higher the intuition. From 370 to 390, pure reason tended to suppress intuition; but above that figure, intuition returned to combine with reason.

Between 390 and 420, Brunler's subjects seemed to be in the grip of self-criticism and self-doubt. Above 420, the ego gained self-confidence; this is the range of natural leaders. (According to Arthur Young,* Freud, Bertrand Russell and John F. Kennedy are all at 420.)

At 440, the ego begins to fade; such people are inclined to anonymity. Significantly, many great musical interpreters fall within this range—Toscanini, Myra Hess, Artur Schnabel, Fedor Chaliapin. It is equally significant that great clairvoyants—like Edgar Cayce and Eileen Garrett—are found at 480, for a clairvoyant is, after all, a kind of interpreter. (This obviously does not mean that clairvoyants *begin* at 480; we have seen that the basic power of telepathy begins at 320.) Above 500, "genius" begins—defined by Brunler as people who are capable of creating something that will survive their death. Picasso is at 515, Shaw at 518, Scott at 562, and Leonardo at an incredible 720—the highest figure on Brunler's scale—with Giorgione and Michelangelo only just below him. (A surprising number of great painters can be found near the top of the brain scale.)

Brunler's scale seems to reveal a complex dance of human faculties and abilities, weaving and changing places in a process of emergent evolution. It is reminiscent of Yeats's curious analysis of human types called *A Vision*—dictated, he

---

*"The Brain Scale for Dr. Brunler," in *Which Way Out?*, 1980. I am indebted to Dr. Young for sending me material on Brunler.

claimed, by spirits. It raises more questions than it answers; and those who find it impossible to take it seriously as a piece of scientific research may still find it fascinating as psychological analysis of a remarkable range of human beings.

What light does Brunler's scale throw on the nature of psychic abilities? To begin with, it seems to suggest that they are confined to the range—a mere five per cent—of above average individuals. But perhaps the most interesting observation is that the most gifted psychics rank with the great musical interpreters, and only slightly below the genius level. This would certainly help to explain the erratic nature of psychic powers, and why so many of the psychics in this chapter have produced such variable results. A great pianist or singer cannot always be at his best; in fact, it occurs only rarely. And this is often when he feels he can be completely spontaneous. This would explain, for example, why Suzanne Padfield produced such excellent results in the Moscow case, and was only moderately successful in the case of Alison Chadwick—where she may have felt a stronger compulsion to produce results.

It is also worth noting that the level of ego assertion is only just below the level of the interpreters and psychics. Very few psychics in history have been self-effacing, and most of them have had more than a touch of showmanship. This suggests that there is an overlap between the 420 and the 460 range, so that most psychics are—like so many great interpreters—a curious combination of natural gifts and overdeveloped egos. And since a psychic is supposed to be an interpreter, a kind of receiving set, this is bound to give rise to a certain conflict.

But the example of the great interpreters makes us aware that this conflict is *not* inevitable. A pianist or conductor may have his share of artistic temperament, but that does not stop him from producing a good performance at will. And this level of skill is maintained by constant practise for hours every day. One of the reasons that psychics are so much more erratic than pianists is undoubtedly that they tend to be lazy about their gift—to accept it as something natural, which needs no development. What Brunler's scale seems to underline is that psychic gifts are of much the same nature as musical or artistic gifts, and can be developed in the same way. At present, psychics are regarded either as freaks or frauds, and this attitude hardly encourages them to take their gift seriously. Brunler's observations suggest that if they could accept it as a kind of artistic gift, capable of training and development, the days of hit-and-miss results would probably be over, and a psychic would be able to turn in the same high level of performance in the laboratory as a pianist in the concert hall.

But perhaps the most important implication of Brunler's work is that psychic powers should be far commoner than they are, since they are latent in anyone who is above 320 on the Brunler scale. "Executive ESP" ought to be as common as executive talent. And for anyone above the 500 level—anyone with creative powers—it should simply be a matter of activating psychic faculties that are already latent at the 480 level. (I have elsewhere presented evidence that most poets are naturally psychic.*) John Reed Swanton shocked his fellow archaeologists by suggesting that all archaeologists should be willing to make use of psychics. The implications of the Brunler scale are even more startling: all gifted archaeologists are already latent psychics. Brunler's researches imply that psychic powers will eventually be as widely accepted by western man as they are in primitive societies, and used as naturally as he at present uses scientific technology. The psychic detectives of this chapter may be regarded as a crude foreshadowing of the psychic technology of the future.

*The Occult, Chapter 3, "The Poet as Occultist."

POSTSCRIPT

The time has come to attempt to summarize this mass of bewildering facts.

The starting point of this investigation was Buchanan's belief that "the past is entombed in the present," and it has appeared in many different forms throughout the course of this book. Such an idea is not confined to psychics or occultists; the French psychologist and philosopher Pierre Janet was also convinced of it. Professor Henri Ellenberger writes:

> Although he took great care never to mingle philosophical concepts with psychological theories, there is one metaphysical idea that occurs repeatedly in his writings as a kind of *leitmotiv*: the idea that the past of mankind as a whole has been preserved in its entirety in some manner. He went so far as to predict that the time would come when man would be able to travel through the past in the same way that he now travels through the air. "Everything that has existed," he said, "still exists and endures in a place which we do not understand, to which we cannot go." He also said that should the "paleoscope" ever be invented, man would learn extraordinary things about which we do not have the slightest inkling today.*

*Ellenberger: *The Discovery of the Unconscious*, p. 353.

Janet died as late as 1947; it seems a pity that he never learned that the "paleoscope" *had* been discovered by Joseph Rodes Buchanan. But perhaps it was just as well. Janet was a scientist, and he would certainly have felt uneasy about some of the conclusions reached by Buchanan.

This, as we have seen, is the problem. Buchanan's discoveries would undoubtedly have been widely accepted if he had confined himself to experiments with chemicals wrapped in brown paper. When he began using samples of handwriting, he was already posing questions that went beyond the paradigms of science. And when he began using photographs, and talking about precognition, he threw away any chance of being taken seriously.

Yet the lesson that emerges from so many experiments— by Denton, Osty, Geley, Pagenstecher, Tischner, Hettinger, Ossowiecki, Emerson, Tenhaeff, Puharich—is that Buchanan was fundamentally correct. When the same phenomena occur again and again, they must be genuine. The problem is that it seems impossible to find a scientific theory that will fit them all.

One very important point emerges from Pagenstecher's experiments with Maria de Zierold: her conviction that she was somehow able to share the consciousness of Pagenstecher, experiencing his sensations, and that she could form a similar link with objects. It is important because it seems to contradict one of our most fundamental assumptions about consciousness: that it is "private." Could this be where we are making our mistake: in assuming that some artificial limitation of consciousness is a necessary condition for its existence? Mystics have again and again expressed their conviction that "normal" consciousness is somehow sub-normal. One man—R. H. Ward—describing his experiences under dental gas, writes:

> On this occasion it seemed to me that I passed, after the first few inhalations of the gas, directly into *a state of consciousness already far more complete than the fullest degree of ordinary waking consciousness* [my italics].

And similar phrases recur repeatedly in the work of the mystics, reminding us that we are wrong to accept normal consciousness as the unchangeable basis of human existence. It has a thousand different levels; and, what is more, we can move from one level to another.

One of the most familiar forms of heightened consciousness is what Abraham Maslow called the "peak experience," the sudden flash of intense happiness, the feeling that all is well. And the first thing we notice in peak experiences is the heightened sense of *control* over the body and the emotions. This sense of control also brings a sense of *wider* awareness, of distant horizons, as if we were suddenly transported to a mountaintop. In these moments of intensified awareness, it suddenly becomes very easy to see that ordinary consciousness is a rather low-grade product, and that heightened awareness could well entail heightened powers. When this happens, telepathy, clairvoyance and psychometry cease to seem impossible or improbable.

In his book *Patterns of Prophecy*, the American researcher Alan Vaughan describes how he came to have a glimpse of precognition during a "peak experience." He had been playing with a Ouija board, and one day realized to his horror that some entity seemed to have got inside his head; he could hear her voice talking repetitively. He appealed to a friend who understood such matters—probably a medium—who, according to Vaughan, contracted a benevolent entity he calls Z. Z made Vaughan's hand write the message: "Each of us has a spirit while living. Do not meddle with the spirits of the dead." Then Z seemed to cause a surge of vital energy to rise in Vaughan's body, pushing the unwanted spirit out of his brain. "I felt a tremendous sense of elation and physical well-being. The energy grew stronger and seemed to extend beyond my body. My mind seemed to race in some extended dimension that knew no confines of time or space. For the first time, I began to sense what was going on in other people's minds, and, to my astonishment, I began to sense the future through some extended awareness . . ."

So it seems arguable that the natural scepticism most of us feel in the face of extra-sensory perception and the paranormal may be simply due to the poor quality of our everyday consciousness, and the fact that we *take it for granted* as a "norm." We are in the position of the old lady who had never been outside the village in which she was born, and could not really believe that Paris and New York actually existed.

Until scientists recognize that consciousness itself is a variable that governs the range of our perceptions, science is unlikely to be willing to admit the possibility of the paranormal. But this still fails to explain the active hostility of so many scientists—like those on the Committee for the Investigation of Claims of the Paranormal. Rosalind Heywood, a historian of psychical research, probably came close to explaining it when she wrote:

> . . . as time went on, practically all scientifically educated persons found that their fear of ridicule, plus their own very reasonable recoil from the seemingly irrational, was more powerful than alleged facts which did not seem to fit into the scheme of things; so, humanly enough, like the man who refused to look through Galileo's telescope for fear that what he saw would not suit his views, they safeguarded themselves by ignoring the evidence.*

In short, when problems seem to defy our *reason*, we feel threatened, and experience a deep sense of unease and anxiety that produces violent emotions and irrational behaviour.

When I was writing *Poltergeist*, I had a sudden insight into the reason why no amount of laboratory research will ever establish extra-sensory perception as a scientific fact. An old friend, a retired publisher, called on me one evening, and I began telling him about a case I had just been investigating in Pontefract. He raised all the usual objections: inaccurate witnesses, seismic disturbances, mischievous children, and so on. I countered each objection by describing some other case in which it could not possibly apply, and he carefully thought up a new set of objections. After half an hour of this, I could see the basic problem very clearly. I had spent months studying poltergeist phenomena from medieval Germany to modern Brazil, and I had become aware of a *pattern*: that case after case involved the same basic phenomena. And when the pattern could be seen in cases from sixteenth-century France to modern London, it became obvious to me that the phenomena were genuine. My friend was like a man studying a newspaper photograph under a microscope and seeing only dots of printer's ink. The picture cannot be seen except by looking at it with the naked eye. If he had read all the material that I had

*From *Science and ESP* edited by R. J. Smythies, 1967, p. 48.

read, he would have seen the overall pattern, and recognized that it could not be explained in terms of fraud and deception. As it was, he felt—correctly—that his powers of reason were as good as mine, and that he had every right to be sceptical. If I had argued that the right to be sceptical also involves an obligation to study the subject thoroughly before passing judgement, he would have felt that I was being unreasonable. Anyone who has read this book from beginning to end will see that the same argument applies to psychometry. Most of the cases can be criticized; but when they are taken as a whole, a perfectly clear and consistent pattern emerges. What this pattern suggests is that our "normal" picture of the world is falsified by the dullness of our senses and the narrowness of consciousness.

All of this may suggest that a hundred years of psychical research have been a waste of time. But this would be a superficial view. The question to which Sidgwick and Myers hoped to find the answer was: is the universe governed entirely by material laws, or is there room for spirit and free will? "We caught together," said Myers, "the distant hope that Science might in our own age make sufficient progress to open the spiritual gateway which she had been thought to close." For the late nineteenth century, this was the greatest of all questions. If the universe is merely a mechanism, if life itself is a mechanism, then life is meaningless and pointless, and man's belief in the "eternal spirit of the chainless mind" is an illusion. We are living in a Samuel Beckett universe, and would probably do better to lie down and die without wasting further effort. Samuel Butler complained that Darwin had banished God from the universe. Tennyson's *In Memoriam* is a long cry of agony about the meaningless universe presented to us by science. And Schopenhauer and Edouard von Hartmann had already embodied their pessimism in works of enormous power that seemed to demonstrate beyond all doubt that human existence is based on illusion. Their central argument was that life is driven by an immense unconscious will to live, and that consciousness is a mere by-product of this will. Von Hartmann's *Philosophy of the Unconscious* is impressive because it cites hundreds of examples of this instinctive drive in animals, birds and plants, and demonstrates that life itself has purposes that are many times more complex than our crude conscious desires. Does this not prove that we are merely leaves being swept away on a torrent that is far too strong for us?

This is the question that haunted Myers, Sidgwick, Gurney and the rest. They reasoned: if there *is* life after death, if there is telepathy and psychometry and precognition, then Darwin and Haeckel and the rest are grossly oversimplifying the universe. And if they are wrong about this, they could be wrong about other things . . .

So whether telepathy and ESP were accepted by science was, in a sense, beside the point, just as it was beside the point for the early Christians whether the Romans accepted their beliefs. All they really cared about was whether Jesus really died on the cross to give men eternal life: *that* was all that mattered. And in spite of all the problems encountered by the pioneers of the SPR, psychical research did achieve its basic purpose of convincing most of them that there *are* more things in heaven and earth than are dreamt of in Darwin's philosophy.

In fact, a book that appeared in 1920, Gustav Geley's *From the Unconscious to the Conscious*, could be regarded as a monument to the triumph of psychical research. It is a direct attack on that question: is life mere mechanism? He gives careful consideration to the latest scientific views that life is a matter of reflexes and chemical reactions, then turns to what he sees as the basic question: the unconscious mind. For, like Thomson Jay Hudson and Frederick Myers, he sees that this is the real anomaly in the universe of science. He cites the phenomena of hypnosis, of cryptomnesia, of mediumship and materialization, and argues, in effect: if all this is true, then man certainly possesses powers that are far greater than he suspects. Of course, Schopenhauer and von Hartmann also admit this when they admit the existence of the unconscious. But they object that man does not "possess" these powers: they possess *him*. He is a helpless puppet in the hands of his unconscious—a view later taken over by Freud. Then Geley goes to the very heart of the matter. *If* Schopenhauer and Hartmann are right, then their pessimism is justified. But is it really true that there is an "impassable abyss" between the unconscious and the conscious, so that consciousness is condemned to bob around on the surface of life, helpless to exert any real influence? "What!" says Geley. "The divine princi-ple, the will or the unconscious, is to be allowed all potentialities but one, and that is the most important of all—the power to acquire and retain the knowledge of itself.'' Why has the unconscious created consciousness, if not to aid it in this struggle to acquire and retain knowledge of itself?

For Geley, his certainty of the reality of the paranormal is the clinching factor. When a psychometrist holds an object, and deliberately ''reads'' its past, his conscious mind is *making use* of his unconscious. The same is happening when a telepath reads somebody's mind—as Langsner deliberately read Vernon Booher's to solve a murder case. The same is happening when a medium contacts a dead person, and brings back some useful piece of information—as Swedenborg did in the case of the missing receipt. (It is quite beside the point whether he really contacted the dead ambassador, or used some form of unconscious clairvoyance.) In such cases, the unconscious is *obeying* the conscious will, proving that there is no impassable abyss between them, and that the conscious mind is not a helpless slave.

This is the real triumph of psychical research: to have made it possible for an intelligent agnostic to reject finally the pessimism of Schopenhauer and Hartmann, and the materialism of the neo-Darwinians, as simplistic and superficial. The only major question that remains is whether the psychic or the psychometrist really has the power to call upon his unconscious at will. We have seen that, from Mrs. Buchanan and Mrs. Denton to Bob Cracknell and Suzanne Padfield, psychic powers tend to be erratic and to vary from day to day. But then, if Oscar Brunler is correct, this is because most psychics are like concert pianists who are too lazy to practise.

Even as it is, there is abundant evidence to show that psychic powers *will* operate on demand. In the past century, literally dozens of psychics have demonstrated their powers under rigorous laboratory conditions. If scientists refuse to accept it, this is not because the demonstrations are unconvincing, but because they find the whole idea deeply disturbing and disagreeable. This is why many psychics, like Uri Geller and Suzanne Padfield, have become disillusioned with scientists. Ted Bastin has explained Suzanne Padfield's reasons for refusing further tests: ''It is a regrettable fact that the scientific world is not at present capable of providing a panel of investigators who it would entrust with the task of setting tests in such a way that (a) the panel would report faithfully the results of the tests, and (b) the report would be recorded as scientific fact." In which case, it seems a waste of time to try to convince Committees for the Investigation of Claims of the Paranormal, whose real aim is to prove that the paranormal does not exist. It is better to look dispassionately at the facts that have been accumulated since the days of Buchanan, and try to grasp the underlying pattern.

What definite conclusions can we draw from this study? First of all, that good psychometrists and clairvoyants are people whose left brains pick up information from "elsewhere," probably from the right brain. And where does the right brain acquire its information? Again the answer seems clear: from what Hudson called the subjective mind, Myers the subliminal self, and Geley the unconscious. And they in turn seem to receive it from some sort of record that already exists in nature. It is difficult to go further than this; but at present that is unimportant. Instead we should consider Freud's remarks at the end of his essay on telepathy: "Perhaps the problem of thought transference will seem rather trifling to you in comparison with the great world of occult miracles. Yet consider that even this hypothesis already represents a great and momentous step beyond our present viewpoint." In fact, Freud deliberately chose not to take that step. But there is no reason why the rest of us should follow his example.

BIBLIOGRAPHY

Blavatsky, H. P.; *Isis Unveiled; Vol. 1: Science, Vol. 2: Theology;* Theosophical University Press, USA, 1960.

Bond, Frederick Bligh, FRIBA; *The Gate of Remembrance;* Basil Blackwell, Oxford, 1921.

Browning, Norma Lee; *The Psychic World of Peter Hurkos;* Frederick Muller, London, 1972.

Buchanan, Joseph Rodes, MD; *Manual of Psychometry: The Dawn of a New Civilization;* Holman Brothers, Boston, 1885.

Burr, Harold Saxton; *Blueprint for Immortality;* Neville Spearman, London, 1972.

Campbell, John L. and Hall, Trevor H.; *Strange Things;* Routledge & Kegan Paul, London, 1968.

Cooper, Joe; *The Mystery of Telepathy;* Constable, London, 1982.

Cracknell, Robert; *Clues to the Unknown;* Hamlyn Paperbacks, London, 1981.

Denton, William; *The Soul of Things* (3 vols.); Denton Publishing Company, 1873–88.

Douglas, Alfred; *Extra-Sensory Powers—A Century of Psychical Research* ; Gollancz, London 1976.

Durville, H.; *Le Fantôme des Vivants;* Librairie Du Magnétisme; Paris, 1909.

Flournoy, Theodore; *From India to the Planet Mars*; University Books, New York, 1963.

Geley, Gustav; *From the Unconscious to the Conscious,* London, 1920.

Goodman, Jeffrey; *Psychic Archaeology: Time Machine to the Past*; Wildwood House, London, 1978. Putnam's, USA, 1977.

Gowan, John Curtis; *Operations of Increasing Order*; privately published by author, California, 1980.

Graves, Tom and Hoult, Janet; *The Essential T. C. Lethbridge*; Routledge & Kegan Paul, London, 1980.

Hall, Trevor H.;*The Strange Case of Edmund Gurney*; Gerald Duckworth, London, 1964.

Haynes, Renée; *The Society for Psychical Research 1882–1982—A History*; Macdonald, London and Sydney, 1982.

Henslow, George; *Spirit-Psychometry*; Rider & Co., London, 1914.

Hettinger, J., Ph.D.; *Exploring the Ultra-Perceptive Faculty*; Rider & Co., London, 1941.

Hudson, Thomson Jay; *The Law of Psychic Phenomena*; G. P. Putnam, London, 1902; A. C. McClurg, Chicago.

Hurkos, Peter; *Psychic. The Story of Peter Hurkos*; Arthur Barker, London, 1961.

Inglis, Brian; *Natural and Supernatural*; Hodder & Stoughton, London, 1977.

Jones, David; *Visions of Time: Experiments in Psychic Archaeology*; The Theosophical Publishing House, USA and London, 1979.

Kardec, Allan; *The Spirits' Book; Spiritualist Philosophy*; Lake, Livraria, Allan Kardec Editôra, Brazil, 1972.

Knight, David C.; *The ESP Reader*; Castle Books, USA, 1969.

Long, Max Freedom; *The Secret Science Behind Miracles*; De Vorss, California, 1948; *The Secret Science at Work*; De Vorss, California, 1953.

Long, William J.; *How Animals Talk*; Harper, New York and London, 1919.

Maeterlinck, Maurice; *The Unknown Guest*; Methuen, London, 1914.

Manning, Matthew; *The Link: The Extraordinary Gifts of a Teenage Psychic*; Colin Smythe, Bucks, 1974.

Mead, G. R. S.; *Did Jesus Live 100 BC?*; University Books, New York, 1968.

Meade, Marion; *Madame Blavatsky. The Woman Behind the Myth*; G. P. Putnam, New York, 1980.

Moore, R. Laurence; *In Search of White Crows*; Oxford University Press, USA, 1977.

Murphy, Gardner and Ballou, Robert O.; *William James on Psychical Research*; Chatto & Windus, London, 1960.

Myers, F. W. H.; *Human Personality and its Survival of Bodily Death*; University Books, New York, 1961.

Osty, Dr. Eugène; *Supernormal Faculties in Man*; Methuen, London, 1923; *Pascal Forthuny*; Librairie Felix Alcan, Paris, 1926.

Pearsall, Ronald; *The Table-Rappers*; Michael Joseph, London, 1972.

Pollack, Jack Harrison; *Croiset the Clairvoyant*; Doubleday, New York, 1964.

Prince, Walter Franklin; *Noted Witnesses for Psychic Occurrences*; University Books, New York, 1963.

Puharich, Andrija; *Beyond Telepathy*; Anchor/Doubleday, New York, 1962.

Reichenbach, Karl Von; *The Odic Force. Letters on OD and Magnetism*; University Books, New York, 1960; Hutchinson, London, 1926.

Richet, Charles, Ph.D.; *Thirty Years of Psychical Research*; Collins, London, 1923.

Roberts, Estelle; *Fifty Years a Medium*; Corgi Books, London, 1969.

Schwartz, Stephan A.; *The Secret Vaults of Time*; Grosset & Dunlap, New York, 1978.

Scott-Elliot, W.; *The Story of Atlantis and the Lost Lemuria;* The Theosophical Publishing House, London and USA, 1962.

Selous, Edmund; *Thought-Transference (Or What?) in Birds*; Constable, London, 1931.

Shallis, Michael; *On Time*; Burnett Books, London, 1982.

Shepard, Leslie A.; *Encyclopedia of Occultism and Parapsychology* (2 vols.); Gale Research, Michigan, USA, 1978.

Stearn, Jess; *The Sleeping Prophet: The Life and Work of Edgar Cayce*; Frederick Muller, London, 1968.

Steiner, Rudolf; *Goethe the Scientist*; Anthroposophic Press, New York, 1950; *Cosmic Memory*; Rudolf Steiner Publications, USA, 1971; *Rudolf Steiner: An Autobiography*; Steinerbooks, New York, 1977.

Tate, John W.; *Genette is Missing*; David & Charles, Newton Abbot, 1979.

Tischner, Rudolf; *Telepathy and Clairvoyance*; Kegan Paul, Trench, Trubner, London, 1924; Harcourt Brace, New York, 1925.

Vyvyan, John; *A Case Against Jones: A Study of Psychical Phenomena*; James Clark, London, 1966.

Wallace, Alfred Russel; *Miracles and Modern Spiritualism*; George Redway, London, 1896.

Wassermann, Jacob; *Caspar Hauser. The Enigma of a Century*; Rudolf Steiner Publications, New York, 1973.

Wilson, Ian; *Mind Out of Time?*; Gollancz, London, 1981.

Wolman, Benjamin B.; *Handbook of Parapsychology*; Van Nostrand Reinhold, USA and London, 1977.

Woodrew, Greta; *On a Side of Light*; Macmillan Publishing, New York; Collier Macmillan, London, 1981.

Young, Arthur M.; *Which Way Out and Other Essays*; Robert Briggs Associates, San Francisco, 1980.

INDEX OF NAMES